Academic Librarianship in Canada

Academic Librarianship in Canada
Post-COVID Perspectives in a Neoliberal Era

Edited by
Jessica E. Shiers, Harriet M. Sonne de Torrens, Joanna Szurmak, and Meaghan Valant

Library Juice Press
Sacramento, CA

Copyright 2024

Published in 2024 by Library Juice Press.

Litwin Books
PO Box 188784
Sacramento, CA 95818

http://litwinbooks.com/

This book is printed on acid-free paper.

Publisher's Cataloging in Publication
Names: Shiers, Jessica, editor. | Sonne de Torrens, Harriet, editor. | Szurmak, Joanna, editor. |
Valent, Meaghan, editor.
Title: Academic librarianship in Canada : post-COVID perspectives in a neoliberal era / Jessica E.
Shiers, Harriet M. Sonne de Torrens, Joanna Szurmak, and Meaghan Valant, editors.
Description: Sacramento, CA : Library Juice Press, 2024. | Includes bibliographical references and
indexes.
Identifiers: LCCN 2024941125 | ISBN 9781634001694 (acid-free paper)
Subjects: LCSH: Academic libraries – Canada – Administration. | Academic libraries – Canada –
Reorganization. | Academic libraries – Canada – Personnel management. | Academic libraries –
Canada – Social aspects.
Classification: LCC Z675.U5 A23 2024 | DDC 027.70971--dc23
LC record available at https://lccn.loc.gov/2024941125

Contents

vii   List of Figures

1   Introduction

7   The Fate of North American Area Studies Collections in the Pandemic and Post-Pandemic Era What is Good for the Goose May Choke the Gander
Miguel A. Torrens

39   What is the Problem with Academic Libraries?: Problematization as Political Construct
Jennifer Dekker

67   Perpetuating a Gendered Profession: An Empirical Deconstruction of the Job Openings for Academic Librarians at the University of Toronto from 1985 to 2021
Guenther Lomas, Jessica Shiers, Harriet M. Sonne de Torrens, Joanna Szurmak, and Meaghan Valant

97   Information Literacy is not Scalable: A Call to Re-envision IL Teaching in the Academy
Esther Atkinson and Sheril Hook

121   Tits, Texts, and Talk: The Neoliberal Shaping of Academic Librarians' Work
Eva Revitt

139   The Proletarianization of Academic Librarianship
Sam Popowich

169   Restructuring an Academic Library without Due Process at the Ontario College of Art and Design University
James Forrester & OCAD U Colleagues

195   Index

Tables

Page			
94	Table 1	Masculine and Feminine Terms in Gender-Decoder by Danielle Gaucher, Justin Friesen, and Aaron C. Kay.
95	Table 2	Subset of Words from S. Tang Lexicon Identified in Gender Analysis of Librarian Postings
96	Table 3	Terminology used in Postings for Level of Qualifications (NER)
97	Table 4	Managerial Responsibilities: Terminology (NER)
99	Table 5	Pedagogical Responsibilities (NER)

Figures

Page			
77	Figure 1	Total Number of Postings by UTL Chief Librarian 1985-2021 (Plot A1). Copyright authors.
77	Figure 2	Total Number of Postings by Librarian Rank, 1985-2021 (Plot A2). Copyright authors.
78	Figure 3	Feminine Language Score Over Time, 1985-2021 (Plot I3). Copyright authors.
78	Figure 4	Feminine Language Score Over Time by Librarian Rank (Plot I6, see previous Plot I3). Copyright authors.
79	Figure 5	Masculine Language Score Over Time. Copyright: authors.
79	Figure 6	Masculine Language Score Over Time by Librarian Rank. Copyright authors.
79	Figure 7	Neutral Language Score Over Time. Copyright authors.
79	Figure 8	Neutral Language Score Over Time by Librarian Rank. Copyright authors.
80	Figure 9	Level of Experience Qualifiers Over Time. Copyright authors.
81	Figure 10	Managerial NER Terminology Over Time. Copyright authors.
81	Figure 11	Managerial NER Terminology Over Time by Librarian Rank. Copyright authors.
82	Figure 12	Pedagogical NER Terminology Over Time. Copyright authors.
82	Figure 13	The 'Teaching' and 'Instruction' Terms Over Time. Copyright authors.
87	Figure 14	The 'Teaching' and 'Instruction' Terms Over Time by Rank. Copyright authors.

Introduction

In keeping with the corporate values that have come to guide policy making in a wide variety of government and institutional settings, university administrations have for several decades sought to redefine education as a for-profit activity, one in which scholarship and academic principles are largely of secondary importance. Much attention has been focused on the consequences for faculty members, who are now obliged to focus on quantity of output rather than on quality, and on the steady erosion of the long-standing tradition of collegial governance. Less visible has been the simultaneous assault on academic libraries. Yet the gradual transformation of academic libraries from sites of scholarly research into service operations with increasingly hierarchical organizations has been integral to the imposition of corporate, frequently called "neoliberal," values and priorities in institutions of higher education, at the expense of intellectual pursuits, academic principles, and collegial processes. This transformation of academic libraries impacts teaching, scholarship, and research in academic communities. All essays in this volume touch upon these unwelcome yet often unremarked upon changes, foregrounding different ways in which the "corporate turn" has hollowed out rich scholarly and collegial traditions.

Before introducing the essays in this volume, it might be useful to define and explore the term "neoliberalism" itself. Like that other dreaded term, capitalism, neoliberalism is used almost exclusively by its critics. What is it, thus, that one is opposing when one identifies and decries something as "neoliberal"? And what do we mean by it even as we use it here as the thread with which we bind together our critiques of academic librarianship in the pre- and post-pandemic era? Kevin Vallier, an American philosopher who has written extensively about social trust in the United States, pointed out in his analysis that the term "neoliberalism" is often used in "popular and pejorative"[1] ways rooted in the well-known work of David Harvey.[2] Harvey has been a significant influence on negative academic analyses of neoliberal socioeconomic phenomena inspiring scholars such as Simon Springer, then at the University of Victoria, who titled his 2016 paper at an international geography conference "Fuck Neoliberalism".[3]

It is difficult to compete with Springer's panache and pithiness, or his level of profanity, but it is also possible to find a more scholarly expression of his ideas in a wide-ranging volume he co-edited[4]. In the book, Springer, along with a cast of co-editors and authors, situate neoliberalism's roots and evolving spaces of influence and dominance, including diverse geographic locations, sociocultural contexts, and disciplinary and institutional domains. Springer et al. define neoliberalism as "a means of identifying a seemingly ubiquitous set of market-oriented policies as being largely responsible for a wide range of social, political, ecological and economic problems. […] At a very base level we can say that when we make reference to 'neoliberalism', we are generally referring to the new political, economic, and social arrangements within society that emphasize market relations, re-tasking the role of the state, and individual responsibility."[5] Reading between the lines, then, it is likely that a misunderstanding and a negative valuation of what markets are or do, may play a role in the scholarly reaction to the term "neoliberalism." It is also clear that along with it, scholars have observed, and reacted to, inappropriate or forced insertions of what were perceived to be market principles into spheres of life in which their values have been traditionally unwelcome.

---

1. Kevin Vallier, "Neoliberalism," in *The Stanford Encyclopedia of Philosophy*, ed. Edward N. Zalta and Uri Nodelman (Stanford, CA: Metaphysics Research Lab, Stanford University, 9 June 2021), para. 9 section 1. Retrieved from https://plato.stanford.edu/archives/sum2021/entries/neoliberalism/.

2. David Harvey, *A Brief History of Neoliberalism* (Oxford: Oxford University Press, 2007).

3. Simon Springer, "Fuck Neoliberalism—Simon Springer" ("Simon Springer" YouTube account, 2016). Streaming Video, 21:50. From the author's reading of his paper titled "Fuck Neoliberalism" at the annual conference of the Association of American Geographers (AGE2016) posted by the author, April 6, 2016. https://youtu.be/jNMakfcZzAo.

4. Simon Springer, Kean Birch, and Julie MacLeavy, *The Handbook of Neoliberalism*, Routledge Handbooks Online (Abingdon: Routledge, 21 Jun 2016).

5. Simon Springer, Kean Birch, and Julie MacLeavy, "Introduction," in *The Handbook of Neoliberalism*, Routledge Handbooks Online (Abingdon: Routledge, 21 Jun 2016), para 3-4.

Vallier defines neoliberalism as "the philosophical view that a society's political and economic institutions should be robustly liberal and capitalist but supplemented by a constitutionally limited democracy and a modest welfare state."[6] The "capitalism" in this definition may be best characterized as the free-market economy calibrated towards protecting freedoms while promoting economic prosperity. Jessica Whyte, an Australian political philosopher and theorist, showed that while a values-driven civil discourse became sophisticated under neoliberalism, it became further divorced from the political realm[7]. This is relevant to our discussion because most critiques of neoliberalism paint it as driven purely by greed and competition, hence not supporting the development of humane or communitarian values. It may be more prudent, however, to hypothesize, along with Whyte, that neoliberalism's approach to moral issues supported dichotomous thinking while precluding more granular, or finessed, responses.

When a phenomenon appears to be as vast as neoliberalism seems to be, however, one might be in danger of finding it everywhere, and branding everything with its mark. When it becomes ubiquitous, a label might lose its utility in helping its users to distinguish, discern, learn, and predict. Instead, its continued use runs the risk of demonizing everything it touches. In this volume, the authors strive to strike a balance between analytical detachment and passionate advocacy. Just as analysis without experiential insight is likely to miss significant inflection points, passion without perspective is likely to advocate a "burn it all down" approach. When the latter is the best solution, however, it is the insight and historical perspective of a thorough analysis that can help individuals and organizations to avoid repeating the mistakes that led to the conflagration. Such insights and perspectives inform the essays in this volume.

This collection of essays examines the consequences of the strengthening of neoliberal values—largely understood as corporate values at odds with the collegial spirit of scholarship—within academia and academic libraries. Academic librarians have struggled to retain their professional rights and fulfill their responsibilities to teaching and research in an increasingly complex and technocratic environment. In

---

6   Vallier, "Neoliberalism," in *The Stanford Encyclopedia of Philosophy*, para. 1.

7   Jessica Whyte, *The Morals of the Market: Human Rights and the Rise of Neoliberalism* (New York: Verso, 2019).

doing so, librarians have sought to resist the imposition of corporate performance metrics to benchmark productivity and output within the academic workplace, and corporate restructuring ideas intended to disrupt the scholarly and collaborative ethos.

James Forrester examines the shifting terrain of the neoliberal landscape that led to the demise of core academic principals at Ontario College of Art & Design University's new identity as an academic university and the national response that resulted from administrators' uninformed decisions. Miguel Torrens reviews how the recent emphasis on e-resource priorities and rhetoric over print within academic libraries, which peaked during COVID-19, is an on-going threat to the collection development of area studies, equity, diversity, and inclusivity. Jennifer Dekker identifies the current administrative trend to strategically problematize areas within academic libraries to facilitate organizational changes that do not align with academic governance or values. Sam Popowich traces the deliberate expansion of market labour relations in academia and how this has contributed to the deprofessionalization of academic librarianship. Eva Revitt demonstrates how key institutional and professional documents such as collective agreements, structure librarians' work as library work and not as professional academic pursuits. Esther Atkinson and Sheril Hook examine how the pedagogical work of academic librarians, often framed as 'support' rather than 'teaching', has been consistently dismissed or nullified to the detriment of student learning. Lastly, the content analysis of thirty years of job postings at the University of Toronto by Guenther Lomas, Jessica Shiers, Joanna Szurmak, Harriet Sonne de Torrens and Meaghan Valant traces how gendered language has infiltrated the profession within the University of Toronto. The results display institutional and professional association influences in the perpetuation of gendered inequities.

Together, the chapters reveal and restate many of the struggles noted by each of the authors, showing how neoliberal corporate creep has infected, if not soured, many of the nuanced relationships between the university, library administration and academic librarians. Critiquing what they think are features of neoliberalism, the authors—one hopes—criticize more specifically not its poorly defined and amorphous reach, but what grew into its poorly articulated lacunae: scientism, corporatism, cronyism, and technocracy.

Bibliography

Harvey, David. *A Brief History of Neoliberalism*. Oxford: Oxford University Press, 2007.

Springer, Simon. "Fuck Neoliberalism—Simon Springer." YouTube account. Streaming Video, 21:50. From the author's reading of his paper titled "Fuck Neoliberalism" at the annual conference of the Association of American Geographers (AGE2016) posted by the author, April 6, 2016. Retrieved from https://youtu.be/jNMakfcZzAo.

Springer, Simon, Kean Birch, and Julie MacLeavy. "Introduction." In *The Handbook of Neoliberalism*. Routledge Handbooks Online. Abingdon: Routledge, 2016. Retrieved from https://www.routledgehandbooks.com and https://doi.org/10.4324/9781315730660

Vallier, Kevin. "Neoliberalism." In *The Stanford Encyclopedia of Philosophy*, edited by Edward N. Zalta and Uri Nodelman (Stanford, CA: Metaphysics Research Lab, Stanford University, 9 June 2021), para. 9 section 1. https://plato.stanford.edu/archives/sum2021/entries/neoliberalism/

Whyte, Jessica. *The Morals of the Market: Human Rights and the Rise of Neoliberalism*. New York: Verso, 2019.

The Fate of North American Area Studies Collections in the Pandemic and Post-Pandemic Era
What is Good for the Goose May Choke the Gander

Miguel A. Torrens[1]

As North American university libraries closed down and stopped user access to their print collections when the COVID-19 crisis developed, they prioritised their efforts on the provision of electronic resources to continue to support teaching, learning and research.[2] When library operations collapsed one by one when the lockdowns were implemented, academic libraries started to plan alternative strategies to fulfill their mission. The early iterations of the lockdown brought about a near closure to library operations; libraries sent their personnel home and tried to devise means and ways of operating in the new pandemic environment. The obvious first steps addressed the immediate need to deliver content to faculty and students. Initially, there was a high and uncertain learning curve as to how to handle access and delivery, since no one had a thorough understanding of how the virus was transmitted. Questions arose as basic as whether

---

1 Miguel A. Torrens is a collections specialist for Philosophy, Italian Studies, Latin American and Spanish Studies with over forty years of service at the University of Toronto, Canada. He served as a subject consultant for Spanish and Portuguese Languages and Literatures, and Latin American Studies at the Oxford University Library Services in 2007-2008.

2 Exceptionally, and only for the purpose of this article, Mexico is not included in the term 'North America'.

print materials would need to be quarantined or disinfected after use, and if so, how was this to be done and for how long? There were no ready answers. Scientific knowledge was not yet able to answer these questions.

Faced with these dilemmas many North American university libraries considered the obvious: electronic content can be delivered to faculty and students without any such considerations. As a matter of fact, many such libraries had already been building electronic resources for decades, so the model existed and was workable to a certain extent. Some of the required content, especially articles in journals, was already being accessed online by the users, and libraries had already acquired electronic access rights, often replacing their print predecessors. Users knew that there were limitations in the versatility of the electronic formats available but, depending on their needs, were willing to accept some of those shortcomings on a temporary basis or, as in the case of undergraduate students, in exchange for more efficient and comfortable access.

A somewhat similar situation was in place with e-books, although in this case many more pedagogical issues related to the format had long been discussed, such as the ability of the users to work effectively with the format of e-books, the learning ratios when compared with the print format, the maneuverability of handling the basic processes of reading and studying text (marking text excerpts, referential moves, etc.) were often raised among users, pedagogues and psychologists. Those reservations notwithstanding, the e-books were being seen as temporarily efficient—if not effective—replacements for the printed book, therefore becoming the format of choice in academic libraries, especially favoured among administrators.[3] As the lockdowns developed, continued e-content became the obvious solution to the access problem. It was an easy fix to an urgent problem in academia. Many library administrators began immediately to initiate plans to replace all printed materials with their e-format equivalent when available. Initially collection development departments across North America were directed to stop all print acquisitions immediately and concentrate on e-format acquisitions. After all, it was a model working very well in

---

3   Alec Mullender and James Marnie, "Now You See It, Now You Don't: The Disappearing Collection of Western University's D. B. Weldon Library," *Canadian Journal of Academic Librarianship* 6, (2020): 1-15. Similar trends have been occurring at the University of Toronto, with the closure of the professional library at the Faculty of Information Studies in the iSchool in 2019.

general in the STEM (Science, Technology, Engineering and Mathematics) areas of academia, so, why not extend it to the Humanities and Social Sciences? Even though some of the faculty and students in the latter disciplines may have generally been considered less adaptable to the technology—a much maligned myth and argument—they should be able to adapt when absolutely necessary. Needs must!

What was not initially obvious in this unconditional move to e-content was that North American academic institutions needed and used resources that are generated globally. This is in marked contrast to the STEM areas that depended chiefly on North American and some Western European resources, where the production of e-content is often the rule, whereas many areas of study, teaching and research in the Humanities and Social Sciences need materials from regions of the world where e-content generation is feeble, format-limited or practically non-existent. This article examines the publishing and scholarship issues exposed by the COVID-19 pandemic in area studies in the Humanities and Social Sciences.

Area Studies and the E-book

Area studies in North America is often understood as the development of serious academic research in areas, which were originally of political and military strategic interest to the United States, thereby originally an off-shoot of the Office of Strategic Services (OSS) and, later, the Central Intelligence Agency (CIA) investigations. With the growth of graduate studies at universities such as Columbia, Harvard, Princeton, Stanford, the Carnegie Foundation, etc., research centres focused on area studies. Khosrowjah argues that one ought to hark back to the Orientalism theories of Michel Foucault and Edward Said, and to Antonio Gramsci's Cultural Hegemony, for the roots of area studies, which can be traced to the colonial and imperial expansions of Western European nations (Belgium, England, France, Germany, Italy, the Netherlands and Spain) around the globe.[4] Since the 1940s, whatever their origins may be, area studies have expanded into ubiquitous extensions of North American academic institutions, and thus

---

[4] For a brief history of this topic see Hossein Khosrowjah, "A Brief History of Area Studies and International Studies," *Arab Studies Quarterly* 33, no. ¾ (2011): 131–42; David Ludden, "The Territoriality of Knowledge and the History of Area Studies," University of Pennsylvania (1997) Accessed August 1, 2021. https://www.sas.upenn.edu/~dludden/areast1.htm.

required subject specialist librarians with language expertise and cultural knowledge specific to their areas in order to support these complex library collections.[5] In addition, as noted in the ACRL statement (Appendix 1) and the SALALM Resolution: Collection Development in the Time of COVID-19 (Appendix 2), area studies, as well as, "voices of Black, indigenous, LGBTQ, and transnational authors, which are so critical to advancing the research and learning of the region and their diasporas" will be impacted by digital priorities. It is in the nature of the materials, as exposed by the circumstances of the pandemic era on area studies, that we need to focus on at this critical point.

As many North American university libraries started re-formulating or implementing collection development policies and practices that assigned top priorities to the acquisition of e-resources over print, professionals in area studies, faculty as well as subject specialist librarians, soon realised the long-term dangers and deleterious effects of those policies and practices on their fields of study. Individuals, as well as representative associations in these fields, were faced with the reality of an existing abysm between the e-resources in the mainstream and the STEM subjects versus those in area studies. As noted by the Council on East Asian Libraries' (CEAL), the North American Coordinating Council on Japanese Library Resources (NCC) and the Society of Chinese Studies Librarians (SCSL) *Statement on Collection Development and Acquisition Amid the COVID-19 Pandemic*, "the publication output in area studies is largely—and in some places exclusively—in print" (Appendix 3).

Area studies in North American universities generally include Africa, Central and Eastern European, Eurasian, East Asian Studies, Latin America and the Caribbean, the Middle East (and former Arabic, Jewish, Islamic Studies and the Ancient Middle East) and Asia, in particular Southeast Asia (China, Japan, North Korea, South Korea, Taiwan, Hong Kong, Thailand), groupings that may adopt different headings depending on the institution (e.g.: Asia-Pacific, etc.). The availability of e-resources in those areas is uneven. There is a marked tendency of very low returns in statistical analyses pertaining to the availability across

---

5 Xiang Li and Tang Li, "The Evolving Responsibilities, Roles, and Competencies of East Asian Studies Librarians: A Content Analysis of Job Postings from 2008 to 2019," *College & Research Libraries* 82, no. 4 (2021): 474–89, doi: 10.5860/crl.82.4.474.; Thea Lindquist and Todd Gilman, "Academic/Research Librarians with Subject Doctorates: Data and Trends 1965-2006," *Libraries and the Academy* 8, no. 1 (2008): 31–52. doi: 10.1353/pla.2008.0008.

all of them. "Digital monographs and access to these materials vary widely among East Asian regions"[6] even though some observers perceive that the market has increased in the past years, "the proportion of East Asian language monograph titles available in digital format remains small."[7] This and other sources reveal the tremendous differences in actual access to East Asian e-content brought about by innumerable and uneven variations in the discovery, digital rights management restrictions in Asia, and the sharing and licensing terms applied to the resources across the different regions: "East Asian countries' copyright restrictions, or varying vendors' business models, prevent the access of resources via interlibrary loan (ILL) and document delivery (DD), effectively decreasing the access to knowledge, particularly of those smaller collections that have to heavily rely on ILL/DD from larger collections" (Appendix 4, CEAL, NCC, SCSL).

Additionally, country or regional statistics do not specify whether or not the e-book can be distributed and accessed through a library, as is the case in the misleading statistics for much of Western Europe, where most of the e-books are in formats that exclude their public access in North American university libraries, or are the re-publications of earlier printed books in e-format. Hence, the real figures reflecting total publication out-put are in single-digit percentages. For example, a statistical analysis of the overall e-book production in Western Europe was only 7% of the total publishing industry in 2015, with significant differences between countries; the largest numbers were from the UK.[8] When the e-book statistics are scrutinized, the majority of the 7% is actually in the category of romance, bestsellers and thrillers, none of which comprise core genres in academic collections.[9] In a Statista graph representing the global e-book revenue for 2016, the aggregated totals for Central and Eastern Europe, Latin America and Middle East-Africa (Statista's grouping) are practically invisible,

---

6   Yao Chen, Jude Yang and Tomoko Bialock, "Demystifying East Asian Language Monograph Publishing: Contemplations on the Current Status, Challenges, and Opportunities," *The Journal of Academic Librarianship* 47, no. 4 (2021): 6. Accessed August 1, 2021. doi: 10.1016/j.acalib.2021.102370.

7   Chen, Yang, and Bialock, "Demystifying East Asian Language Monograph Publishing."

8   Michael Kozlowski, "The State of the European eBook Market," (blog) March 16, 2017. https://goodereader.com/blog/e-book-news/the-state-of-the-european-ebook-market.

9   Rüdiger Wischenbart, "European e-book Barometer: A Report on Digital Consumer Publishing in Germany, Italy, The Netherlands and Spain," (2018). Accessed August 1, 2021. https://libranda.com/wp-content/uploads/2018/10/eBook_Barometer_2018.pdf.

amounting to approximately 3% of the North American figure.[10] Again, the 3% does not represent academic publishing but rather the total of all e-book output, most of which would not be part of any North American academic library collection. Hidden in the statistical barrage of numbers is the reality that much of the world is alien to the production of academic research material in a library-friendly electronic format.[11]

Area Studies Collections and the Pandemic

After the initial stumbling and falls during the COVID-19 pandemic, North American university libraries in general reacted with a decisive implementation of policies to re-start their collection development practices supporting the teaching, learning and research at the institutions they serve, as expected. Those practices, however, involve many individuals, publishers, distributors and agents outside the library and university systems, whose reaction to the crisis varied greatly. It would not be possible here to go into detail about all of them, their reaction levels or state of readiness, but it ought to be noted that all of them are partners (approval plan vendors, aggregators, etc.) of the library without whom our diverse collections could not exist. In the specific case of area studies, it tends to get more complicated as the vendors for an area or part of an area, as for example Latin America vs. Mexico, must themselves do their own collection work with the country's publishers, smaller vendors, individual bookstores, etc., all of whom are part of the complex acquisitions network essential to collection development in area studies at the post-secondary level. These vendors have often been partners of the library for many years, in fact for decades, and are part of the symbiotic relationship academic institutions have with them. Just as their successful survival and well-being is essential to our institutional operations, so too it should be noted that our research collections could not exist without their support and expertise.

Collection librarians in area studies were quick to realise the putative dangerous effects of the e-centered collection practices that were

---

10   Statista, "Global e-book Revenue from 2009 to 2016 by Region," Accessed August 1, 2021 from the website https://www.statista.com/statistics/280249/global-e-book-revenue-by-region/ .

11   Lesley Pitman, "Digital Resources for Area Studies," in *Supporting Research in Area Studies: A Guide for Academic Libraries*, (Boston: Elsevier Science & Technology, 2016), 55-68.

being implemented early in the COVID-19 crisis. Those fears and concerns were brought to their professional area studies associations at both the regularly scheduled meetings and those urgently called ad-hoc to address the dire needs at hand. Among the many international organisations representing area studies the International Studies Association (ISA) lists no less than ninety such organisations, covering areas ranging a range of specialized topics (e.g.: the Portuguese Political Science Association or the Kazakhstan International Relations Association), to those covering continental areas (e.g.: the European International Studies Association or the Seminar on the Acquisition of Latin American Library Materials), to those with a global scope (e.g.: Association des Internationalistes).[12] Prompted by the grave consequences perceived by their members some of these area studies organisations met during the summer months of 2020. Statements were issued highlighting the flaws, gaps and inequities associated with the dominant rhetoric in the management of collections at post-secondary institutions.

The Association of College & Research Libraries (ACRL), an organisation that represents over 10,000 members, issued a Statement on Equity, Diversity, Inclusion, and the Print Collecting Imperative (Appendix 1) in October 2020 in which it recommended "that North American research libraries continue to collect and preserve valuable print materials, even as the global COVID-19 crisis and associated financial circumstances may compel them to shift, at least temporarily, to digital formats where available." [13] The ACRL shared "the apprehensions vis-à-vis vulnerable categories of important materials liable to be marginalized or excluded by a rapid and sweeping shift towards collecting models that categorically privilege electronic formats."

Professional academic librarians have a responsibility to understand the long-term ramifications of adopting digital primacy over print, the demise of core academic principles of equity, inclusivity and unfettered access to knowledge in scholarship, and how, ultimately, if threatened could result in a disservice to the communities we serve and support. The ACRL statement makes it clear the long-term damage

---

12   ISA, https://www.isanet.org/ Accessed March 4, 2023.

13   Association of Colleges and Research Libraries (ACRL), "ACRL Statement on Equity, Diversity, Inclusion, and the Print Collecting Imperative," Accessed August 2, 2021. https://www.ala.org/acrl/sites/ala.org.acrl/files/content/acrlissues/ACRL_Print_Collecting_Statement.pdf.

that prioritizing e-resources based on economies of scale over print materials will have on the advancement of scholarship and research in the second paragraph which stresses the reliance on market forces and how that will "perpetuate the marginalization of perspectives not traditionally well represented in research and higher education in North America" and thus "reinforcing legacy political, ideological, and cultural hegemony".

The ACRL acknowledged that its apprehensions and concerns had already been expressed by a number of area studies organisations, including those from the "Seminar on the Acquisition of Latin American Library Materials (SALALM) in their SALALM Resolution: Collection Development in the Time of Covid-19 (Appendix 2); the Middle East Librarians Association (MELA) (Appendix 4); the Committee on South Asian Libraries and Documentation (CONSALD) (Appendix 5); the Collaborative Initiative for French Language Collections (CIFNAL), the German-North American Resources Partnership (GNARP), and the Slavic East European Materials Project (SEEMP) in their joint statement (Appendix 6); the Committee on Libraries and Information Resources of the Association of Slavic East European and Eurasian Studies (ASEEES CLIR);[14] the Council on East Asian Libraries (CEAL), the North American Coordinating Council on Japanese Library Resources (NCC), and the Society of Chinese Studies Librarians (SCSL) (Appendix 3); the statement by the Committee on Research Materials on Southeast Asia (CORMOSEA) (Appendix 7); and the statement Equity and Access in Higher Education and Academic Libraries Amid the COVID-19 Pandemic signed by many institutions and professional bodies.[15]

The ACRL statement (Appendix 1) further notes "the related potential for damage to research collections" and the fact that "e-resource licensing agreements" do inhibit "inter-institutional cooperative collection development arrangements and inter-institutional resource sharing" which is "critical for ensuring equal access to research materials." Furthermore "a shift of focus to center on digital formats risks perpetuating the marginalization or suppression in North American library

---

14 Andy Spencer et al., "ASEEES CLIR Statement on Collection Development in the time of COVID-19", accessed March 4, 2023, https://sites.google.com/site/aseeesclir/.

15 Joint Area Task Force Members, "Equity and Access in Higher Education and Academic Libraries amid the COVID-19 Pandemic," July 31, 2020, accessed March 4, 2023, https://www.eastasianlib.org/newsite/wp-content/uploads/2020/08/Equity-and-Access-in-Higher-Education-and-Academic-Libraries-Final-August-17.pdf.

collections of traditionally under-represented North American populations" such as "African American, Indigenous, Jewish, Latinx, LGBTQ+, and other communities ... outside of mainstream publishing and distribution structures."

The ACRL statement ends with a strong recommendation: "ACRL therefore strongly urges academic and research libraries to take a deliberate, measured approach to any shift, temporary or permanent, toward an e-centric collection development model, an approach that balances fiscal exigencies with equity, diversity, and inclusion imperatives; takes full stock of the important research and teaching that cannot be accommodated through electronic resource collecting alone; and ensures support for continued print collecting in relevant areas." (Appendix 1)[16]

The Reality of Here and Now

In conclusion, then, some of the re-formulation and implementation of collection development practices that favour the selection and acquisition of e-resources over print during the COVID-19 pandemic, as well-intentioned they may have been in the rush to respond to immediate needs, have overlooked the obvious, that is, the indisputable fact that e-resources do not exist at a significant level in area studies to support the library mission, and that serious gaps are developing in the collections in these areas. Furthermore, as our acquisitions of the indispensable supporting print materials drop, serious issues of equity and diversity arise, as e-resources that represent the established and more North American based subjects and disciplines to the detriment of the area studies, clearly contradicting the recently publicised claims and statements made in favour of equity, diversity and inclusivity (EDI), as articulated in the ACRL statement above. Moreover, the extraordinarily high costs of collecting e-resources has raised some serious questions about sustainability, scope and equity issues in area studies, as noted by the statements issued by members of the Asian associations (CEAL, NCC, SCSL): "the focus on the acquisition of electronic resources has a strenuous impact on the overall acquisition budget of libraries of all sizes but putting particularly

---

16 ACRL, "ACRL Statement on Equity, Diversity, Inclusion, and the Print Collecting Imperative," accessed October 23, 2022, https://www.ala.org/acrl/sites/ala.org.acrl/files/content/acrlissues/ACRL_Print_Collecting_Statement.pdf. See Appendix 1.

medium-size and small-size print collections at risk of survival and contributing to a greater knowledge divide."[17]

A final point to be made on the subject of eroding area studies collection development is the on-going tendency in many North American university libraries to greatly reduce or totally eliminate the specialisation of collection development expertise in these areas. As stated in the introduction to this article, the format preferences that may have suited the STEM collection areas in academic research libraries cannot and ought not be directly transferred to the Humanities and Social Sciences collections. Indeed, what may have been good for the goose may instead choke the gander.

---

[17] The Committee on South Asian Libraries and Documentation (CONSALD), "Consald Statement on Collection Development, Access, and Equity in the Time of COVID-19." Accessed October 23, 2022. http://www.consald.org/covid.html.

Appendix 1

ACRL Statement on Equity, Diversity, Inclusion, and the Print Collecting Imperative[18]

In keeping with its Core Commitment to Equity, Diversity, and Inclusion, ACRL recommends that North American research libraries continue to collect and preserve valuable print materials, even as the global COVID-19 crisis and associated financial circumstances may compel them to shift, at least temporarily, to digital formats where available. ACRL shares the apprehensions vis-à-vis vulnerable categories of important materials liable to be marginalized or excluded by a rapid and sweeping shift towards collecting models that categorically privilege electronic formats, apprehensions expressed by the Seminar on the Acquisition of Latin American Library Materials (SALALM) in their Collection Development and Equity in the Time of Covid-19 Task Force Resolution; the Middle East Librarians Association (MELA); the Committee on South Asian Libraries and Documentation (CONSALD); the Collaborative Initiative for French Language Collections (CIFNAL), the German-North American Resources Partnership (GNARP), and the Slavic East European Materials Project (SEEMP) in their joint European Studies Statement on Collection Development, Access, and Equity in the Time of COVID-19; the Committee on Libraries and Information Resources of the Association of Slavic East European and Eurasian Studies (ASEEES CLIR) Statement on Collection Development in the time of COVID-19; the Statement on Collection Development and Acquisition Amid the COVID-19 Pandemic signed by the Council on East Asian Libraries (CEAL), the North American Coordinating Council on Japanese Library Resources (NCC), and the Society of Chinese Studies Librarians (SCSL); a statement published by the Committee on Research Materials on Southeast Asia (CORMOSEA); and the Equity and Access in Higher Education and Academic Libraries Amid the COVID-19 Pandemic statement signed by representatives of many institutions and professional bodies.

All these statements identify troubling consequences of a sweeping shift in research libraries toward a collecting paradigm of digital

---

18 Association of College and Research Libraries, "ACRL Statement on Equity, Diversity, Inclusion, and the Print Collecting Imperative," accessed December 29, 2023. http://www.ala.org/acrl/sites/ala.org.acrl/files/content/acrlissues/ACRL_Print_Collecting_Statement.pdf.

primacy as a monolithic and permanent response to the formidable, but temporary, unforeseen challenges of the COVID-19 crisis. Many of the efficiencies being advocated by library administrations rely on consolidation of acquisitions processes and expansion of arrangements with large-scale commercial partners. The business models of these vendors are predicated on economies of scale that privilege materials for which there are well established markets within the academy. Such reliance on market forces is wont to perpetuate the marginalization of perspectives not traditionally well represented in research and higher education in North America; it risks reinforcing legacy political, ideological, and cultural hegemony and subalternity by reproducing them in the representation of the world compiled in collections that support North American research and teaching. Specifically, the aforementioned statements address the following circumstances and the related potential for damage to research collections in the context of a broadly adopted collecting paradigm centered around electronic formats:

- the continued prevalence of print in many regional publishing ecosystems and the lack of digital publishing and distribution infrastructure for materials issuing from those regions;
- international intellectual property complexities that prevent, hinder, or complicate acquisition and use of existing electronic editions where available, including preventing or hindering the long-term preservation of those electronic materials via third-party arrangements such as LOCKSS, CLOCKSS, and PORTICO;
- the necessity for a healthy ecosystem of specialized vendors with intensive regional expertise to identify and capture research-valuable content likely to elude the broader collecting enterprises of less specialized vendors; and
- e-resource licensing agreements' inhibition of inter-institutional cooperative collection development arrangements and inter-institutional resource sharing critical for ensuring equal access to research materials for the full range of researcher populations.

These same liabilities exist within the Anglo-American publishing and distribution sphere, and a shift of focus to center on digital formats risks perpetuating the marginalization or suppression in North American library collections of traditionally under-represented North American populations and perspectives as well. Important periodical and monographic output of Mexico, as well as of African American, Indigenous, Jewish, Latinx, LGBTQ+, and other communities in North America, remain outside of mainstream publishing and distribution structures and are likely to be overlooked by large-scale, general-scope electronic content aggregators.

\

CRL therefore strongly urges academic and research libraries to take a deliberate, measured approach to any shift, temporary or permanent, toward an e-centric collection development model, an approach that balances fiscal exigencies with equity, diversity, and inclusion imperatives; takes full stock of the important research and teaching that cannot be accommodated through electronic resource collecting alone; and ensures support for continued print collecting in relevant areas.

Appendix 2

SALALM Resolution: Collection Development in the Time of Covid-19[19]

In light of the COVID-19 situation and budgetary reductions, libraries are implementing policies focusing primarily on digital formats, SALALM expresses the following concerns regarding challenges in the collection development eco-system for Latin American and Caribbean Studies:

1. Whereas, the majority of publications from Latin America and the Caribbean are print-only, and are not available in electronic formats, as UNESCO's CERLALC reports in *El espacio iberoamericano del libro* see https://urldefense.proofpoint.com/v2/url?u=https-3A__cerlalc.org_wp-2Dcontent_uploads_2019_04_EIL2018-5F2.pdf&d=DwMF-g&c=lhMMI368wojMYNABHh1gQQ&r=vhefRqjEPtALKxJMmFEM9g&m=NVKo7CPE7fe75YlMB6JnRzQ3p3joCZvm-0HORnrzHhf0&s=08X3uQsc1pMyKXd_qQ03D8HuXO0VtrF-rzUfphmiYqc&e=.

2. Whereas, e-preferred collection development policies will exclude non-English language materials and Latin America and Caribbean cultural and scholarly production, including the voices of Black, indigenous, LGBTQ, and transnational authors, which are so critical to advancing the research and learning of the region and their diasporas in the United States;

3. Whereas, a sudden shift away from research materials only available in print not only threatens the integrity of diverse library collections, but also places a dedicated network of local vendors of scholarly and ephemeral research materials at risk of closure;

4. Whereas, these regional vendors are important because of their expertise in specific regions and they provide access to necessary and unique materials for learning, teaching and research needs of library users that would be overlooked by larger vendors based outside of the region;

---

19 Seminar on the Acquisition of Latin American Library Materials (SALALM), "SALALM Resolution: Collection Development in the Time of Covid-19," accessed October 23, 2022. http://salalm.org/content.asp?admin=Y&contentid=485.

5. Whereas, pioneering cooperative Open Access models such as SciELO https://scielo.org/en/ and RedALyC https://www.redalyc.org/ have made scholarly journals from the region widely available for over two decades, yet a gap for monographs still exists;

Be it resolved, that Seminar for the Acquisition for Latin American Library Materials (SALALM), on behalf of its members:

1. Urges libraries to continue acquiring print material through a network of regional vendors, often the only available sources, and thereby not limit diversity in scholarly collections.

2. Encourages collaboration and further discussion with other organizations working with international collections at a national and international level, such as the Africana Librarians Council, Council on East Asian Libraries or the Middle East Librarians Association, among others.

3. Advocates for continued and increased support for Open Access initiatives in Latin American and Caribbean countries through the Latin American Materials Project (LAMP), Latin Americanist Research Resources Project (LARRP), SALALM's Award for Institutional Collaborative Initiatives, and other existing collaborative Open Access projects.

Appendix 3

CEAL Statement on Collection Development and Acquisition Amid the COVID-19 Pandemic (in collaboration with the NCC and the SCSL)[20]

Amid the COVID-19 Pandemic: In Collaboration with the North American Coordinating Council on Japanese Library Resources (NCC) and the Society of Chinese Studies Librarians (SCSL) Approved by the CEAL Executive Board on August 13, 2020
Endorsed by the Association for Asian Studies on August 31, 2020

The COVID-19 crisis has unleashed a new operational and budgetary ecosystem in which the sudden and complete lack of access to print and non-digitized materials, albeit temporary, has resulted in an increase in the need for provision of resources in electronic formats. Budget cuts are anticipated, and while many institutions have not yet released their budgets for the current, and or, upcoming fiscal year, the acquisition of resources in electronic formats has been prioritized, and libraries are increasingly implementing or reformulating policies that focus on the acquisition of digital content for the time being.

Based on the knowledge that the publication output in area studies is largely—and in some places exclusively—in print, concerns regarding equity, representation and access in collection development have been raised by peer library associations in the form of statements such as those of the Seminar on the Acquisition of Latin American Library Materials' (SALALM) Resolution, the Middle East Librarians Association's (MELA) Statement on Collection Development, Access, and Equity in the Time of COVID-19, and the Committee on South Asian Libraries and Documentation's (CONSALD) Statement on Collection Development, Access, and Equity in the Time of COVID-19.

While we have observed the growth of electronic content over the years in East Asia, a large percentage of the overall publication output remains as print-only. It is also worth noting that there are enormous discrepancies in the availability of electronic contents among the

---

20 Council on East Asian Libraries, " CEAL Statement on Collection Development and Acquisition Amid the COVID-19 Pandemic," accessed December 29, 2023. https://www.eastasianlib.org/newsite/ceal-covid19-statement/

individual countries and regions within East Asia (including Tibet), as well as within individual disciplines. In addition to the insufficient volume of scholarly content in digital format, technological limitations of the platforms present challenges to scholars' engagement with many of the resources, making print collections indispensable to the East Asian studies scholarly community.

The members of the Council on East Asian Libraries (CEAL), the North American Coordinating Council on Japanese Library Resources (NCC) and the Society of Chinese Studies Librarians (SCSL) are committed to maintaining the breath, diversity and integrity of collections by advocating for the implementation of collection development policies that are congruent with those principles. In addition to the shared concerns raised by SALALM, MELA, and CONSALD on the implementation of e-preferred collection development policies, we would like to express the following concerns:

- Whereas the focus on the acquisition of electronic resources has a strenuous impact on the overall acquisition budget of libraries of all sizes but putting particularly medium-size and small-size print collections at risk of survival and contributing to a greater knowledge divide.

- Whereas East Asian countries' copyright restrictions, or varying vendors' business models, prevent the access of resources via interlibrary loan (ILL) and document delivery (DD), effectively decreasing the access to knowledge, particularly of those smaller collections that have to heavily rely on ILL/DD from larger collections.

- Whereas the standard expectation for terms of use of e-books, as well as ownership of contents and perpetual access rights cannot be guaranteed due to the restrictions imposed by the publishing cultures and copyright provisions of East Asian countries.

- Whereas the acquisition of materials in print is the only way to salvage knowledge and information that would be otherwise doctored, lost or unavailable as a result of censorship

- Whereas the integrity of collections and quality of scholarship will be negatively impacted. due to the insufficiency of scholarly content available in commercial e-book platforms, as well as the lack of representation of regional and niche (specialized) collections in platforms that libraries are able to license.

- Whereas the technological limitations in East Asian platforms curtail researchers' ability to engage with and manipulate data.

- Whereas the lack of quality metadata that oftentimes not only becomes the largest impediment to the discovery of resources but also demands more attention from library staff of all levels to properly acquire, describe and make resources discoverable.

With the above in mind, the CEAL, the NCC, and the SCSL urge libraries to:

- Reassure that e-preferred collection development policies implemented temporarily during the pandemic are not meant to be prescriptive for long-term collection development practices.

- Exercise flexibility in the implementation of collection development policies to allow for balanced collection development practices that adequately address the needs for print and electronic formats.

- Rely on the expertise and advice of professional librarians who are better informed of the conditions of the publishing environments of the areas and disciplines they develop and support.

- Commit to protect the acquisition of print materials, as well as the personnel responsible for making them discoverable and accessible, as an effort to ensure the inclusion of non-traditional publications that are often regarded to offer the most poised critique of mainstream voices and perspectives.

- Continue to support the work of vendors and smaller publishers who are vital to the building of diverse, specialized library collections and whose survival is critical to the academic enterprise.

- Support and advocate for Open Access (OA) initiatives via the collaboration of North American and East Asian partners to bring to light our unique and specialized collections while minimizing the reliance on commercial entities to make them available.

- Encourage a collaborative, cross-institutional approach in developing best practices for license negotiations of East Asian resources that systematically address the issues outlined in this document.

Task Force Membership

- Fabiano Rocha, University of Toronto (Co-Chair)
- Hong Cheng, University of California, Los Angeles (Co-Chair)
- Chengzhi Wang, Columbia University (CEAL/Committee on Chinese Materials Representative)
- Chiaki Sakai, Columbia University (CEAL/Committee on Japanese Materials Representative)
- Jude Yang, Yale University (CEAL/Committee on Korean Materials Representative)
- Xiuying Zou, Claremont Colleges (SCSL Representative)
- Haruko Nakamura, Yale University (NCC Representative)
- Hana Kim, University of Toronto (ex-officio)

About the Council on East Asian Libraries (CEAL)

CEAL is a committee of the Association for Asian Studies. CEAL is the largest international professional organization in the field of East Asian Studies librarianship. It was founded in 1958 as the Committee on Development and Acquisition.

Appendix 4

MELA Statement on Collection Development, Access, and Equity in the Time of COVID-19

by *Middle East Librarians Association (MELA)*[21]

The COVID-19 pandemic has introduced significant operational and financial challenges for libraries and other institutions committed to preservation and access for documentary heritage.

As library specialists engaged in the work of collection development and collection access in support of the study and appreciation of the communities, cultures, and languages of the Middle East (Southwest Asia), North Africa, and their diasporas, we in the Middle East Librarians Association (MELA) share the concerns around equity, representation, and access raised by our colleagues in the Seminar on the Acquisition of Latin American Library Materials (SALALM) in their Task Force Resolution issued 10 June 2020.

---

[21] Middle East Librarians Association (MELA), "MELA Statement on Collection Development, Access, and Equity in the Time of COVID-19," Accessed October 23, 2022. https://www.mela.us/2020/06/22/mela-statement-on-collection-development-access-and-equity-in-the-time-of-covid-19/

Appendix 5

Committee on South Asian Libraries and Documentation (CONSALD)[22]

July 17, 2020

The Committee on South Asian Libraries and Documentation (CONSALD) recognizes the tremendous work of the Collection Development and Equity in the Time of Covid-19 Task Force in the crafting of the Seminar on the Acquisition of Latin American Library Materials (SALALM) Resolution, as well as the substantive and important response by the Middle East Librarians Association (MELA).

We share the concerns articulated by both groups surrounding the vulnerability of print materials and the economies that support their production, as well as the potentially exclusionary impact of e-preferred collection policies. We strongly advocate for the continued support of Open Access initiatives, and the preservation of funding and expert staffing required to acquire and process materials from these regions.

Like Latin America, the Caribbean, the Middle East, and other areas of focused study, South Asia has had its own experience of the impact of COVID-19 since the beginning of 2020. Over the last several months, South Asians have been grappling with the pandemic and the associated violence caused by the pendulation of lockdowns and subsequent quick reopenings that disproportionately affect at-risk groups, including forced migrations. In addition, the recent natural disaster, Cyclone Amphan, in the Bay of Bengal has compounded already precarious and unprecedented circumstances. These events have touched every aspect of the economy of scholarly and cultural production, from creation, to publication, to dissemination of works.

Therefore, CONSALD endorses the SALALM Resolution and MELA response, and asks libraries to consider the following addenda:

1. Whereas, most U.S. and Canadian-based South Asian Studies collections rely heavily, if not exclusively, on the Library of Congress

---

[22] Committee on South Asian Libraries and Documentation (CONSALD), "CONSALD Statement on Collection Development, Access, and Equity in the Time of COVID-19," accessed October 23, 2022. http://www.consald.org/covid.html

Cooperative Acquisitions Programs, SACAP (New Delhi) and PIA-CAP (Islamabad), for acquisitions of print and other physical media from South Asia, and the full impact of COVID-19 on LCCAP's staffing, collecting, and distribution remains unknown;

2. Whereas, acquiring materials from South Asia also relies on experienced regional suppliers to locate and distribute materials, and these vendors often additionally facilitate cataloging and shipping of materials purchased at a distance and during acquisitions trips in South Asia;

3. Whereas, commercial electronic resources from South Asia, when available, are not well suited to library lending and interinstitutional resource sharing, and in the rare cases that they are, licenses can be difficult to negotiate across languages, national boundaries, and jurisdictions; moreover, they also present the potential for permanent loss of content if access to subscriptions ceases;

4. Whereas much of the cultural and intellectual heritage of South Asia held in libraries and archives across the world is unavailable to scholars in South Asia and elsewhere;

5. Whereas, no one institution can collect, describe, provide access, and preserve the breadth and depth of scholarly output from South Asia;

On behalf of its members, CONSALD:

- Urges libraries to preserve the budgets and staffing workflows necessary for participation in the Library of Congress Cooperative Acquisitions Programs, and urges the Library of Congress to continue robust support of these Overseas Office initiatives and staff members;

- Urges libraries to support South Asia-based vendors whose accrued expertise, supply networks, and specialized services are in danger due to loss of livelihood for an extended period;

- Urges the continued acquisition of commercial print resources and non-commercial ephemera despite recent shifts to e-preferred strategies;

- Urges libraries to begin and/or continue robust investment in innovative Open Access initiatives in South Asia and North America, such as the South Asia Open Archives (SAOA); to support projects that archive born-digital content; and to foster digital scholarship that brings resources and knowledge about South Asia to diverse audiences;

- Urges libraries to fund and support collaborative and interdependent efforts (e.g., South Asia Open Archives [SAOA], the South Asia Materials Project [SAMP], and the South Asia Cooperative Collection Development Workshop [SACOOP]) that maximize the potential for research on South Asia from broad disciplinary perspectives; these initiatives reduce duplication in LC profiles and encourage the development of niche collections that are critical for diversity in the collective collection;

- Urges libraries to invest funds, time, and staffing to support the development of metadata and academy-owned infrastructure to facilitate the discovery of shared resources and to provide more evenly distributed access inter-institutionally and internationally, including controlled digital lending in times of crisis.

In the face of significant challenges to research due to limitations on resource circulation, lack of access to libraries and archives, and reduced ability to travel, we furthermore encourage enhanced partnerships and dialogue amongst the community of South Asia scholars and librarians. CONSALD continues to strengthen communication with its parent organization, the South Asia Council of the Association of Asian Studies, and CONSALD's members welcome opportunities to liaise with academic and archival partners. By working together, we will weather the difficulties prompted by COVID-19 and continue working towards inclusive, discoverable, and accessible South Asia collections.

Appendix 6

"European Studies Statement on Collection Development, Access, and Equity in the Time of COVID-19," Issued by The Collaborative Initiative for French Language Collections (CIFNAL), German-North American Resources Partnership (GNARP), and Slavic and East European Materials Project (SEEMP)[23]

August 20, 2020

In response to the SALALM resolution "European Studies Statement on Collection Development, Access, and Equity in the Time of COVID-19" issued on August 17, 2020.

In light of the COVID-19 situation and budgetary reductions, libraries are implementing collecting policies focused primarily on digital formats. The following represents an endorsement and expansion of the Seminar on the Acquisition of Latin American Library Materials (SALALM) Collection Development and Equity in the Time of Covid-19 Task Force Resolution (link is external)issued 10 June 2020—an endorsement and expansion of that resolution by library specialists engaged in the work of collection development and access to support the study of the communities, cultures, and languages of Europe. Members of the three Europe-focused programs administered by the Center for Research Libraries—the Slavic and East European MaterialsProject (SEEMP), https://www.crl.edu/area-studies/seemp/membership-information the Collaborative Initiative for French Language Collections (CIFNAL) https://www.crl.edu/programs/cifnal, the German-North American Resources Partnerships (GNARP) https://www.crl.edu/programs/gnarp—share the concerns around equity, representation, and access raised by our SALALM colleagues, and hereby reaffirm those concerns as they pertain to the long-term availability to North American researchers and teachers of the documentary record of the peoples, languages, and cultures of Europe—an extensive and enormously diverse geographic category having eastern and western

---

23 Centre for Research Libraries, "European Studies Statement on Collection Development, Access, and Equity in the Time of COVID-19," Accessed October 23, 2022. https://www.crl.edu/news/european-studies-statement-collection-development-access-and-equity-time-covid-19-issued-cifnal.

divisions; numerous national and subnational cultures and languages representing many ethnic categories and language families; porous shared boundaries with Africa and Asia; and an abiding cultural and linguistic consanguinity with Latin America.

We list here seven concerns surrounding current challenges and vulnerabilities in the collection development ecosystem for European Studies and scholarship originating from Europe, and three related resolutions.

1. Whereas, the majority of publications from Europe are available in print only, and cannot be licensed to North American libraries in electronic formats, and many of the ebooks that are available come with unacceptable DRM restrictions, unsustainable price models, and moving walls, hindering access to timely and useful content;

2. Whereas, collection development policies privileging ebooks generally exclude non-English language materials and a significant portion of the cultural and scholarly production from the region, including small independent presses and the voices of marginalized, minority and vulnerable communities, new social movements, and transnational authors, which are so critical to advancing research of and learning about the linguistic and cultural diversity of the European continent;

3. Whereas, the inability to lend and borrow European ebooks inter-institutionally further reduces access to critical resources available across North American libraries and directly undermines the numerous existing shared print and other cooperative collecting partnerships formed to guarantee adequate representation of the linguistic, ethnic, and cultural diversity of the European continent;

4. Whereas the output of small, independent, print-only publishers outside mainstream distribution networks in countries with legacies and/or current practice of authoritarian publishing and media control (including many in Eastern Europe and the territories of the former Soviet Union) represents a crucial category for North American collections supporting research and teaching focused on those regions, and an e-centric collection model jeopardizes adequate capture and preservation of these critical categories;

5. Whereas, a sudden shift away from collecting research materials available only in print not only threatens the integrity of diverse library collections, but also places a dedicated network of local vendors of scholarly and ephemeral research materials at risk;

6. Whereas, these vendors are important because of their expertise in specific regions and local publishing practices, and the access they provide to necessary and unique materials for learning, teaching and research that would be overlooked by larger vendors based outside of the region;

7. Whereas, while pioneering cooperative Open Access models such as the European Commission's OpenAIRE(link is external) https://explore.openaire.eu/, OpenEdition(link is external) https://www.openedition.org/ in France, REDIB(link is external) https://www.redib.net/home in Spain, OA2020(link is external) https://oa2020.org/ organized by the Max Planck Digital Library in Germany, and other initiatives have made scholarly journals from the region widely available, a gap for open monographs still exists across Europe;

Be it resolved, that the Collaborative Initiative for French Language, and the German-North American Resources Partnerships, and the Slavic and East European Materials Project, on behalf of their members:

A. Urge North American libraries to continue acquiring European print material through a network of regional vendors, often the only available sources, and thereby not limit diversity in scholarly collections.

B. Encourage collaboration and further discussion with other organizations working with international collections at a national and international level, such as the Africana Librarians Council, other divisions of the Center for Research Libraries, Council on East Asian Libraries, Middle East Librarians Association, the East Coast Consortium of Slavic Library Collections, the Pacific Coast Slavic and East European Library Consortium, the MidWest Slavic and Eurasian Library Consortium, the Association for Slavic East European and Eurasian Studies Committee on Libraries and Information Resources, and the Seminar for the Acquisition for Latin American Library Materials (SALALM), among others.

C. Advocate for continued and increased support for Open Access initiatives in European countries through the Center for Research Libraries' Collaborative Initiative for French Language Collections, German-North American Resources Partnership, Slavic and East European Materials Project, and other existing collaborative projects.

Appendix 7

CORMOSEA Statement on Collection Development, Access, and Equity in the Time of COVID-19[24]

Task force members

Judith Henchy, Carol Mitchell, Jeffrey Shane (convener and chair), and Virginia Shih.

The Committee on Research Materials on Southeast Asia (CORMOSEA) acknowledges the substantial contributions of the Seminar on the Acquisition of Latin American Library Materials (SALALM) for its pathbreaking resolution entitled Collection Development in the Time of COVID-19 on June 11, 2020, and subsequent statements by the Middle East Librarians Association (MELA) on June 22, 2020, and the Committee on South Asian Libraries and Documentation (CONSALD) on July 17, 2020.

CORMOSEA shares the same priorities, challenges, concerns, and issues regarding the scholarship, curatorship, and stewardship of the ecosystem of print and electronic resources, and the economies to support publishing in the midst of the current pandemic. We fully endorse open access initiatives and continue to advocate for library administrative support in assuring the diversity, equity, inclusion, and access to Southeast Asia scholarly resources in the United States and beyond. This statement outlines the specific challenges of collecting library resources on Southeast Asia, the collective measures that CORMOSEA will take as an international studies consortium, and those areas of national and international collaboration for which we depend on our library administrations for support.

---

24 Committee on Research Materials on Southeast Asia, "CORMOSEA Statement on Collection Development, Access, and Equity in the Time of COVID-19," Accessed October 23, 2022. https://cormosea.files.wordpress.com/2020/09/cormosea-statement-on-collection-development-2.pdf.

State of the Field: Challenges to Collecting for Southeast Asian Studies

Southeast Asia is the smallest community of Title VI-funded National Resource Centers. Its boundaries include exclusively less-commonly taught languages with some of the lowest language enrollments institutionally, such as Hmong, and nine important national languages taught at various U.S. institutions, and the annual Southeast Asian Studies Summer Institute (SEASSI) consortium.

Despite the low profile of its core learning community, Southeast Asia and Southeast Asian Studies have a large and important impact across a wide range of scholarly fields, and provide case studies of considerable interest to undergraduates across disciplines on global and social issues such as: war, ethnic conflicts, terrorism, human trafficking, human rights, gender and education equality, environmental change, public health, migration, poverty, and food security, to name a few.

The Library of Congress Jakarta office manages the Cooperative Acquisitions Program for Southeast Asia (CAP-SEA) and its sub-offices in Bangkok, Kuala Lumpur, and Manila. CAP-SEA acquires materials published in 11 Southeast Asian countries for its participating libraries in the U.S. and beyond based on subject profiles or circular title lists. However, many institutions also rely upon supplementary vendors, and the market networks that are referred to in other statements as imperiled in the current COVID-19 crisis. Onsite acquisition trips have always played a critical role in ensuring that fugitive materials are represented in our collections. Because of the linguistic diversity of the region—with over a dozen major national languages and hundreds of regional languages and scripts—Southeast Asia library collections have a history of collaboration through CORMOSEA and SEASSI.

Due to the shortage of MLIS Southeast Asia catalogers in the field, and the relatively low institutional priority of Southeast Asia collections, most libraries have hired non-MLIS library professionals, para-professionals, or student assistants to perform the Southeast Asia cataloging work, resulting in a lack of professional cataloging leadership nationally. The Library of Congress Jakarta Office offers cataloging records for Southeast Asian language materials that participating libraries acquire through CAP-SEA. However, most institutions maintain large cataloging backlogs, particularly for less-commonly collected languages, such as Burmese or Javanese. Other libraries rely on outsourcing cataloging for Burmese, Thai, and Vietnamese language materials to improve users' access to the ongoing backlogs.

Many CORMOSEA institutions rely heavily on graduate students from the region to assist in selecting and cataloging Southeast Asian language materials. Although much remains unknown, it is very likely that fewer Asian language materials.

Southeast Asia and the Institutional Responses to COVID-19

Difficulties resulting from COVID-19 have exacerbated access inequities within our institutions, particularly disadvantaging international programs such as Southeast Asian Studies, for which fewer digital resources exist, beyond the mainstream press and English language texts that serve lower level undergraduate teaching. Upper level undergraduate, professional and graduate programs require access to library resources that are currently only available in print or analog formats, including monographs, journals, newspapers on microfilm, historical data sources, and archival and special collections.

Besides the long-standing destabilizing effect of electronic journal prices, the post-COVID trend towards electronic monograph access for the general undergraduate curriculum will have the long-term effect of undermining print markets and distribution networks by diverting library resources. This trend has been adequately referenced in other statements mentioned above.

Recent national discussions around issues of equity and diversity have highlighted the need for increasing emphasis on unique institutional resources that represent minority views and cultures, bringing such resources into the scholarly mainstream and recognizing their importance to histories of disadvantaged American ethnic communities, including Southeast Asian and Pacific Island American histories. In this quest to enhance access to unique and archival sources, we recognize the need to consider access practices and rights regimes that differ from the standard copyright and licensing schema that dominate North American/European library models.

As a cooperative organization, CORMOSEA will:

- Enlist the support of relevant funding institutions—the U.S. Department of Education Title VI, American Overseas Research Centers, and the Henry Luce Foundation—to coordinate response and advocacy work in collaboration with library administrators to ensure that the role of library collections in research and teaching remain prominent in national debate.

- Continue to strengthen our communication with the Southeast Asia Council of the Association of Asian Studies, and its various country studies groups, and with academic partners in the region for collaborative initiatives, such as expanding the *Bibliography of Asian Studies* to include the increasing volume of open access journals published in the region, in exchange for expanded access to the *Bibliography* within the region.

- Collaborate with the Library of Congress offices in the region by leveraging the language and in-country expertise of CAP-SEA, together with the specialized subject and language knowledge of CORMOSEA librarians, to identify new materials for purchasing, and to ensure a cooperative model for the processing of materials into OCLC in a timely manner.

- Collaborate with the Southeast Asian Studies Summer Institute (SEASSI), the Southeast Asia Digital Library (SEADL), and the recently Luce-funded Graduate Education and Training in Southeast Asia Studies (GETSEA) to maximize our strengths for resources sharing and scholarly support.

- Partner with the Center for Research Libraries and its Southeast Asia Materials Project (SEAM) on increasing digital access to its SEAM holdings and consortial licensing of materials from the region beyond our standard institutional purchasing practices.

- Connect with international stake-holding institutions (libraries, archives, and museums) interested in creating Southeast Asia born-digital and intangible cultural heritage resources for online resource sharing through linked open data and innovative rights management.

- Seek administrative support to ensure that the significant challenges of Southeast Asian languages are represented in the American Library Association and the Library of Congress national discussions, as libraries move to BIBFRAME and linked open data, enabling more seamless access to Southeast Asia resources across formats and discovery tools.

- Reach out to the HathiTrust Digital Library, JSTOR, Artstor, Ithaka S+R, and Portico for collaborative strategies in incorporating Southeast Asian vernacular materials in those national digital depositories for institutional subscription access to and preservation of facilitated national Southeast Asia collections.

Bibliography

Association of Colleges and Research Libraries (ACRL). "ACRL Statement on Equity, Diversity, Inclusion, and the Print Collecting Imperative." Accessed August 2, 2021. https://www.ala.org/acrl/sites/ala.org.acrl/files/content/acrlissues/ACRL_Print_Collecting_Statement.pdf.

ACRL, "ACRL Statement on Equity, Diversity, Inclusion, and the Print Collecting Imperative." https://www.ala.org/acrl/sites/ala.org.acrl/files/content/acrlissues/ACRL_Print_Collecting_Statement.pdf. See Appendix 1.

Centre for Research Libraries, "European Studies Statement on Collection Development, Access, and Equity in the Time of COVID-19." Accessed October 23, 2022. https://www.crl.edu/news/european-studies-statement-collection-development-access-and-equity-time-covid-19-issued-cifnal.

Chen, Yao, Jude Yang and Tomoko Bialock. "Demystifying East Asian language monograph publishing: Contemplations on the current status, challenges, and opportunities." *The Journal of Academic Librarianship* 47, no. 4 (2021): 6. doi:10.1016/j.acalib.2021.102370.

International Studies Association (ISA). Accessed March 4, 2023. https://www.isanet.org/

Joint Area Task Force Members. "Equity and Access in Higher Education and Academic Libraries amid the COVID-19 Pandemic." (July 31, 2020). Accessed March 4, 2023. https://www.eastasianlib.org/newsite/wp-content/uploads/2020/08/Equity-and-Access-in-Higher-Education-and-Academic-Libraries-Final-August-17.pdf.

Khosrowjah, Hossein. "A Brief History of Area Studies and International Studies." *Arab Studies Quarterly* 33, no. ¾ (2011): 131-142.

Kozlowski, Michael. "The State of the European eBook Market." (March 16, 2017). Blog, https://goodereader.com/blog/e-book-news/the-state-of-the-european-ebook-market.

Li, Xiang and Tang Li. "The Evolving Responsibilities, Roles, and Competencies of East Asian Studies Librarians: A Content Analysis of Job Postings from 2008 to 2019." *College & Research Libraries* 82, no. 4 (2021): 474-489. doi: 10.5860/crl.82.4.474

Lindquist, Thea and Todd Gilman. "Academic/Research Librarians with Subject Doctorates: Data and Trends 1965-2006." *Libraries and the Academy* 8, no. 1 (2008): 31-52. doi: 10.1353/pla.2008.0008.

Ludden, David. "The Territoriality of Knowledge and the History of Area Studies." University of Pennsylvania (1997). Accessed August 1, 2021. https://www.sas.upenn.edu/~dludden/areast1.htm.

Middle East Librarians Association (MELA). "Statement." Accessed October 23, 2022. https://www.mela.us/2020/06/22/mela-statement-on-collection-development-access-and-equity-in-the-time-of-covid-19/.

Mullender, Alec and James Marnie. "Now You See It, Now You Don't: The Disappearing Collection of Western University's D.B. Weldon Library." *Canadian Journal of Academic Librarianship* 6, (2020): 1-15.

Pitman, Lesley. "Digital Resources for Area Studies." *Supporting Research in Area Studies: A Guide for Academic Libraries*. (Boston: Elsevier Science & Technology, 2016): 55-68.

Seminar on the Acquisition of Latin American Library Materials (SALALM). "Statement on SALALM Resolution: Collection Development in the Time of COVID-19." Accessed October 23, 2022. http://salalm.org/content.asp?admin=Y&contentid=485.

Spencer, Andy et al. "ASEEES CLIR Statement on Collection Development in the time of COVID-19." Accessed March 4, 2023. https://sites.google.com/site/aseeesclir/.

Statista. "Global e-book revenue from 2009 to 2016 by region." Accessed August 1, 2021. https://www.statista.com/statistics/280249/global-e-book-revenue-by-region/

The Committee on South Asian Libraries and Documentation (CONSALD), "CONSALD Statement on Collection Development, Access, and Equity in the Time of COVID-19." Accessed October 23, 2022. http://www.consald.org/covid.html

Wischenbart, Rüdiger. "European e-book barometer: A report on digital consumer publishing in Germany, Italy, The Netherlands and Spain." (2018). Accessed August 1, 2021. https://libranda.com/wp-content/uploads/2018/10/eBook_Barometer_2018.pdf.

What is the Problem with Academic Libraries?
Problematization as Political Construct

Jennifer Dekker

> "...a problem is a problem only if it can have a solution; to talk about anything else is a waste of time."[1]

Introduction

Have you noticed how often we talk about problems in academic libraries? In my workplace alone, we have discussed the problems of filling associate university librarian positions, managing the overwhelming number of print books in the stacks, budget cuts, how to make the library truly accessible for people with disabilities, and student mental health—and these are only a few of the problem identified in the past week! Problems abound. But what exactly is a problem and how does something—or someone—get defined as a problem? Whose definition of problem gets adopted in an organization? What are the impacts of labelling something a problem? And do the solutions betray a different view of the problem than what was originally imagined? It is quite often policy solutions that cause us to reflect on what constitutes a problem, especially when a solution does not seem to fit our

---

1 Carol Bacchi is referring critically to the pragmatism of David Dery and Aaron Wildavsky in this quotation. See Carol Bacchi, *Women, Policy and Politics: The Construction of Policy Problems* (London, UK: Sage, 1999), 50.

own understanding of a given problem. We likely all have examples of solutions that forced us to question what the actual problem was.

An often-recurring solution in academic libraries and in the case study presented here, is the re-org (short for the reorganization or restructuring of an academic library). A re-org is a managerial technique that purports to resolve several problems through purposeful redesign of an organization. This redesign can take different forms. For example, one academic library may be re-engineered to achieve a relatively flat reporting structure while another may be redesigned to create fewer overall departments. Organizational structure per se is not the subject here, however. We are instead examining how certain actors engage in problem representation, how problems are disseminated and reproduced in the workplace, as well as the lived effects of policy solutions. As such, I view the re-org to be neither inherently positive nor negative but rather an outcome of a particular way of framing the problem so that it would lead to that specific policy solution.

WPR: What's the Problem Represented to Be?

Carol Bachhi developed a framework for interrogating problems called What's the Problem Represented to Be. She provocatively argues that problems do not exist; that they are political constructions and not empirically verifiable. [2] Instead of using the word 'problem,' Bacchi suggests using 'problem representations' because this formulation makes it clear that we are discussing interpretations of a phenomenon and not verifiable facts.[3] WPR attempts to expose the hidden power and taken-for-granted assumptions that support problem representation.[4] It provides opportunities for insight into unarticulated values embedded both in the problem representation and proposed solutions. Bacchi argues that policy solutions are often depicted by those in power as though they are natural, obvious, and not subject

---

2   Carol Bacchi, "Deploying a Post Structural Analytic Strategy: Political Implications. Presented at the 2017 Contemporary Drug Problems Conference Keynote: Carol Bacchi," Helsinki, Finland, 2017, video, 4:33, https://www.youtube.com/watch?v=JTZ8nsu3NhA.

3   Bacchi, *Deploying a Poststructural Analytic Strategy*.

4   Mike Allen, ed., "Critical Analysis," in *The SAGE Encyclopedia of Communication Research Methods* (Thousand Oaks, CA: SAGE Publications, Inc, 2018), doi: 10.4135/9781483381411.n109.

to debate, yet they are designed to address problem representations that are neither inevitable nor infallible.[5]

WPR is based on a Foucauldian analysis of power that asks "who becomes the problem representers, whose representations get taken up, and whose voices remain unheard."[6] Careful attention to discourse—the "practices that systematically form the objects of which they speak"—is central to the method.[7] WPR examines who is entitled to speak, what is spoken, and the objects, subjects, and realities that are constructed through speech acts. Finally, WPR evaluates the lived effects of policy proposals, whether and how a particular solution is harmful or helpful and who is harmed or helped. A WPR analysis consists of six main questions:

- Q1—What's the 'problem' represented to be in a specific policy or policy proposal?

- Q2—What presuppositions or assumptions underpin this representation of the 'problem'?

- Q3—How has this representation of the 'problem' come about?

- Q4—What is left unproblematic in this problem representation? Where are the silences?

- Q5—What effects are produced by this representation of the 'problem'?

- Q6—How / where has this representation of the 'problem' been produced, disseminated and defended? How has it been (or could it be) questioned, disrupted and replaced?[8]

The final stage of analysis is to apply questions one through six to oneself, to reveal and understand one's own assumptions and values

---

5   Carol Bacchi and Susan Goodwin, "Making Politics Visible: The WPR Approach," in *Poststructural Policy Analysis: A Guide to Practice*, eds. Carol Bacchi and Susan Goodwin (New York: Palgrave Macmillan US, 2016): 13–26, doi: 10.1057/978-1-137-52546-8_2.

6   Bacchi, *Women, Policy and Politics*, 39.

7   Bacchi, 40.

8   Carol Bacchi, "Introducing the 'What's the Problem Represented to Be?' Approach," in *Engaging with Carol Bacchi. Strategic Interventions and Exchanges*, eds. Angelique Bletsas and Chris Beasley (Adelaide: University of Adelaide Press, 2012): 21–24, https://library.oapen.org/bitstream/handle/20.500.12657/33181/560097.pdf.

in the critique of the problem representation. Bacchi insists on the intellectual honesty that self-interrogation elicits. One must identify and scrutinize potential forms of domination, limitations, or repercussions of one's own problem representations as an integral element of WPR.[9]

The Case Study and its Neoliberal Context

The current study examines a problem representation at the University of Ottawa (Ontario, Canada) library which eventually led to a re-org. The University of Ottawa, with a full-time enrollment of approximately 47,000 students, is a large university in Canada's most populous province. Most universities in Canada continue to receive slightly more than half of their operating budgets from taxation but now rely on other funds like endowments, tuition, research funds, funding from private companies, interest on investments, and charitable donations to make up for operating shortfalls.[10] Canadian postsecondary institutions are subject to the same pressures thrust on international counterparts, particularly in the United Kingdom, the United States, Australia, and more recently, East Asia.[11] Such pressures are not limited to higher education but are part of the transformation of public infrastructure and services since the 1970's widely referred to as neoliberalism. Some of the expressions of neoliberalism in the postsecondary sector include administration and financial logics and techniques such as defunding programs whose graduates do not typically have high salaries.[12] There are also decreasing rates of public funding which forces institutions to increase private sources of revenue such as tuition fees and donations, stagnant or declining salaries for workers as a proportion of overall spending, over-reliance

---

9 Bacchi and Goodwin, "Making Politics Visible," 40.

10 Stephanie Ross, Larry Savage, and James Watson, "University Teachers and Resistance in the Neoliberal University," *Labor Studies Journal* 45, no. 3 (2020): 227-249, 229, doi: 10.1177/0160449X19883342.

11 Ben Kunkler, "Australian Universities Are Finance Investors With a Side Hustle in Education," *Jacobin* (magazine), September 2021, https://jacobinmag.com/2021/09/australia-universities-neoliberalism-speculation-finance-real-estate-international-students; Jung Cheol Shin and Yangson Kim, "Changing Patterns of Higher Education Governance Under Neoliberalism: Global and East Asian Perspectives," in *Higher Education Governance in East Asia: Transformations under Neoliberalism* (Singapore: Springer Singapore, 2018): 223–41.

12 Anna Fazackerley, "Ministers Could Limit Student Numbers on Lower-Earning Arts Degrees in England," *The Guardian*, October 23, 2021, sec. Education, https://www.theguardian.com/education/2021/oct/23/ministers-could-limit-student-numbers-lower-earning-art-degrees.

on precarious workers, and an infantilizing audit culture that focuses on metrics, managerial control, and performance outcomes.[13] These techniques and themes permeate academic library culture and literature as well, where topics such as "proving the value" of the academic library, or "doing more with less" are routine. Neoliberal practices have been widely employed in academic libraries with varying degrees of fervour, depending on the country.[14] Some of the most familiar are increasingly hands-on management, performance metrics, budget reductions, outsourcing, automation, and just-in-time service delivery.[15] Although re-orgs have not typically made the list of neoliberal forms in academic library literature, a 2019 conference hosted by the Canadian Association for University Teachers (CAUT) featured panels, discussions, and activities related to how to push back against re-orgs that negatively affect the culture or work for librarians and archivists and often lead to more managerial techniques, reductions in staffing, and employer manipulations of collective agreements and collegial governance structures.[16]

The Academic Library Policy Universe

In this chapter, policy refers to a set of decisions made by political actors that is intended to influence, change, frame, or solve a particular problem representation. When we hear the word policy we often think of "Big-P" policy—that is federal or provincial level public policy.[17] Laws, rules, and regulations passed by elected officials such

---

13 Jo Littler, *Against Meritocracy: Culture, Power and Myths of Mobility* (London: Routledge, 2017), doi: 10.4324/9781315712802; Henry A. Giroux, *Neoliberalism's War on Higher Education*, 2nd ed. (Chicago: Haymarket Books, 2020).

14 Petra Düren et al., "Effects of the New Public Management (NPM) and Austerity in European Public and Academic Libraries," *Journal of Library Administration* 59, no. 3 (2019): 342–57, doi: 10.1080/01930826.2019.1583019.

15 Petra Düren, Ane Landøy, and Jarmo Saarti, "New Public Management and Libraries: A Success Story or Just an Excuse for Cost Reduction," *Library Management* 38, no. 8/9 (2017): 477–87, doi: 10.1108/LM-01-2017-0005; Karen P. Nicholson, "'Being in Time': New Public Management, Academic Librarians, and the Temporal Labor of Pink-Collar Public Service Work," *Library Trends* 68, no. 2 (2019): 130–52, doi: 10.1353/lib.2019.0034.

16 A recent exception to the dearth of library literature to feature re-orgs as part of neoliberal reforms is the publication of Lydia Zvyagintseva and Tim Ribaric, "No Justice, Only Struggle: Academic Restructuring and Library Labour in Authoritarian Capitalism," *Canadian Journal of Academic Librarianship* 8 (2022): 1–24, doi: 10.33137/cjal-rcbu.v8.38423. The authors argue that library re-orgs are part of authoritarian capitalism.

17 Annette L. Gardner and Claire D. Brindis, *Advocacy and Policy Change Evaluation: Theory and Practice* (Stanford, CA: Stanford Business Books, 2017).

as progressive tax policies are one example of Big-P policy. However, "Small-P" policies operate on the organizational level and can include institution-specific policies, guidelines, internal decisions, and memoranda.[18] An important distinction between these two forms of policy is that while the public usually demands Big-P policy change to address issues that they think are important, Small-P policy making is less transparent or accountable to those affected by resulting policies. In the workplace for example, a small, select group of actors with decision-making power can change the conditions and structures of work for a much larger number of subjects who have little influence regarding the issues that policy solutions would purport to address. Workplace wellness policies are an instance of Small-P policy meant to address the problem of stress in the workplace. These policies, however, can create harm by deflecting responsibility for healthy and safe workplaces onto workers themselves. Cederström and Spicer found that privatizing and individualizing workplace stress through a wellness program actually had a negative impact on worker health because the issue of stress as a collective, whole workplace issue was whitewashed by the policy solution that viewed the problem as one of individual choices rather than as one of collective responsibility.[19] If the message that health and safety is a private issue rather than an employer responsibility is repeated and rationalized by influential and powerful people, that message becomes difficult to question and workers may ultimately internalize the problematization. WPR can help workers see the genealogy of problem representations which can provide tools for questioning and disrupting harmful policies.

Local policies are not created in isolation but are part of larger policymaking systems at international, federal, provincial, and local levels. In Canada, the policy directions of the Canadian Association of Research Libraries (CARL), the Canadian Knowledge Research Network (CKRN), and provincial associations ultimately filter down to individual institutions. At the time of writing, CARL's policies focused on "Capacity strengthening," which includes "Supporting leadership and workforce development across the broad spectrum of competencies required for success in contemporary research libraries," and "Measure impact," whose mandate includes developing "new indicators and

---

18   Gardner and Brindis, *Advocacy and Policy Change*, 22-23.

19   Carl Cederström and André Spicer, *The Wellness Syndrome* (Cambridge: Polity Press, 2018).

approaches" to demonstrate library value, among others. [20] Through these policy areas, CARL encourages a program of intensive measurement, performance outcomes, idealized worker profiles, and emphasizes control and quantification of resources to demonstrate the value of academic libraries. While these national level policies could and should be subject to a WPR analysis, I mention the policy environment here to remind readers that policies are not always developed locally to address the immediate environment but sometimes trickle down from outside institutions, funders, and governments.

Another sphere of influence is professional and academic literature in the field of Library and Information Studies. It contributes to constructing the realities in which academic libraries operate and can provide much needed symbolic and emotionally resonant justifications for certain problem representations. One especially poignant article was recommended by the Organizational Renewal Team (ORT) at the University of Ottawa during my analysis of the case study. [21] The author compared two libraries in the future: one thrived because of significant change engineered through an organizational review (described as "difficult, time-consuming, and emotionally draining work") and the other atrophied because it only changed a modest amount.[22] The message was clearly communicated; if a library does not radically restructure and change, it will inevitably meet its demise.

Other English-language articles advocating specific problem representations that resulted in library re-orgs cited repetitive and familiar concerns such as technological determinism where library workers describe having no agency in the face of overwhelming changes in technology. Others included an almost fetish-like obsession with the efficiencies to be gained from streamlining services and departments (especially library collections and acquisitions), the crushing effects of budget cuts and lack of options for responding to them, ever-changing student expectations that library workers feel they must respond to, unrelenting workloads, the urgent need to consolidate cataloguing and collection development departments, the desire for

---

20 "CARL Strengthening Capacity Committee—Terms of Reference," CARL-ABRC, November 2022, https://www.carl-abrc.ca/wp-content/uploads/2023/01/Strengthening-Capacity-Committee-Comite-sur-laccroissement-de-la-capacite-.pdf; "Measure Impact," CARL-ABRC, n.d., https://www.carl-abrc.ca/measuring-impact/.

21 The ORT was a group of workers selected by administration to make recommendations for a re-org.

22 Mary Ann Mavrinac, "A Tale of Two Libraries," Library Journal 138, no. 15 (2013): 30-32.

measurable performance targets, obstructive organizational design, frequent staff turnover, and poor communication between different library units.[23] The literature frequently conveyed a sense of crisis and a lack of control as key aspects of the problem representation. The typical response to these 'problems' was a desire for more power over workers and their labour processes including increased quantitative performance targets, the consolidation of departments, staff reductions, and the elimination of superfluous administrative layers. Many of the solutions to the problem representations were either full- or small-scale library re-orgs.

Academic library policy networks (such as CARL and CRKN) that postulate distinctive ways of problematizing combined with the professional literature (affording assumed expertise, practical rationality, and symbolism) provide decision-makers with the raw materials required for problem representations that can be difficult to critique because of the familiar and taken-for-granted symbols and language they employ. WPR can unpack these constructed realities, reveal what their purposes are within a policy proposal, and provide openings for other voices to be heard and alternative options to be considered. In the following section, we consider WPR and how to apply it.

The WPR Method

Since problem representations are often strategically hidden in policy solutions, Bacchi suggests working backward from a solution.[24] Although Bacchi developed WPR for analysis of policy texts, she notes that it could equally be applied to non-textual forms of problem representations such as buildings or ceremonies, which highlights the

---

23 Daureen Nesdill, April Love, and Maria Hunt, "From Subject Selectors to College and Interdisciplinary Teams," *Science & Technology Libraries* 29, no. 4 (2010): 307–14, doi: 10.1080//0194262X.2010.523308; Pauline Dewan and Michael Steelworthy, "Incorporating Online Instruction in Academic Libraries: Getting Ahead of the Curve," *Journal of Library & Information Services in Distance Learning* 7 (2013): 278–96, doi: 10.1080/1533290X.2013.804020; Sandra Barstow, David Macaulay, and Shannon Tharp, "How to Build a High-Quality Library Collection in a Multi-Format Environment: Centralized Selection at University of Wyoming Libraries," *Journal of Library Administration* 56 (2016): 790–809, doi: 10.1080/01930826.2015.1116336; Sarah Tusa, "Perspectives on Library Reorganization," *Serials Review* 45, no. 3 (2019): 163–66, doi: 10.1080/00987913.2019.1644483; Marwin Britto and Kirsten Kinsley, eds., *Academic Libraries and the Academy: Strategies and Approaches to Demonstrate Your Value, Impact, and Return on Investment*, Volume Two (Chicago, Ill: Association of College and Research Libraries, 2018).

24 Bacchi, *Deploying a Poststructural Analytic Strategy*.

flexibility of the method.²⁵ The case study presents a greater volume of textual documents than can be analysed in a single chapter however, so my focus will be on a limited selection of texts. The group of workers given the responsibility of recommending a new organizational design for the library—the ORT—created a central website and nearly 200 pages of published documentation over its various phases.²⁶ The *Phase I Final Report* provides the mandate and justification for the project:

> ...recommander un ou plusieurs modèle(s) organisationnels pour la Bibliothèque de l'u Ottawa qui lui permettra de renforcer sa capacité à se concentrer sur les priorités stratégiques et de répondre aux nouveaux besoins en évolution du corps enseignant, des chercheurs et des étudiants en matière de recherche et de services.²⁷

Translated, the goal was to recommend an organizational model to assist the library in strengthening its capacity to focus on strategic priorities and to respond to new and evolving needs of teaching faculty, researchers, and students as regards research and services. The Phase I Final Report is 107 pages and consists of an Executive summary, an introduction, a primer on organizational structure and design, an analysis of the former organizational structure, a description of the proposed organizational model, a section on roles and responsibilities, an explanation of major changes from the previous structure, a conclusion, references, and appendices. The appendices include recommendations for implementation, a section on aligning library priorities and the proposed model, the project's Phase I plan, and an interim report. The Phase I Final Report was authored by the ORT, which consisted of five librarians, two library technicians, and one manager who is not a librarian. They were selected according to the following criteria: three must be members of Library Council, three must be members or nominees of the Supervisors' Committee (non-librarian

---

25 Carol Bacchi, "Drug Problematizations and Politics: Deploying a Poststructural Analytic Strategy," *Contemporary Drug Problems* 45, no. 1 (2018): 3–14, doi: 10.1177/0091450917748760.

26 Stéphane Cloutier et al., "University of Ottawa Library Organizational Renewal—Phase I (Research, Analysis, and Recommendations) Interim Report" (Ottawa, ON: University of Ottawa Library, August 2016), https://uottawa.libguides.com/ld.php?content_id=25590891.

27 Stéphane Cloutier et al., "University of Ottawa Library Organizational Renewal Phase I (Research, Analysis, and Recommendations) Final Report" (Ottawa, ON: University of Ottawa, November 2016), https://apuobibliolib.wordpress.com/2021/11/22/organizational-renewal-final-report-phase-i/.

management or management-selected staff); and one must be a member of the senior administration.[28] While other library workers were afforded "engagement strategies"—opportunities for specific types of participation—the ORT members chose what to include in the report and whose opinions would be represented therein.[29] The Chair of the ORT reported on a bi-weekly basis to the "project sponsor" (the University Librarian) throughout the re-org.[30]

WPR Questions

Q1 *What's the 'problem' represented to be in a specific policy or policy proposal?*

The *Phase I Final Report* provides the context for the policy proposal: "We seek an organizational structure that will allow us to strengthen our capabilities, maximize our capacity to meet our strategic goals, and improve the effectiveness of our day to day operations. The new structure must allow for agility, flexibility, and responsiveness to change."[31] An unavailing grouping of words at first glance—abstract, imprecise, and oddly inspirational—sets the stage for the policy solution. But even at this early stage, we pick up various messages including that the current structure does not provide opportunities to strengthen capabilities or meet goals, and that it is less effective than it could be. Furthermore, the organization is assumed to be lethargic and intransigent. Two other sections of the document reveal a more focused problematization. First, although the library has changed in response to external environmental factors in previous years, it has only done so incrementally (the suggestion being that incremental change has been inadequate). The second and more elaborate explanation is the "divisional" structure of the organization, which is the "main impediment to coordinating and rationalizing services, spaces, staff, and policies."[32] The ORT therefore proposed to eliminate libraries with a faculty affiliation such as the Law library and Education

---

28 "UOttawa Library—Organizational Redesign Roadmap," November 17, 2015, https://uottawa.libguides.com/ld.php?content_id=18934370.

29 Cloutier et al., "Interim Report."

30 Cloutier et al., "Final Report," 46.

31 Cloutier et al., "Final Report," 4, para 2.

32 Cloutier et al., "Final Report," 12.

Resource Centre as separate organizational entities so that "services, spaces, staff, and policies"—also known as library functions—could be streamlined and prioritized. This change was justified because distinctive administrative structures for each library were deemed inefficient and an "impediment to progress."[33] Other supporting reasons were that managers in each library created redundancy and increased administrative costs; it was difficult to consolidate the management of collections; the subject liaison model lacked integration and was characterized by a duplication of effort; and finally, the independence of subject liaison librarians was said to be inconsistent with interdisciplinarity in the research environment.[34] These are the problem representations:

1. the former library organization was sluggish, redundant, and inefficient;

2. the former divisional structure of the organization was costly and too decentralized;

3. subject liaison roles were obstacles to achieving efficiencies and standardization and did not support interdisciplinary research.

Q2 *What presuppositions or assumptions underpin this representation of the 'problem'?*

Ross and Savage note that the neoliberal university is in a state of perpetual restructuring, requiring an ever-growing administrative workforce to perform constant strategic planning and assessment.[35] Universities have adopted the principles of private sector management using techniques that keep workers "insecure and destabilized," and prepared to accept increasing responsibility in the name of service excellence and competitiveness.[36] When viewed according to the governing logic of neoliberalism, the problem representation in Q1 assumes that subject-focused, decentralized, and independent library support undermines efficiency and requires extensive overhaul. A second

---

33 Cloutier et al., "Final Report," 12.

34 Cloutier et al., "Final Report," 13-14.

35 Stephanie Ross and Larry Savage, "Work Reorganization in the Neoliberal University: A Labour Process Perspective," *The Economic and Labour Relations Review* 32, no. 4 (2021): 495–512, doi: 10.1177/10353046211003635.

36 Ross and Savage, "Work Reorganization," 502.

assumption is that efficiency is stable, desirable, and measurable. The report states, "Efficiency is an organizational goal with a focus on inputs, use of resources, and costs…" and "Effectiveness is an organizational goal with a focus on outputs, products, or services."[37] The concept of efficiency rests largely on positivist thinking which is often associated with reductionism, quantification, and the assumption that an objective reality can be understood and perceived with the human senses. Its epistemological opposite is often considered to be constructivism which acknowledges phenomena as socially constructed rather than observable through empirical study. Within the report, the concept of efficiency appears as though it is independent of the people who work in the library and would not differ according to staffing levels or individual capabilities. As a result of centering efficiency as a structuring value and goal, the report views tailored or unique services, collections, and staff as inefficient and therefore problematic. What are missing however, are definitions and benchmarks of efficiency. Related to the logic of efficiency is that of standardization. Standardization reduces or eliminates differences to achieve efficiency. The report views standardization, consolidation, and centralized control over resources as the means of achieving desired efficiencies. It states that the freedom to "do things differently" is a "significant source of inefficiency" (without providing any examples of how), an "impediment to progress, and no longer sustainable when considering the Library as a whole."[38] The idea that custom or specialized service and support and separate administrative units such as the Law Library or the Education Resource Centre evokes the recent dismantling of Laurentian University where among other serious restructuring activities, its president terminated agreements with the federated institutions of Huntington University, Thorneloe University, and the University of Sudbury in order to provide a "more efficient delivery model" and intensify resources into programs that allegedly drew more students.[39] Similarly, Zvyagintseva and Ribaric noted that in a major restructuring at the University of Alberta, 17 faculties have been

---

37 Cloutier et al., "Final Report," 8.

38 Cloutier et al., "Final Report," 12.

39 Laurentian University, "Laurentian Federation Relationship Terminated," *Letter from the President*, April 1, 2021, https://laurentianu.info/laurentian-federation-relationship-terminated/.

collapsed into only three colleges, and that Augustana, Native Studies, and Campus Saint Jean were dropped from the organizational chart.[40]

Q3 How has this representation of the 'problem' come about?

This is perhaps the most interesting and revealing question in the case study. Reading through the entire *Phase I Final Report*, it became obvious that an assessment of the former organizational structure did not occur until after the re-org was launched. Which means that the decision to restructure was made prior to examining whether a re-org would even be appropriate. Evidence points to documentation having been created to justify a re-org rather than investigate whether such a radical solution was needed. Moreover, the ORT never performed an assessment of the library prior to the re-org that would establish a baseline for the functions that were targeted in the exercise, nor were any quantitative data ever made available to the ORT. How could improvements be proven without conducting pre- and post-re-org evaluations? Earlier, I suggested that the policy context may have been a factor and indeed several Canadian academic libraries had recently been subjected to re-orgs. CARL's policy areas at the time of the re-org were emphasizing strategies similar to the case study (especially with respect to the centralization of collection management), and peer institutions may have performed re-orgs as a way to gain efficiencies or cut budgets. It would seem that the problem representation was internally inconsistent with the policy solution.

Q4 What is left unproblematic in this problem representation? Where are the silences?

The most remarkable silence was the lack of basis for determining that a re-org was a necessary policy solution to the problem representation. The website created to communicate the re-org to an outside audience stated that its goals were to "sharpen our strategic focus and to improve our organizational effectiveness and efficiency."[41] However, since there were no data provided on how effective or efficient the library was, it is impossible to know whether the organizational structure needed change and how organizational effectiveness

---

40 Zvyagintseva and Ribaric, "No Justice, Only Struggle," 12.

41 Liz Hayden, "Renouvellement organisationnel / Organizational Renewal: FAQ," accessed December 29, 2021, https://uottawa.libguides.com/OrganizationalRenewal/faq.

and efficiency would be improved. Also silenced in the *Phase I Final Report* and official documents were dissenting perspectives, notably from library workers. The union however did meet with librarians and collected feedback with respect to how librarians were coping with the re-org, discussed below in Q5, but the ORT did no similar exercise. In fact, since the re-org, there has never been an evaluation of its impacts or achievements which is a notable silence given that its stated goals were related to library operations.

Q5   *What effects are produced by this representation of the 'problem'?*

While it is tempting to introduce competing perspectives of the problem representation, the focus in this question is on the discursive and lived effects that the problem representation creates. Both contribute to the governing of the workplace and operate through norms, rules, and practices.[42] All parties maintain these structures by tacitly reproducing them day after day—but library administration has a more visible, decisive, and directive role. The following pages describe certain lived effects of the problematization related to the policy solution.

When originally asked about their work environment, library workers communicated a desire for greater autonomy and complained about poor communication throughout the library including an intranet that was considered disorganized and unwieldy.[43] Some stated having difficulty knowing who performed what role, especially as people changed positions. Others noted that the library was overly hierarchical, and that management obstructed certain collaborative initiatives.[44] Under-staffing was also felt to be a problem as the library tried to spread itself too thin in developing new programs and service areas without having enough workers. A striking example was when 13 support staff positions were eliminated in 2009-2010, but remaining workers were told that "because of our rapid expansion, we must accomplish more despite our limited resources."[45] This feedback points to workers wanting to be seen and heard; to their desire for tools to understand and communicate about the workplace, to have more

---

42   Bacchi, "Drug Problematizations and Politics," 3-14.
43   Cloutier et al., "Interim Report," 42.
44   Hayden, "Renouvellement organisationnel / Organizational Renewal: FAQ."
45   Cloutier et al., "Final Report," 79. Author translation.

control over their work, and for the organization to be adequately staffed before embarking on ambitious projects. However, rather than focus on the change that workers wanted, library administration embarked on a wholescale re-org. As a result, the union representing librarians was approached for assistance. It published feedback from its "Listening Tour" report as follows:

> The Listening Tour took place as the Library was nearing the end of a multi-year reorganization process affecting all positions. The impact of the reorganization continues to be felt and the APUO continues to assess its impact for the longer term. ... Many librarian members felt that their workloads increased over the course of the reorganization insofar as their regular duties continued apace while they had to take on the additional work of participating in the reorganization process. Some members found themselves doing the work of two positions, essentially taking on new responsibilities while "covering off" their old positions. For others, completing their tasks often translated into having to work considerably longer hours—including evenings and weekends—than stipulated in their employment contracts.
>
> Indeed, some of the changes flowing from the library reorganization have resulted in many librarians being assigned new and additional disciplinary or subject responsibilities and, in turn, a corresponding increase in the work needed to support and resource students and faculty in their research and teaching. Others have seen their responsibilities shift and reported feeling "demoted" as work they perceive to be of high value or as a key priority shifted to other positions or were seemingly downgraded as a result of shifts in the focus of their positions. The reorganization has also led to increases in the administrative responsibilities taken on by some members, who now find themselves working with, or managing new teams with new priorities while struggling with a lack of clarity about their roles and responsibilities. As members are increasingly asked to take on new responsibilities, there does not seem to be a corresponding decrease in what they are no longer responsible for, leaving librarians noticing an increase in their workload. This, in

turn, has impacted the amount of time they can devote to their professional, academic service and scholarly activities.[46]

It should be noted that the feedback from the Listening Tour would only reflect the views of librarians and not library staff who are represented by a different union. Librarians were told that the re-org would increase capacities, efficiencies, and organizational flexibility, yet in the paragraphs above, they are demoralized by the ongoing under-staffing of the library. Not having enough workers created a high-pressure environment: there was an increased quantity of work, individuals had more areas of responsibility, and there was less time for scholarly or service activities that could provide a sense of accomplishment. Librarians mentioned the frustration over shifting responsibilities—whether that meant adding new tasks or a change in the perceived value of duties performed previously. Added to these emotional challenges was the need to adjust to a new organizational structure. Librarians were struggling psychically as well as emotionally: constructing new identities post re-org, making time to learn or add new responsibilities, while also attempting to maintain or augment competency through activities such as conferences, research, and making service contributions to their profession. Though not captured in the union's report, there were several meetings in which librarians expressed resentment at the standardization of their positions and the fact that many were transformed into entry-level positions when previously they had required more skill and education. Complexity and decision-making were often eliminated from librarian roles despite individuals in those roles having considerable training and experience in positions that had been more demanding. Some librarians were insulted and frustrated by their transformed positions.

Q6 *How/where has this representation of the 'problem' been produced, disseminated and defended? How has it been (or could it be) questioned, disrupted and replaced?*

Much of the problem representation was made in the Phase I Final Report, as well as at library town hall meetings where all staff were present, in Library Council meetings, through other focused meetings,

---

46 Association of Professors of the University of Ottawa, "Report of the 2019 Listening Tour on the Issue of Workload," (Ottawa, ON: Association of Professor of the University of Ottawa, 2021), https://apuo.ca/wp-content/uploads/2021/11/Workload-Report-Final.pdf.

a website, interviews, activities, and consultant-led workshops. The project was defended in the upper administrative decision-making bodies at the university, as well as in Library Council—one of the few spaces available for librarians to contribute well-informed critique, as most other venues were either information sessions, brainstorming meetings, or were not intended as spaces for constructive feedback. Many library workers initially supported the re-org, perhaps hopeful that it might improve areas they had identified as needing attention including organizational communication, increasing workloads, obstructive management, under-resourcing, and greater demands for technology-enhanced collections and services. But workers did not seek a re-org; there was no evidence something so radical was required and the analysis of the former organizational structure did not begin until the re-org was already underway. Nonetheless, the policy proposal was only occasionally questioned in Library Council and alternatives, if suggested, were not seriously considered. Workers were disadvantaged in terms of questioning, disrupting, or suggesting alternatives. One familiar concept that prevents critique is 'vocational awe' which rests on the assumption that libraries are inherently good and even heroic institutions; that they protect democracy and freedom of expression; that they welcome the most marginalized among us; that they are righteous or safe spaces and are thus beyond reproach—even when labour practices exploit the passion of library workers.[47] Another factor is the tacit requirement for "library nice" behaviour where gendered and racialized oppression demands that workers conform to rigid forms of workplace civility because levels of niceness are more highly valued than skill, experience, and education.[48] Davis Kendrick also revealed an ingrained expectation that workers shall not voice negative opinions or critiques of workplace culture.[49] Similarly, Freedman found that many academic librarians conflate congeniality for

---

47 Fobazi Ettarh, "Vocational Awe and Librarianship: The Lies We Tell Ourselves," *In the Library with the Lead Pipe* (blog), January 10, 2018, https://www.inthelibrarywiththeleadpipe.org/2018/vocational-awe/; Fobazi Ettarh and Chris Vidas, "'The Future of Libraries:' Vocational Awe in a 'Post-COVID' World", *The Serials Librarian* 82, no. 1-4 (2022): 17-22, doi: 10.1080/0361526X.2022.2028501.

48 Kaetrena Davis Kendrick, "Leaving the Low Morale Experience: A Qualitative Study," *Alki: The Washington Library Association Journal* 37, no. 2 (2021): 9-24, 18, https://wala.memberclicks.net/assets/Alki/Alki_July2021_FINAL.pdf. Note that CARL also prioritizes adaptation, collaboration, communication, engagement, and participation as part of its 'core' competencies for research librarians. See CARL Competencies Working Group, "Competencies for Librarians in Canadian Research Libraries" (CARL-ABRC, September 2020), https://www.carl-abrc.ca/wp-content/uploads/2020/09/Competencies-Final-EN-1-2.pdf.

49 Kendrick, "Leaving the Low Morale Experience," 9–24.

collegiality to the detriment of a truly collegial work environment.[50] Finally, general factors related to the neoliberal workplace prevent librarians from mounting critique. These include time poverty and the obvious risks to careers, especially for recently hired and equity-deserving individuals or those precariously employed.[51] In addition, a librarian might be hopeful about a sabbatical or promotion application, it might be time for an annual review, or they might require a letter of reference. Being openly critical of library administration can have serious repercussions on careers. In reflecting on how to make constructive and honest feedback more possible, the ORT might have considered the "subjective, trust, or emotional factors" for why workers may not have been open and honest with their feedback and why they might not have supported the re-org despite not openly opposing it.[52] Further, the quality of feedback that the ORT collected and selectively shared, as well as the ways in which workers were asked to participate were highly controlled and opposition could easily be whitewashed by those with an interest in and receiving benefits for continuing the project. Finally, language used to frame the problem representation made it nearly impossible to critique. When an organization, process, or department is labelled inefficient, lethargic, ineffective, and redundant by a group of employees selected and supported by the central administration, who will defend it?

Interrogating the Self[53]

The preceding analysis is based on my experiences as an academic librarian at the University of Ottawa Library as a mid-career, unionized, non-administrative library worker who values academic and professional autonomy. My direct participation in the re-org was limited due to my term as President of the Association of Professors of the

---

50 Shin Freedman, "Collegiality Matters: How Do We Work With Others?" in *Proceedings of the Charleston Library Conference*, 377-385 (SC: Charleston, 2009). https://docs.lib.purdue.edu/charleston/2009/Management/2/.

51 Maggie Berg and Barbara Karolina Seeber, *The Slow Professor: Challenging the Culture of Speed in the Academy*. (Toronto: University of Toronto Press, 2017); Nicholson, "Being in Time."

52 Nancy B. Turner, "When Numbers Are Not Enough: Using Assessment toward Organizational Change," in *Academic Libraries and the Academy: Strategies and Approaches to Demonstrate Your Value, Impact, and Return on Investment*, edited by Marwin Britto and Kirsten Kinsley, 520–2. Volume Two (Chicago, Ill: Association of College and Research Libraries, 2018), 9.

53 The following section follows Bacchi's six questions without specifically stating each question.

University of Ottawa (APUO) from 2015-2017, the period during which much of the re-org planning occurred. I rarely had opportunities to attend meetings or presentations related to the exercise. After two years as union President, I took a twelve-month academic leave where I performed no professional activities related to my role as a librarian, which ensured even more distance from the re-org. In 2019, I returned to a workplace that was in the final phase of restructuring. However I noted almost immediately that the re-org appeared to have manifested some of the unattractive elements identified by Ross and Savage in their discussion of work reorganization in the neoliberal university.[54] These included a loss of autonomy for many librarians, the development of a more powerful centralized administration, an increased number of mid-level managers, heightened pressure for a greater number of meetings with no clear objectives, and new attempts at performance measurement (which colleagues have so far successfully thwarted).

This tension between my advocacy for the professional autonomy of librarians and the reality of labouring daily in a system that provides me with certain possibilities for making improvements to it, is embedded in this analysis. My longstanding engagement with my union and the CAUT has intensified my critique of the ways in which universities are managed in Canada—especially with respect to the rise of corporatization and neoliberalism. There are too many examples to list here, but I will provide a few that readers may find familiar. First, the proliferation of sub-contractors and part-time workers: whether in the classroom, in the cafeteria, cleaning offices, or doing payroll, part-time and contract workers tend to earn lower wages and have access to fewer benefits than those in full-time, continuing employment. Second, the student debt crisis in Canada. One fall term, a colleague and I asked dozens of students how many hours a week they worked to afford their university costs. The lowest number was 17 and the highest was 40. Students work far too many hours every week to pay tuition because of provincial defunding of the postsecondary system. Lastly, the ballooning of upper administration: most universities have vastly increased the numbers of vice-presidents, vice-deans, and other senior administrative positions (including three additional Associate University Librarian positions in my own workplace since the re-org)

---

54   Ross and Savage, "Work Reorganization."

while the number of full-time, regular positions remains the same and the number of precarious workers increases. This is a very expensive choice, and one which students and workers often challenge. These few examples demonstrate some of the characteristics of the neoliberal university against which individuals, especially those deeply committed to their unions and / or to social justice and organizations such as CAUT are systematically battling. Because of changes I have witnessed in universities over the past twenty years, my positioning as a rank-and-file worker, my experience as a union activist, and my skeptical nature, I always viewed the problem representation that led to the re-org with a very critical eye. I rejected and continue to reject the notion that skilled library workers with considerable expertise in their field should perform standardized tasks as though complexity leads to excessive time wastage and lack of efficiency. I question the need for intrusive, hands-on, infantilizing styles of management and performance evaluation which have taken root since the re-org. I advocate for academic and professional autonomy even when odds are stacked so firmly against it. Ultimately, the re-centering of academic and professional autonomy requires the rejection of neoliberalism and corporatism, an overhaul of the taxation system so that universities can operate with consistently reliable and adequate funding, and a major shift in the way the public understands and values education in society. These are not likely to occur soon, so in the meantime, approaches that focus on achievable goals are usually preferable. The compromise I have found is to assert the rights that workers have within the existing system and to push for more capacity for collective critique. WPR is one technique that might assist in this goal.

Approximately 200 pages of text were published in support of the re-org project at one time or another as well as the creation of a central website. These converged to construct a certain reality, a specific 'problem', and one single solution—the re-org. One of the overarching messages from the documentation was that faculty-affiliated libraries and specialist librarians were far too independent and therefore inefficient. The ORT suggested that tasks be fragmented, separated into small parts, and consolidated in various positions so that job descriptions were focused on a single function rather than on providing many services centred on a discipline. As someone with many family members who worked in the Canadian automotive industry, this reminded me of the factory floor where workers perform the same repetitive task all day because it is cost-effective. Both the standardization of tasks and the fragmentation of labour—stripping the "whole" of academic librarianship into parts that different workers in various departments perform routinely are strategies to increase productivity—or in the nomenclature of the Phase 1 Final Report—increase capacity and efficiency. Unique or time-consuming work such as reference service, collection development or cataloguing, where every interaction is different, are "artifact[s] of the print-dependent world," and anyone who works in an academic library today knows what happens to print: it is moved off campus or discarded.[55] Yet studies going back more than 50 years validate findings that a scientific approach to management which upholds "managerial authority, worker specialism, clear divisions of labour, rules and regulations, and a separation of conception and execution" creates inefficiency and worker alienation.[56] They also affirm that autonomous worker groups guided by clear boundaries provide greater worker satisfaction, increased efficiencies, and higher quality of life.

A classic example of the demise of specialist labour is that of craftspeople in the medieval period.[57] They formed guilds to restrict entry into their crafts, self-regulated their professions through collective standards, innovated their own practices from within, and in so doing, carefully protected their work. Early in the twentieth century however, industrial capitalists pierced through the tightly protected guild system—which later became trade unions—and chipped away at specialized craft processes until they could be broken down into smaller, simpler tasks that could be performed by cheaper workers.[58] There is a strong parallel in this example to the disaggregation of librarianship where outsourcing of labour to less costly workers—whether technicians or private companies for outsourcing—is a common occurrence. Other impacts that flowed from the breakdown of the guild and trade unions was the availability of previously specialized knowledge to the management sphere, the restructuring of work into more

---

55 Cheryl LaGuardia, "What Do We Need to Stop Doing? A Survey | Not Dead Yet," *Library Journal* (June 23, 2016): 4. https://www.libraryjournal.com/story/what-do-we-need-to-stop-doing-a-survey-not-dead-yet.

56 David Guest, Angela Knox, and Chris Warhurst, "Humanizing Work in the Digital Age: Lessons from Socio-Technical Systems and Quality of Working Life Initiatives," *Human Relations* 75, no. 8 (2022): 1461–82, doi: 10.1177/00187267221092674.

57 Ross and Savage, "Work Reorganization."

58 Ross and Savage, 497.

operationally efficient units, and the alienation of workers from their own labour who no longer had control over their work or working conditions.

Like craft workers, the independence of subject liaison librarians was attacked by the ORT and labelled inefficient: "an impediment to progress, and no longer sustainable."[59] The Phase I Final Report stated that "positions that support specialized scholarly needs are modeled on the highly independent liaison approach despite the scope and interdisciplinarity of these positions. Our current structure positions librarians to be independent operators in a world of connectedness."[60] Prior to the re-org, subject liaison librarians, especially those working in faculty-affiliated libraries, had relatively insulated relationships with instructors and students, substantial control over their work and contributions to educational programs, considerable familiarity with departments' research and teaching areas, and could be selective regarding what to share with the rest of the organization.

However, the ORT advocated for a different model of librarianship, specifying that no one librarian would be a single point of contact for a specific department, school, or faculty; their work could be done individually or in teams according to what library users preferred instead of the librarian using their professional judgment regarding how to perform tasks. Librarians were now expected to transfer their knowledge beyond department and faculty boundaries to allow for "better" service and partnerships with instructors and students.[61] Note however that librarians have little professional agency in this new way of operating.

Conclusion

This chapter illustrates how WPR might activate worker critique where policy solutions—be they re-orgs, equity strategies, wellness programs, or anything else—do not seem to fit the problems they claim to address. WPR provides the tools to systematically interrogate messages and policy solutions that are framed and coded in language and symbols that subjects are not expected to question. In academic

---

59   Cloutier et al., "Final Report," 12.

60   Cloutier et al., "Final Report," 14. Emphasis original.

61   Cloutier et al., "Final Report," 19.

libraries, these policy solutions can range from very specific things such as how to catalogue collections to very broad policies such as how to use space or make a building accessible. Policy proposals are typically presented as helpful ways to address challenges, but thorough attention to proposals can reveal who and what decision-makers think the problems really are and open space for further debate. In the case study, the problem representations included statements that the former library organization was sluggish, redundant, and inefficient; the former divisional structure of the organization was costly and too decentralized; that subject liaison roles were obstacles to achieving efficiencies and standardization and were inconsistent with interdisciplinary research. WPR helped to unpack these problematizations and reveal that subject liaison librarian roles and faculty-affiliated libraries that offered specialized support and services were the main problems for administrators. The language of organizational efficiency and agility was used to construct the idea that the entire library was inefficient; to create a problem that required a particular solution.

Readers should remember that re-orgs are a technique that employers use to destabilize workers and control their labour, so any re-org proposal ought to be seriously examined by affected workers and their unions.[62] Many academic libraries have recently or are currently being reorganized with the most drastic example being the Ontario College of Art and Design University (OCAD U) library where several positions disappeared from the organizational chart altogether.[63] WPR is one tool that can help workers reveal what underlies problem representations so that we may better defend our work and our institutions against the ongoing crush of neoliberal reforms, and take back some of the agency that the past few decades have stolen from workers.

---

62 Ross and Savage, "Work Reorganization."

63 Brenda Austin-Smith and David Robinson, "Re: Decision to Terminate Four Senior Librarians," letter to Ana Serrano on behalf of CAUT, May 14, 2021, https://www.caut.ca/latest/2021/05/caut-objects-decision-lay-four-senior-librarians-ocad-university.

Bibliography

Association of Professors of the University of Ottawa. 2021. "Report of the 2019 Listening Tour on the Issue of Workload." Ottawa, ON: Association of Professor of the University of Ottawa. https://apuo.ca/wp-content/uploads/2021/11/Workload-Report-Final.pdf.

Austin-Smith, Brenda, and David Robinson. 2021. "RE: Decision to Terminate Four Senior Librarians and Eliminate Two Library Positions at OCAD U." CAUT. Accessed July 18, 2022. https://ocadfa.ca/wp-content/uploads/2021/05/CAUT-to-A.-Serrano-OCAD-re.-decision-to-terminate-4-senior-librarians-and-2-library-positions-at-OCADU-2021-05-14.pdf.

Bacchi, Carol. *Women, Policy and Politics: The Construction of Policy Problems.* London, UK: Sage, 1999.

Bacchi, Carol. "Introducing the 'What's the Problem Represented to Be?' Approach." In *Engaging with Carol Bacchi. Strategic Interventions and Exchanges*, edited by Angelique Bletsas and Chris Beasley, 21–24. Adelaide: University of Adelaide Press., 2012. https://library.oapen.org/bitstream/handle/20.500.12657/33181/560097.pdf.

Bacchi, Carol. "Drug Problematizations and Politics: Deploying a Poststructural Analytic Strategy." *Contemporary Drug Problems* 45, no. 1 (2018): 3–14. doi: 10.1177/0091450917748760.

Bacchi, Carol, and Susan Goodwin. "Making Politics Visible: The WPR Approach." In *Poststructural Policy Analysis: A Guide to Practice*, edited by Carol Bacchi and Susan Goodwin, 13–26. New York: Palgrave Macmillan US, 2016. doi: 10.1057/978-1-137-52546-8_2.

Barstow, Sandra, David Macaulay, and Shannon Tharp. "How to Build a High-Quality Library Collection in a Multi-Format Environment: Centralized Selection at University of Wyoming Libraries." *Journal of Library Administration* 56, no. 7 (2016): 790–809. doi: 10.1080/01930826.2015.1116336.

Berg, Maggie, and Barbara Karolina Seeber. *The Slow Professor: Challenging the Culture of Speed in the Academy.* Toronto: University of Toronto Press, 2017.

Britto, Marwin, and Kirsten Kinsley, eds. *Academic Libraries and the Academy: Strategies and Approaches to Demonstrate Your Value, Impact, and Return on Investment.* Volume Two. Chicago, Ill: Association of College and Research Libraries, 2018.

CARL-ABRC. "CARL Strengthening Capacity Committee—Terms of Reference," November 2022. https://www.carl-abrc.ca/wp-content/uploads/2023/01/Strengthening-Capacity-Committee-Comite-sur-laccroissement-de-la-capacite-.pdf.

CARL-ABRC. "Measure Impact." https://www.carl-abrc.ca/measuring-impact/.

CARL Competencies Working Group. "Competencies for Librarians in Canadian Research Libraries." CARL-ABRC, September 2020. https://www.carl-abrc.ca/wp-content/uploads/2020/09/Competencies-Final-EN-1-2.pdf.

"CAUT Letter RE: Decision to Terminate Four Senior Librarians and Eliminate Two Library Positions at OCADU." Accessed July 18, 2022. https://ocadfa.ca/blog/2021/05/15/caut-letter-re-decision-to-terminate-four-senior-librarians-and-eliminate-two-library-positions-at-ocadu/.

Cederström, Carl, and André Spicer. *The Wellness Syndrome*. Cambridge: Polity Press, 2018.

Cloutier, Stéphane, Liz Hayden, Margo Jeske, Katrine Mallan, Catherine McGoveran, McKinnon, Christian, Anthony Petryk, and Thomas Rouleau. "University of Ottawa Library Organizational Renewal—Phase I (Research, Analysis, and Recommendations) Interim Report." Ottawa, ON: University of Ottawa Library, 2016. https://uottawa.libguides.com/ld.php?content_id=25590891.

Cloutier, Stéphane, Liz Hayden, Margo Jeske, Katrine Mallan, Catherine McGoveran, McKinnon, Christian, Anthony Petryk, and Thomas Rouleau. "University of Ottawa Library Organizational Renewal Phase I (Research, Analysis, and Recommendations) Final Report." Ottawa, ON: University of Ottawa, 2016. https://apuobibliolib.wordpress.com/2021/11/22/organizational-renewal-final-report-phase

"Critical Analysis." In *The SAGE Encyclopedia of Communication Research Methods*, 295–96. Edited by Mike Allen. Thousand Oaks, CA: SAGE, 2018. doi: 10.4135/9781483381411.n109.

Deploying a Poststructural Analytic Strategy: Political Implications. Presented at the 2017 Contemporary Drug Problems Conference Keynote: Carol Bacchi. 2017. Helsinki, Finland. https://www.youtube.com/watch?v=JTZ8nsu3NhA.

Dewan, Pauline, and Michael Steelworthy. "Incorporating Online Instruction in Academic Libraries: Getting Ahead of the Curve." *Journal of Library & Information Services in Distance Learning* 7, no. 3 (2013): 278–96. doi: 10.1080/1533290X.2013.804020.

Düren, Petra, Stéphane Goldstein, Ane Landøy, Angela Repanovici, and Jarmo Saarti. "Effects of the New Public Management (NPM) and Austerity in European Public and Academic Libraries." *Journal of Library Administration* 59, no. 3 (2019): 342–57. doi: 10.1080/01930826.2019.1583019.

Düren, Petra, Ane Landøy, and Jarmo Saarti. "New Public Management and Libraries: A Success Story or Just an Excuse for Cost Reduction." *Library Management* 38, no. 8-9 (2017): 477–87. doi: 10.1108/LM-01-2017-0005.

Ettarh, Fobazi. "Vocational Awe and Librarianship: The Lies We Tell Ourselves." *In the Library with the Lead Pipe* (blog). January 10, 2018, https://www.inthelibrarywiththeleadpipe.org/2018/vocational-awe/.

Ettarh, Fobazi, and Chris Vidas. "The Future of Libraries:" Vocational Awe in a "Post-COVID" World, *The Serials Librarian*, 82, no. 1-4 (2022): 17-22, doi: 10.1080/0361526X.2022.2028501.

Fazackerley, Anna. "Ministers Could Limit Student Numbers on Lower-Earning Arts Degrees in England." *The Guardian*, October 23, 2021, sec. Education. https://www.theguardian.com/education/2021/oct/23/ministers-could-limit-student-numbers-lower-earning-art-degrees.

Freedman, Shin. "Collegiality Matters: How Do We Work With Others?"*Proceedings of the Charleston Library Conference*, 377-385. SC: Charleston, 2009. https://docs.lib.purdue.edu/charleston/2009/Management/2/.

Gardner, Annette L., and Claire D. Brindis. *Advocacy and Policy Change Evaluation: Theory and Practice*. Stanford, CA: Stanford Business Books, 2017. https://web-p-ebscohost-com.proxy.bib.uottawa.ca/ehost/ebookviewer/ebook?sid=7ad6db58-945f-441f-83fb-010ecf7f87e9%40redis&vid=0&format=EB.

Giroux, Henry A. *Neoliberalism's War on Higher Education*. 2nd ed. Chicago: Haymarket Books, 2020.

Guest, David, Angela Knox, and Chris Warhurst. "Humanizing Work in the Digital Age: Lessons from Socio-Technical Systems and Quality of Working Life Initiatives." *Human Relations* 75, no. 8 (2022): 1461–82. https://doi.org/10.1177/00187267221092674.

Hassel, Anke. "Public Policy." In *International Encyclopedia of the Social & Behavioral Sciences*, edited by James D. Wright, 2nd ed., 569–75. Amsterdam: Elsevier, 2015. http://www.sciencedirect.com/science/article/pii/B978008097086875029X.

Hayden, Liz. 2016. "Renouvellement Organisationnel / Organizational Renewal: FAQ." Accessed December 28, 2021. https://uottawa.libguides.com/OrganizationalRenewal/faq.

Kendrick, Kaetrena Davis. "Leaving the Low Morale Experience: A Qualitative Study." *Alki: The Washington Library Association Journal* 37, no. 2 (2021): 9–24.

Kunkler, Ben. "Australian Universities Are Finance Investors With a Side Hustle in Education." *Jacobin*. September 2021. https://jacobinmag.com/2021/09/australia-universities-neoliberalism-speculation-finance-real-estate-international-students.

LaGuardia, Cheryl. "What Do We Need to Stop Doing? A Survey | Not Dead Yet." *Library Journal*, Opinion. June 23, 2016. https://www.libraryjournal.com/story/what-do-we-need-to-stop-doing-a-survey-not-dead-yet.

Laurentian University. "Laurentian Federation Relationship Terminated." *Letter from the President*, April 1, 2021. https://laurentianu.info/laurentian-federation-relationship-terminated/.

"Library's Organizational Renewal Project." Accessed November 10, 2021. https://biblio.uottawa.ca/en/about/projects/library-organizational-renewal.

Littler, Jo. *Against Meritocracy: Culture, Power and Myths of Mobility*. London: Routledge, 2017. doi: 10.4324/9781315712802.

Mavrinac, Mary Ann. "A Tale of Two Libraries." *Library Journal*, September 15, 2013.

Nesdill, Daureen, April Love, and Maria Hunt. "From Subject Selectors to College and Interdisciplinary Teams." *Science & Technology Libraries* 29, no. 4 (2010): 307–14. doi: 10.1080/0194262X.2010.523308.

Nicholson, Karen P. "'Being in Time': New Public Management, Academic Librarians, and the Temporal Labor of Pink-Collar Public Service Work." *Library Trends* 68, no. 2 (2019): 130–52. doi: 10.1353/lib.2019.0034.

Ross, Stephanie, and Larry Savage. "Work Reorganization in the Neoliberal University: A Labour Process Perspective." *The Economic and Labour Relations Review* 32, no. 4 (2021): 495–512. doi: 10.1177/10353046211003635.

Ross, Stephanie, Larry Savage, and James Watson. "University Teachers and Resistance in the Neoliberal University." *Labor Studies Journal* 45, no. 3 (2020): 227–49. doi: 10.1177/0160449X19883342.

Shin, Jung Cheol, and Yangson Kim. "Changing Patterns of Higher Education Governance Under Neoliberalism: Global and East Asian Perspectives." In *Higher Education Governance in East Asia: Transformations under Neoliberalism*, 223–41. Singapore: Springer Singapore, 2018.

Turner, Nancy B. "When Numbers Are Not Enough: Using Assessment toward Organizational Change." In *Academic Libraries and the Academy: Strategies and Approaches to Demonstrate Your Value, Impact, and Return on Investment*, edited by Marwin Britto and Kirsten Kinsley, Vol. Two: 520–29. Chicago, Ill: Association of College and Research Libraries, 2018.

Tusa, Sarah. "Perspectives on Library Reorganization." *Serials Review* 45, no. 3 (2019): 163–66. doi: 10.1080/00987913.2019.1644483.

"UOttawa Library–Organizational Redesign Roadmap." 2015. https://uottawa.libguides.com/ld.php?content_id=18934370.

Winter, Richard. "Academic Manager or Managed Academic? Academic Identity Schisms in Higher Education." *Journal of Higher Education Policy and Management* 31, no. 2 (2009): 121–31. doi: 10.1080/13600800902825835.

Perpetuating a Gendered Profession
An Empirical Deconstruction of the Job Openings for Academic Librarians at the University of Toronto from 1985 to 2021

Guenther Lomas, Jessica Shiers, Harriet M. Sonne de Torrens, Joanna Szurmak, and Meaghan Valant

Introduction

Gender discrimination within academic librarianship has deep roots in the history of the profession and female labour in Canada that can be traced back to the early decades of the twentieth century and to the development of the professional educational programs for librarianship.[1] The history of academic librarianship at the University of Toronto (U of T) has remained a relatively silent partner in the published histories of the University, the University of Toronto Library (UTL) system and the seven affiliated colleges (Innis College, New College, St. Michael's College, Trinity College, University College, Victoria College

---

1 Lorne Bruce, "Professionalization, Gender, and Librarianship in Ontario, 1920-75," *Library & Information History* 28, no. 2 (2012): 117-34; Harriet Sonne de Torrens, "Academic Librarianship: The Quest for Rights and Recognition at the University of Toronto," in *In Solidarity: Academic Librarian Labour Activism and Union Participation in Canada*, edited by Jennifer Dekker and Mary Kandiuk, 81-102, 314-324 (Sacramento, CA: Library Juice Press, 201). In the nineteenth century, academic librarianship was a male occupation. In 1876, Melvil Dewey noted, "[t]he time has at last come when a librarian may, without assumption, speak of his occupation as a profession," see M. Dewey, "The Profession," *American Library Journal* I (1876): 5-6. The last quarter of the nineteenth century was when library work was professionalized, with the visible signs of library schools opening (first in 1887) and organization of the American Library Association in 1876, see Joanne E. Passet, "Men in a Feminized Profession: The Male Librarian, 1887-1921," *Libraries & Culture* 28, no. 4 (1993): 385-402, 386; Lorne D. Bruce, "From Library Work to Library Science: Forming Canadian Librarianship, 1920-1960," Partnership: *The Canadian Journal of Library* and *Information Practice and Research* 14, Iss. 1 (2019): 1-41. doi:10.21083/partnership.v14i1.4752

and Woodsworth College).[2] In some respects, this is surprising, given that U of T is one of the largest and oldest post-secondary institutions in Canada (established in 1849) and with a global library collection, built by librarians, that rivals the top major Ivy League collections in North America. The UTL system has consistently employed the largest number of librarians in Canada compared to other post-secondary institutions. Librarians are appointed in the forty-two libraries on three campuses and support the teaching and research requirements of "over 300 graduate programs, with more than 70 professional programs, and about 700 undergraduate degree programs. There are more than 15 million volumes in 341 languages in the 42 libraries."[3]

From a broader perspective, however, the relatively silent history of U of T librarianship corresponds to the low profiles that librarians have had on Canadian academic campuses and to the way academic libraries are considered expensive cost centres rather than pivotal academic units of knowledge, an increasingly prominent ideology within the corporatization of academia.[4] In the last thirty years (1991 to 2021), 74% of the librarians holding full-time positions at the University of Toronto have consistently been female. This exceeds the understood average of 69.5% females in the *Association of Research Libraries Annual Salary Survey 2021*.[5]

The statistical evidence of predominantly female librarians over the decades at the University of Toronto raises equity questions. It is known, for example, in other female dominated professions, such as nursing, teaching, and social media jobs, that men receive higher salaries compared to their female counterparts.[6] Similar findings have been reported in the library profession with male librarians receiving higher salaries

---

2   Robert H. Blackburn, *Evolution of the Heart: A History of The University of Toronto Library up to 1981* (Toronto: University of Toronto Press, 1989).

3   The description of the UTL system is from the job posting, Associate Librarian, Collections and Research Services (Librarian III), at the University of Toronto Mississauga, February 2021.

4   Lisa Sloniowski, "Affective Labor, Resistance, and the Academic Librarian," *Library Trends* 64, no. 6 (2016): 645-666.

5   University of Toronto, *Facts & Figures, (2010 to 2021)*, https://data.utoronto.ca/facts-and-figures/ The publication no longer lists part-time librarians; Anam Mian, ARL Annual Salary Survey 2021, Association of Research Libraries, https://doi-org.myaccess.library.utoronto.ca/10.29242/salary.2021.

6   Shiliang Tang, "Understanding Unconscious Bias by Large-scale Data Analysis" (PhD diss., University of California, 2019), 78.

than their female counterparts.[7] Low morale in the workplace increases the risk of professionals seeking employment in other sectors, as has been recently observed in the diminishing numbers in the Canadian nursing profession.[8] At U of T librarians' minimum salaries are below faculty, teaching stream and comparable non-unionized managerial ranks, even though many librarians have, in addition to the professional master's degree in information studies, advanced degrees in management, law, the sciences, the humanities and the social sciences.[9] In addition, it has been shown that men are drawn to stereotypical female occupations because there is a view that there are more opportunities for promotion given the gender biases, which, in turn, reinforces the gender discrimination.[10] Stereotypes, as the historically feminized profession of librarianship, are especially suited to justifying these inequalities.[11]

Given the consistently high percentage of female librarians in the UTL system, the researchers were interested in determining to what extent gendered language has been incorporated into the job advertisements.

---

7   Nicole Eva, Mê-Linh Lê, John Sheriff, "Less Money, Less Children, and Less Prestige: Differences between Male and Female academic Librarians," *Journal of Academic Librarianship* 47 (2021), 1-11 (p. 5). doi: https://doi.org/10.1016/j.acalib.2021.102392 ; Eva O. Arceo-Gomez, Raymundo M. Campos-Vazquez, Raquel Y. Badillo and Sergio Lopez-Araiza, "Gender Stereotypes in Job Advertisements: What do They Imply for the Gender Salary Gap?," *Journal of Labor Research* 43 (2022), 65–102.

8   Meredith Schwartz, "Women's Work: What If No One Wants To Work (Here) Anymore?," *Library Journal* 147, Iss. 10 (2022): 6; for the recent feminization of social media employment, see B. E. Duffy and B. Schwartz, "Digital "Women's Work?": Job Recruitment Ads and the Feminization of Social Media Employment," *New Media & Society* 20, no. 8 (2018): 2972-2989. doi: https://doi.org/10.1177/1461444817738237

9   In the 2018 Canadian Association of Professional Academic Librarians census notes that academic librarians in Canada in addition to the required masters degree in Information Studies, 56.85% have a second masters degree, 3.27% a third masters degree, 10.63% have a PhD, 13.29% have an additional professional degree (law, etc.) and 45.19% have additional certificates and diplomas, https://capalibrarians.org/wp/wp-content/uploads/2019/03/2018_Census_March_24_2019.pdf

10 Ben Lupton, "Explaining Men's Entry into Female-Concentrated Occupations: Issues of Masculinity and Social Class," *Gender, Work, and Organization* 13, no. 2 (2006): 103–28.

11 Aaron C. Kay, Szymon Czaplinski and John T. Jost, "Left-right Ideological Differences in System Justification following Exposure to Complementary Versus Noncomplementary Stereotype Exemplars," *European Journal of Social Psychology* 39 (2009): 290–98. doi:10.1002/ejsp.500; Nicolas Kervyn, Vincent Y. Yzerbyt, Charles M. Judd and Ana Nunes, "A Question of Compensation: The Social Life of the Fundamental Dimensions of Social Perception," *Journal of Personality and Social Psychology* 96, no. 4 (2009): 828-842; Danielle Gaucher, Justin Friesen, and Aarun C. Kay, "Evidence that Gendered Wording in Job Advertisements Exists and Sustains Gender Inequality", *Journal of Personality and Social Psychology* 101, issue no. 1 (2011): 109-128.

Words have meaning, conscious or subliminal.[12] This study uses content analysis to examine 355 academic librarian job openings that were advertised from 1985 to December 2021 and issued by the libraries in the University of Toronto Library (UTL) system. During this 36-year period, the UTL system has had two Chief librarians, 1) Carole Moore (1985-2011) and 2) Larry Alford (2011-present), henceforth referred to as CL1 and CL2.[13] The year of transition (2010-2011), when the leadership changed from CL1 to CL2, surprisingly, introduced decisive turning points in the results of the analysis of the job advertisements.

This study examines the use of gendered and stereotypical language in librarian job ads at the University of Toronto. First, we examine hiring trends in entry-level job postings over time. Second, we examine the extent to which gendered language is used in job ads for librarians. Third, we investigate the degree of undervalued managerial and pedagogical responsibilities in the librarian job ads at the University.

Literature Review

Content analysis of job advertisements has been used in library science studies dating back to the 1950s. Studies have focused primarily on job changes within the profession. A few cases have explored the effects of listing character traits in job ads, as well as the hiring trends of subject specialists, digital or electronic librarians, technical services and other specialized areas of academic librarianship.[14] Few studies, however, have focused on a single Canadian institution over a lengthy period of time and even fewer have employed artificial intelligence as a tool for analyzing the content of the postings.

---

12 Tang, "Understanding Unconscious Bias."; Gaucher et al., "Evidence that Gendered Wording in Job Advertisements Exists,"; Rayla E. Tokarz, Tati Mesfin, "Stereotyping Ourselves: Gendered Language Use in Management and Instruction Library Job Advertisements," *Journal of Library Administration* 61, no. 3 (2021), 301-311 (p. 301).

13 John Papadopoulos, "New UofT Chief Librarian," *Slaw: Canada's Online Legal Magazine*, August 3, 2011. https://www.slaw.ca/2011/08/03/new-uoft-chief-librarian/

14 Rayla E. Tokarz, "Creative, Innovative and Collaborative Librarians Wanted: The Use of Personality Traits in Librarian Job Advertisements," *Library Philosophy and Practice* (2019): 1-21. https://digitalcommons.unl.edu/libphilprac/2463 ; Akhilesh K. S.Yadav, "Key Skills and Competencies of LIS Professionals in the Digital Library Environment: A Content Analysis of Job Advertisements," *Library Management*; Bradford 43, Iss. ½ (2022): 50-65; Ildiko Kovacs and Kornelia Vamosi Zarandne, "Digital Marketing Employability Skills in Job Advertisements—Must Have Soft Skills for Entry-Level Workers: A Content Analysis," *Economics & Sociology* 15, Iss. 1 (2022): 178-192.

Gender analysis of librarians' job postings has been an active area of research for the past twenty years.[15] Especially in recruitment practices, which some researchers suggest are responsible for reinforcing gender biases.[16] The subject of ideal personality traits for librarians has been of interest to some researchers for the past decade, with mixed perspectives from candidates, who in some cases were less attracted to positions which emphasize these traits.[17] Interestingly, in the Gender-Decoder, discussed below and used for previous analysis of librarians' job postings, there is a pronounced emphasis on personality characteristics in the lexicon utilized.

Technology has played an increasingly prominent role in the assessment of gendered language in postings.[18] This study's application of artificial intelligence (AI) to the content analysis of the job advertisements, however, is relatively unique, as there have been few similar studies undertaken. This may be due to the size of datasets available for most studies. AI has been used primarily to examine the automation of library resources, legal significance and services, library operations and the supporting role of librarians in the use of AI in academic communities.[19] There is little scholarship on the use of AI in the

---

15   Ronald Beaudrie and Robert Grunfeld, "Male Reference Librarians and the Gender Factor," *Reference Librarian* 33 (1991): 211-213; Lupton, "Explaining Men's Entry into Female-Concentrated Occupations,"; Adeola Adesoji Arinola and F. Oyewusi, "Gender Influence on Managerial Efficiency of Academic Librarians in Nigeria," *Gender and Behaviour* 7, no. 1 (2009): 2317-2329. doi: 10.4314/gab.v7i1.45048 ; Gaucher et al., "Evidence that Gendered Wording in Job Advertisements exists ,"; Tang, "Understanding Unconscious Bias."

16   Inger Askehave and Karen Korning Zethsen, "Gendered Constructions of Leadership in Danish Job Advertisements," *Gender, Work and Organization*, Vol. 21 No. 6 (November 2014): 531-545.

17   Janine Bosak and Sabine Sczesny, "Am I the Right Candidate? Self-Ascribed Fit of Women and Men to a Leadership Position," *Sex Roles* 58, Iss. 9-10 (2008): 682–688. https://doi.org/10.1007/s11199-007-9380-4; Susan A. Henricks and Genevieve M. Henricks-Lepp, "Desired Characteristics of Management and Leadership for Public Library Directors as Expressed in Job Advertisements," *Journal of Library Administration* 54, no. 4 (2014): 277-290, doi: 10.1080/01930826.2014.924310; Lisa Kristina Horvath and Sabine Sczesny, "Reducing Women's Lack of Fit with Leadership Positions? Effects of the Wording of Job Advertisements," *European Journal of Work and Organizational Psychology* 25, no. 2 (2016): 316-328.

18   Gaucher et al., "Evidence that Gendered Wording in Job Advertisements Exists,"; Tang, "Understanding Unconscious Bias."

19   Sofia Pr. Grigoriadou, "Artificial Intelligence Law and Management for E-Libraries," *Journal of Internet Law* 25 Iss. 10 (2022): 1, 3-9; Sandy Hervieux and Amanda Wheatley, *The Rise of AI: Implications and Applications of Artificial Intelligence in Academic Libraries*. ACRL Publications in Librarianship Ser., vol. 78 (Association of Colleges and Research Libraries, 2022); Sandy Hervieux and Amanda Wheatley, "Perceptions of Artificial Intelligence: A Survey of Academic Librarians in Canada and the United States," *Journal of Academic Librarianship* 47 (2021): 1-11; Geneva Henry, "Research Librarians as Guides and Navigators for AI Policies at Universities," *Research Library* no. 299 (2019): 47-66.

content analysis of academic librarian positions, except for the following studies. In 2011 the Gender-Decoder, which was created by Danielle Gaucher, Justin Friesen, and Aaron C. Kay includes two brief lists of masculine and feminine words (Table 1).[20] The same Gender-Decoder was used by Tokarz and Mesfin in their analysis of gendered language in management and instruction library job advertisements in 2021.[21] The Gender-Decoder is available to use online to check the language in job postings.[22] Based on Gaucher et al., earlier work, Shiliang Tang at the University of California in 2019 created a comprehensive list of gendered terms, masculine, feminine, as well as, neutral.[23] The Tang lexicon was extracted from 17 million job postings on LinkedIn (2005-2016) which were analyzed to create a large dataset of gendered terminology.[24] Based on the Gaucher et al Gender-Decoder and the two online bias classification systems, Textio and Unitive, Shiliang Tang at the University of California in 2019 designed similar algorithms, "two scalable algorithms that match the same metrics" using similar methodologies to assess the language in the LinkedIn postings.[25] As a result, words were listed in different gender score ranges for adjectives and verbs: Strongly Masculine, Masculine, Slightly Masculine, Neutral, Slightly Feminine, Feminine, and Strongly Feminine.[26] Despite an increase in the participation of women in the workforce, Tang's text analysis of gender biases in 17,376,448 LinkedIn job advertisements (from 2005 to the end of 2016) demonstrates that significant biases remain within certain professions. "People still hold strong gender stereotypes."[27] The Tang lexicon became the basis for the gendered language analysis undertaken in this study.

In terms of the two areas of responsibilities, management and instruction, it is generally acknowledged that management responsibilities in job postings are imbued with masculine language and is embedded

---

20 Gaucher et al., "Evidence that gendered wording in job advertisements exists."
21 Tokarz and Mesfin, "Stereotyping Ourselves."
22 The Gender Decoder, https://gender-decoder.katmatfield.com/.
23 Tang, "Understanding Unconscious Bias," 144-149.
24 Tang, 76.
25 Tang, 79-82.
26 Tang, 144-149.
27 Tang, 134.

with masculine discourses and practices.[28] Teaching has gradually lost some of its prestige in academia with increased class sizes, workloads and administrative responsibilities in the neoliberal academy.[29] With this development academic librarianship has been undergoing a transition which has contributed to a shift in emphasis on more teaching responsibilities and collaboration with faculty.[30] Within the history of the University of Toronto, the term "teaching" has been exclusively reserved for faculty (tenure and teaching streams), as noted in the revisions made to the University of Toronto Art (1971, 1978).[31] Neither libraries nor librarians are mentioned in the revised act, even though they were a core part of the previous 1971 University of Toronto Act revisions. Librarians are designated as staff. As a result, the depreciative value of pedagogy for librarians has been relegated to the lower rungs of the hierarchical ladder of academia, resulting in the fortification of a further internal gendered stratification within academia.[32] Even though there has been an increased acknowledgement of the role of teaching, there is no known study on the professional-level contributions to stratifying, therefore, devaluing teaching within librarianship

---

28 Rosemary Deem, 'New Managerialism' and Higher Education: The Management of Performance and Cultures in Universities in the United Kingdom,' *International Studies in Sociology of Education* 8, Iss. 1 (1998): 47-70. https://doi.org/10.1080/0962021980020014.

29 Margaret Thornton, "The Changing Gender Regime in the Neoliberal Legal Academy," *Zeischrift für Rechtssoziologie (The German Journal of Law and Society)* 33, no. 2 (2014): 235-251.

30 Joyce Lindstrom and Diana D. Shonrock, "Faculty-Librarian Collaboration to Achieve Integration of Information Literacy," *Reference and User Services Quarterly* 46, no. 1 (2006): 18-23 (p. 18); Annamary Consalvo, Gina M. Doepker, Vandy Dubre and Joanna Neel, "Librarian-Faculty Collaboration for Literacy Courses: Promoting Better Learning for Preservice Teachers," *Language and Literacy* 24, Iss. 3 (2022): 107-130.

31 Lisa Becksford, "Teacher, Librarian, or Both? A Quantitative Investigation of Instruction Librarians' Teacher Identity," *CR&L* 83 no. 3 (2022): 372; Cate Watson, "Narratives of Practice and the Construction of Identity in Teaching," *Teachers and Teaching* 12, no. 5 (2006): 509–26, https://doi.org/10.1080/13540600600832213; David Peele, "Librarians as Teachers: Some Reality, Mostly Myth," *Journal of Academic Librarianship* 10, no. 5 (1984): 267–71; Topsy N. Smalley, "Bibliographic Instruction in Academic Libraries: Questioning Some Assumptions," *Journal of Academic Librarianship* 3, no. 5 (1977): 280–83; Pauline Wilson, "Librarians as Teachers: The Study of an Organization Fiction," *Library Quarterly* 49, no. 2 (1979): 146–62; Robert Zai, "Neither Fish nor Fowl: A Role Theory Approach to Librarians Teaching," *Journal of Library Administration* 55, no. 1 (2015): 1–23, https://doi.org/10.1080/01930826.2014.978680.

32 Tilman Reitz, "Academic Hierarchies in Neo-Feudal Capitalism: How Status Competition Processes Trust and Facilitates the Appropriation of Knowledge," *Higher Education; Dordrecht* 73, Iss. 6 (2017): 871-886. doi:10.1007/s10734-017-0115-3.

by using the term instruction rather than teaching.[33] This appears to be both an institutional, as well as a professional trend that devalues librarians' pedagogical contributions to academic communities.

Entry-level postings figure prominently in the last decades combined with increased experiences and knowledge in the current study. The literature on entry-level positions has concentrated on job skills for different recent graduates and on specific responsibilities, such as the digital environment, systems, and specialized areas.[34] Only a few studies have examined the precariousness of entry-level positions with lower remuneration and proliferation of contract employment and the expectations of higher experience in the profession.[35] Sajni Lacey examined the "financial insecurity, devalued labour" of entry-level positions and determined the complicated precariousness of contract work in libraries. Researchers have found that entry-level positions often require higher levels of experience.[36] There are even fewer studies on how entry-level positions with high expectations for experience and knowledge contribute to the gendered biases and pay-equity issues in the profession.

Methodology

The analysis of the UTL job openings is comprised of three interrelated methodologies in Studies One to Three. Study One presents a time series with an analysis that reviews the number of postings issued

---

33 For the professional use of instruction rather than teaching see, *Information Literacy Instruction, Objectives for: A Model Statement for Academic Librarians* (Jan. 2001); *Instruction Programs in Academic Libraries*, Guidelines for (October 2011); *Framework for Information Literacy for Higher Education* (filed February 2015, approved January 2016).

34 E. C. Tewell, "Employment Opportunities for New Academic Librarians: Assessing the Availability of Entry Level Jobs", *Portal: Libraries and the Academy* 12 no. 4 (2012); 407-423; Claudene Sproles and David Ratledge, "An Analysis of Entry-Level Librarian Ads Published in American Libraries, 1982-2002", *Electronic Journal of Academic and Special Librarianship* 5, nos 2-3 (2004); David Ratledge and Claudene Sproles, "An Analysis of the Changing Role of Systems Librarians" *Library Hi Tech*; Bradford 35, Iss. 2 (2017): 303-311; Joe C. Clark, "What Employers Want: Entry-Level Qualifications for Music Librarians," *Notes* (2013): 472-493.

35 Carli Agostino and Melanie Cassidy, "Failure to Launch: Feelings of Failure in Early Career Librarians," *Partnership* 14 no. 2 (2019): 1-7. doi: https://doi.org/10.21083/partnership.v14i1.5224.

36 Robert K. Reeves and Trudi Bellardo Hahn, "Job Advertisements for Recent Graduates: Advising, Curriculum, and Job-seeking Implications," *Journal of Education for Library and Information Science* 51, Iss. 2 (2010): 103-119; J. Deeken and D. Thomas, "Technical Services Job ads: Changes since 1995," *College & Research Libraries* 67 (2001): 136-145; Penny M. Beile and Megan M. Adams, "Other Duties as Assigned: Emerging Trends in the Academic Library Job Market," *College & Research Libraries* 61 (2000): 336-347; Sproles and Ratledge, "An Analysis of Entry-Level Librarian Ads."

over time during the appointments of CL1 and CL2. Studies Two and Three employ data science methods, including some tools commonly used in artificial intelligence, to examine the gendered language and the creation of thematic lexicons specific to the profession of academic librarianship. Study Two applies the Tang Lexicon, as discussed in the literature review, to the analysis of the language used in the UTL postings. Study Three employs Named Entity Recognition (NER) to examine the use of language in job ads that list management or pedagogical responsibilities. The results of these analyses were plotted in graphs (Figures 1-13).

Preparation of Dataset

Job advertisements were assembled from the online Faculty of Information Job Site, the internal UTL listserv, existing college sites, and the University of Toronto archives. Due to the historically inconsistent advertising practices at U of T for librarians' positions there may be missing job ads in some years. The study undertook no filtering or grouping of the job advertisements.

There is a difference between job postings and job openings. 352 job ads were assembled; three job postings had two job openings each. In order to build a dataset that accurately represents the population of the study, the rows for the postings which had two openings were duplicated in the excel spreadsheet describing all postings. In total the dataset has 355 job openings. Data from the postings was manually parsed and coded on an excel sheet. The following categories were identified: unique id for each posting, title of job, file name of posting (pdf or word or web posting), campus, name of library unit, type of library (college, central system, UTM, UTSC), librarian rank, date (submission deadline, year, month), educational requirements, language requirements and the full text (description under the headings of duties, responsibilities and opportunities). For the analysis all punctuation and capital letters were removed, leaving only the unstructured text of the job openings. This was the basis for all the text analysis. From this a working dataset was compiled.

Librarian Ranks

The University of Toronto has four ranks: Librarian I, II, III, IV. Librarian I is a "probationary appointment, the term of which shall not be less than one year or more than two years."[37] To qualify for appointment or promotion to the rank of Librarian II, "the candidate shall have met the minimum educational requirement and shall have at least one year's professional experience or equivalent."[38] Combined, the job openings at the ranks of Librarian I and I-II total Administration considers the rank of Librarian III as the normal career path and the rank of Librarian IV is conferred to outstanding achievements in the UTL system, profession or University.

Study 1: Annual Time Series Analysis

The 355 postings have the following ranks: Librarian I (n=40), Librarian I-II (n=115), Librarian I-II-III-IV (n=1), Librarian II (n=59), Librarian I-III (n=2), Librarian II-III (n=50), Librarian II-III-IV (n=6), Librarian III (n=25), Librarian III-IV (n=27), Librarian IV (n=13). There are 17 postings without a rank. Entry-level, pre-permanent status (ranks I, II, I-II) total 60% (n=214) of the 355 openings.

Based on the counts of the job openings from 1985 to 2021, the graph has an overall upward sloping trend, despite slowing down between about 2005 and 2011 (Figure 1). The solid black line is a smoothed conditional means time series line plot that displays the total number of job postings per year from 1985 to 2021. The gray band around the solid black line represents the confidence band. This plot includes a vertical red dotted line that is positioned at the year 2011, which separates the two time periods of interest. The first time period, 1985-2011, represents CL1, while the second time period, which runs from 2012 to 2021, denotes the period for CL2.

Figure 2 plots the total number of postings per year per rank. This figure depicts a panel of dots—one for each variation of Librarian rank in the dataset. There are 11 variations for specifying the ranks (I to IV) on the postings: i, i-ii, i-ii-iii, i-ii-iii-iv, ii, ii-iii, ii-iii-iv, ii-iv, iii, iii-iv and iv. The unknown category is a catch-all category for postings with no mention of a rank. There is a rise in postings with the rank of Librarian I from c. 2006 to 2012 and then a decline for the rank of Librarian I

---

37 Definition, article 8 in University of Toronto, *Policies for Librarians*, http://www.governingcouncil.utoronto.ca/policies/lpolicy.htm.

38 Definition, article 9 in University of Toronto, *Policies for Librarians*, http://www.governingcouncil.utoronto.ca/policies/lpolicy.htm.

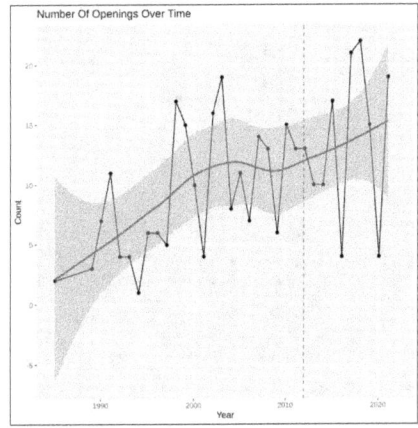

Figure 1 Total Number of Postings by UTL Chief Librarian 1985-2021 (Plot A1). Copyright authors.

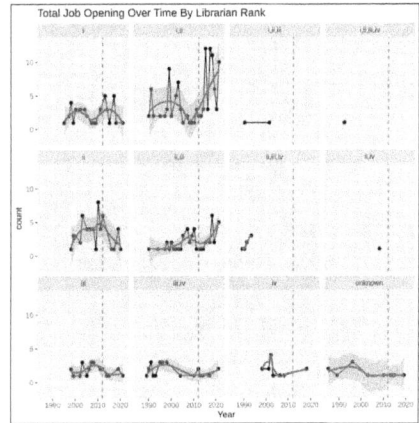

Figure 2 Total Number of Postings by Librarian Rank, 1985-2021 (Plot A2). Copyright authors.

to 2011 to 2021 (Figure 2). Instead, there is a sharp rise of postings with the rank of Librarian I-II from 2010 to 2015 (Figure 2). Combined the entry-level postings with the ranks of I, I-II, II (n=214) which is 66% of the 355 openings.

Artificial Intelligence and Thematic Lexicons

Study 2: Tang Lexicon and the Gender Decoder

To assess the degree to which gendered language was used in all the postings assembled, the Tang Lexicon from the LinkedIn study of 17 million job ads was applied to the full text of the dataset of job openings. Study Two examines the degree of gendered terms (masculine, feminine, neutral) in all the postings. The Tang lexicon, which is more extensive than the Gender Decoder, was used to analyze all the UTL job postings and each rank listed on the postings. The Gender Decoder includes numerous personality traits as part of the lexicon (Table 1). The Tang LinkedIn word clouds had seven categories–strongly masculine, masculine, slightly masculine, neutral, slightly feminine, feminine and strongly feminine.[39] These were simplified into three major categories: masculine, neutral and feminine.

---

39 Tang, "Understanding Unconscious Bias," 144-149.

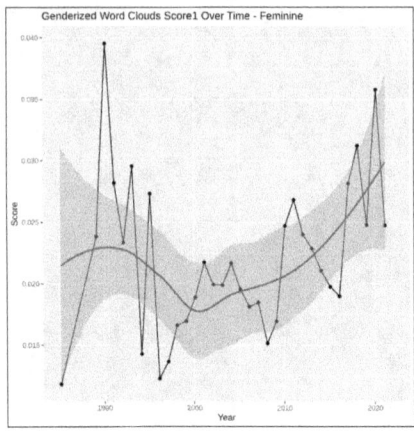

Figure 3 Feminine Language Score Over Time, 1985-2021 (Plot 13). Copyright authors.

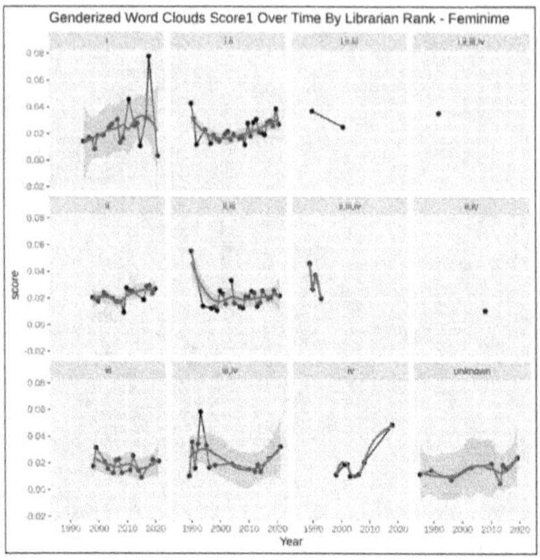

Figure 4 Feminine Language Score Over Time by Librarian Rank (Plot 16, see previous Plot 13). Copyright authors.

The line plot of the feminine score of terms (Figure 3) is the result of analyzing the word clouds from the LinkedIn thesis (Tang). A subset of words from the Tang LinkedIn lexicon of gendered terms were identified in the UTL job postings (Table 2). The analysis involved identifying overlaps between the word clouds in the LinkedIn paper and those in our corpus. The proportion of those overlapping words over the total number of words in each job posting was then calculated. These proportions were then averaged by year, resulting in a time series of scores that are represented in the line plot for the feminine words (Figures 3, 4). The plot (Figure 3) provides a clear visualization of how the proportion of words in the job postings overlap with the LinkedIn paper's word clouds and change over time. The plot displays the degree of feminine terms in the job postings, on average, over time. Between 1995 to 2021 there is a steady rise in the use of feminine language which peaks in 2021 (Figure 3). The rise in feminine language is most pronounced in the librarian ranks of I and II at the lower ranks (Figure 4). Whereas the use of masculine language tends to be relatively flat over time (Figures 5, 6) and the use of neutral language rapidly declines from the year 2000 to 2021 (Figures 7, 8).

Study 3: NER, Spans and Thematic Lexicons

The creation of thematic lexicons began with a preliminary short list of professional terms compiled manually by the researchers. This initial

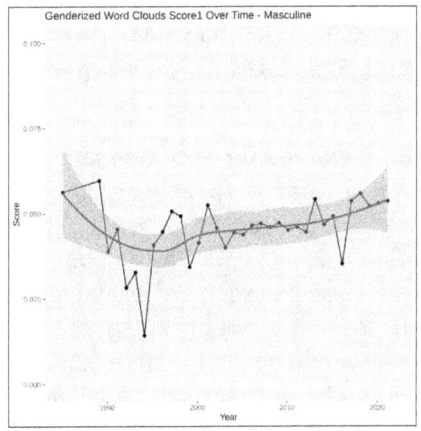

Figure 5 Masculine Language Score Over Time. Copyright authors.

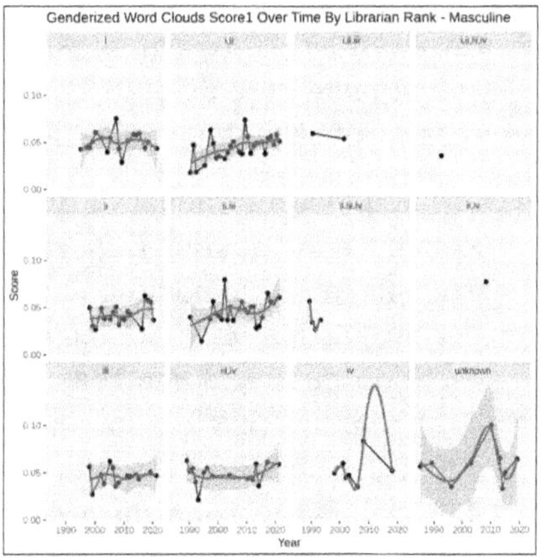

Figure 6 Masculine Language Score Over Time by Librarian Rank. Copyright authors.

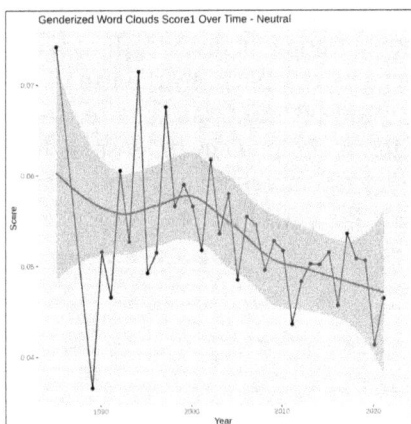

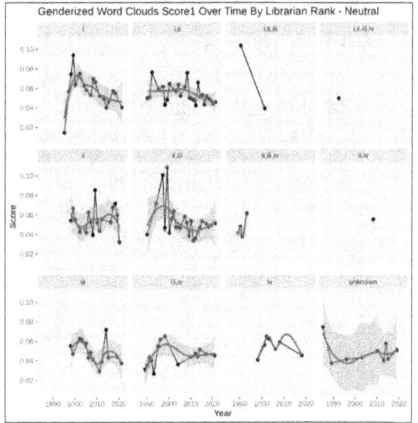

Figure 7 Neutral Language Score Over Time. Copyright authors.

Figure 8 Neutral Language Score Over Time by Librarian Rank. Copyright authors.

basket of terms was used by the AI programming to find related words, thereby, expanding the list of terms in the thematic lexicon. This process, the Named Entity Recognition (NER) in artificial intelligence, compiled a comprehensive set of terms using the library called Spacy. NER is an AI-powered model that auto-highlights words in text after it has been trained on a specific criteria (context-specific), https://spacy.io/universe/project/video-spacys-ner-model-alt. The NER lists for qualifications, managerial and pedagogical responsibilities were reviewed by the researchers. Terms having other meanings than the main theme were deleted from the thematic lexicons. See further discussion of each thematic lexicon below.

To calculate the frequency of a term identified for each thematic lexicon, each job posting is given a total number of 'spans', e. g. 100. For example, a single posting has 2 'spans' (occurrences for HTML), then the proportion for that single posting is 2/100=0.02. This is done for each job posting. Then they are averaged per year. For example, in 2010, there were 3 job postings with these proportions, respectively: 0.01, 0.05, 0.09. Then the value for 2010 would be (0.01 + 0.05 + 0.09)/3 = 0.05. This is the value shown in each cell for each term per applicable year in the plot.

Level of Qualifications Required

The postings lacked consistent references to years of experience except in the postings with the rank of Librarian III. Instead, the degree or level of experience and knowledge were defined by the use of descriptive superlatives and descriptive phrases. AI was used to identify related terms to an initial list of terms compiled by the researchers (Table 3). An analysis was calculated over time according to the lexicon of words. There is a sharp increase in the use of superlative terminology from c. 2010 to 2021.

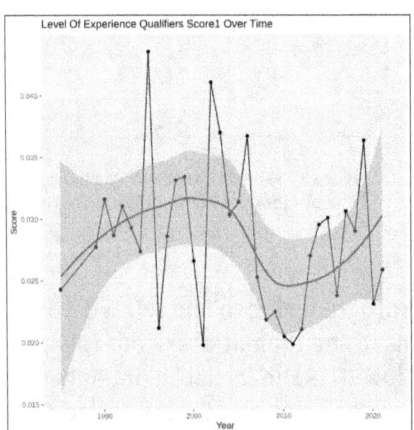

Figure 9 Level of Experience Qualifiers Over Time. Copyright authors.

Managerial Responsibilities

Table 4 lists the NER terms identified denoting managerial responsibilities. The entry-level positions, the majority of postings, demonstrate a steady rise in managerial responsibilities. An analysis was calculated over time (Figure 10) and by rank (Figure 11).

Librarian Rank	Management Score
I	0.0185
I, II	0.0250
I, II, III	0.0337
I, II, III, IV	0.0293
II	0.0281
II, III	0.0336
II, III, IV	0.0335
II, IV	0.0306
III	0.0375
III, IV	0.0424
IV	0.0435

Table

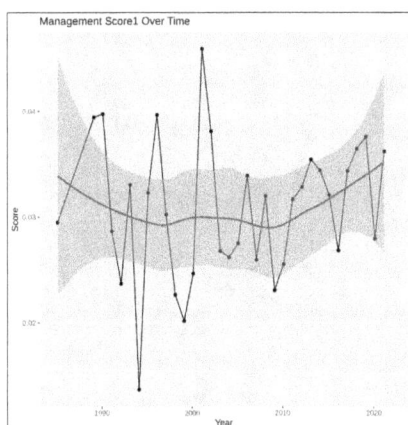

Figure 10 Managerial NER Terminology Over Time. Copyright authors.

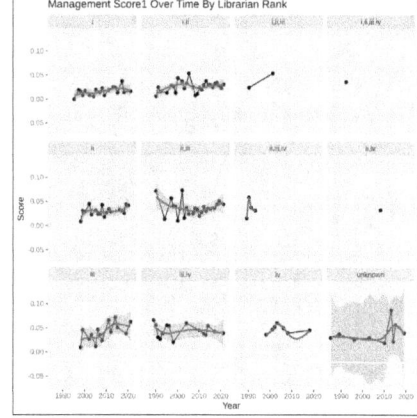

Figure 11 Managerial NER Terminology Over Time by Librarian Rank. Copyright authors.

Managerial responsibilities are a consistent component of librarians' postings. The responsibilities increase with each rank, as indicated in the table above. Note that the management score for librarian rank I is 0.0185, and for librarian rank II is 0.0281. Librarian postings with the rank I-II is at 0.0250, placing this rank closer to librarian rank II than to I. A similar situation exists for the postings with rank II and III. Postings with the rank II-III has a value of 0.0336, which is just slightly higher than the midpoint between II and III (i.e., [0.0281+0.0375]/2 = 0.0328). From this table it was determined that postings with mixed ranks listed, as for example I-II and II-III are biased toward the higher end of the spectrum, thus indicating a higher level of managerial responsibilities.

Pedagogical Responsibilities

The researchers questioned to what degree pedagogical responsibilities were a component of academic librarianship at the University of Toronto. In addition, there was an internal institutional understanding that the term 'teaching' was used for faculty and 'instruction' was the term used for the pedagogical work by librarians, thus segregating the value of the two endeavours. This differed from the gendered associations traditionally applied to the terms. The researchers were interested in determining to what extent the two terms were used or not in the job ads at the University of Toronto.

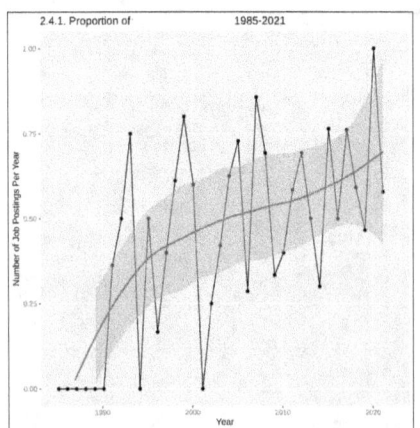 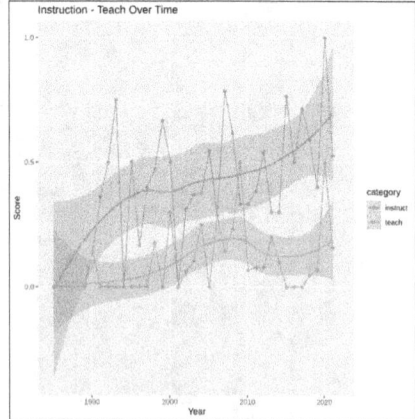

Figure 12 Pedagogical NER Terminology Over Time. Copyright authors.

Figure 13 The 'Teaching' and 'Instruction' Terms Over Time. Copyright authors.

Two methods were adopted to examine the degree of librarians' pedagogical responsibilities in the UTL job postings. The first method employed NER and AI to analyse to what degree the comprehensive pedagogical topic of teaching in librarians' postings had increased or decreased over time. AI was used to create a lexicon of words related to pedagogical responsibilities (Table 5, Figure 12). The second method was an examination of how the two terms, 'teaching' versus 'instruction,' were employed in the postings' language. The researchers pursued an analysis of the terms over time (Figure 13).

Analysis and Results

Institutionalizing a Feminized Profession

The gender analysis of the 355 UTL job openings, using the Tang Lexicon, demonstrates an increased use of feminine language from 1995 to 2021, with a sharp rise from c. 2010 to 2021 under CL2 (Figure 3). The red line signals the transition year, c. 2010, between CL1 and CL2 (Figure 1). There is no doubt that the language utilized in the UTL postings reinforce and perpetuate a gendered profession. To what degree this is a conscious and deliberate decision is unknown. However, it is clear that the institution is supporting an element of professional stereotyping at the lower ranks. The data demonstrates that there is an increased usage of feminine language at the lower, entry-level ranks of librarian I and II and decrease in neutral language (Figs 3-8).

Hiring Practices and Entry-Level Job Advertisements

Contract work is often framed as enabling recent graduates to gain library experience.[40] At the University of Toronto, there are two types of contract jobs. The first, known as contractually limited appointment, has a set end-date. The second is in the permanent status stream, which leads to permanent status, the equivalent of tenure. The *Policies for Librarians* at U of T specifically notes that rank I and even rank

---

[40] Lindsay McNiff and Nicole Carter, "Contract Academic Librarians in Canada: Stories from a Nation-Wide Survey," *Canadian Journal of Academic Librarianship*, Vol 8 (2022); 1-31 (p. 3). https://doi.org/10/33137/cjal-rcbu.v8.38451.

II require only limited professional experience.[41] Of the 355 openings, 155 openings (43.7%) were contractually limited appointments (CLTA), 196 were contractual but in the permanent status stream (55%) and 4 postings had no information.

The analysis of the levels of qualifications required on the UTL job postings does not correspond, however, to the entry-level requirements described in the Policies for Librarians. Overall, the entry-level openings for the ranks of Librarian I, II, I-II (n=218) amount to 61% of all postings (Figs 1-2). The postings with the rank listing of I-II provide opportunities for more qualified individuals to apply and be hired at the rank of Librarian I. As studies have demonstrated, successful candidates obtaining entry-level positions usually have several years of experience.[42] Librarian ranks I and II are equivalent to Assistant Professor, the entry-level position prior to tenure at the University of Toronto. Librarians have four ranks rather than three ranks like the faculty, thus reinforcing a lower salary for a longer period of time in a female profession. By recruiting in the lower ranks, the remuneration for a predominantly female profession remains at a lower level. It takes 3 to 6 years before a librarian in the lower ranks is eligible for permanent status and the rank of Librarian III. This has a long-term and short-term impact on professionals. This is advantageous for the institution from a financial and managerial perspective.[43]

The analysis of the level of qualifications noted in the job postings confirm that the UTL administration is seeking qualified and experienced librarians beyond entry-level, and the descriptions offered in the librarians' policy (Figure 9, Table 3). This is in keeping with the trend that suggests that contract work is becoming more specialized.[44] Regrettably, this results in the devaluation of the expertise of candidates hired. Furthermore, in recent years librarian candidates applying for UTL positions have been told by administrators that they cannot negotiate their starting salaries. This is a specifically administrative bias within

---

41 Definition, articles 8 and 9 in University of Toronto, *Policies for Librarians*, http://www.governingcouncil.utoronto.ca/policies/lpolicy.htm.

42 Tewell, "Employment Opportunities for New Academic Librarians," 420.

43 James S. Chervinko, "Temporary Employees in Academic and Research Libraries" *Journal of Academic Librarianship* Vol 12 No. 4 (1986): 217-20.

44 McNiff and Carter, "Contract Academic Librarians in Canada," 14.

the UTL system that serves to reinforce the lower remuneration of professionals who are predominantly female.

Managerial Responsibilities

Managerialism, an ideology put into practice, has contributed to the UTL hierarchy and a shift of the decision-making authority to a few rather than the expertise of the librarians who work in the specific areas—all justified by the need for efficiency.[45] For example, the disbanding of the Library Council and replacement with the Chief Librarian's Executive Council has had a rippling impact on the role of the library in the community as well as dampening the voices of experts in the UTL system.

For this analysis the AI deduced list of words representing managerial responsibilities demonstrated a consistent inclusion of managerial responsibilities in the library postings from 1995 to 2021, even though most of these postings were not designated as having management responsibilities in the title of the position. There was a decline in the mid-1990s and then a sharp increase of managerial terms from 2010 to 2021, parallel to the rise of feminine gendered language (Figure 9). The latter is an interesting change, especially noteworthy when you consider that the majority of postings from 2010 to 2021 were for the ranks of librarian I and II, the more precarious and less remunerated positions, thus serving to undervalue the managerial responsibilities.

Librarians' Teaching and Pedagogical Contributions

Pedagogical activities and teaching have historically been a continuous component of academic librarianship, beginning in the nineteenth century when U of T faculty were actively involved in the building of the early collections and when the early librarian programs were affiliated with the Ontario Institute of Education. Academic librarians are themselves educators, knowledgeable about specialized areas of research and scholarship, and continually engaged on multiple levels in the education mandate of their communities, as officially first endorsed in 1958 by the Universities Library Section of the Association of College and Research Libraries (ACRL).

---

45 Silvia Vong, "More Critical, Less Managerial: Addressing the Managerialist Ideology in Academic Libraries," *Partnership*, Vol. 16, no. 2 (2021): 1-20.

AI deduced a list of terms representing pedagogical requirements for academic librarians (Table 5). The analysis revealed that pedagogical responsibilities increase steadily from the 1990s through to 2021, with a more upward swing from 2010 onward, confirming the increased role of librarians in the pedagogical mission of the university (Figure 12). This is not surprising given the emphasis on information literacy, development of embedded librarians in faculties, increased teaching, curriculum involvement and librarians' role in the design of pedagogical guides and programs.

At the University of Toronto, a political stratification and division was established between faculty and librarians in the revised University of Toronto Act (1971, 1978).[46] The term teach described the responsibilities of faculty, whereas librarians were designated as 'staff' in the University of Toronto Act. References to the library, which had been part of the previous act, were removed. [47] Furthermore, instruction is the term that has been promoted by the professional library associations, differentiating librarians' pedagogical role from faculty.[48] Consequently, the researchers were interested in understanding how the term 'teach' versus 'instruction' was being used in the UTL job postings. The results show that instruction remains the preferred term with a steady increase in the frequency of the term from the 1990s. Teaching, however, was minimally used during the 1990s, increases in frequency from 2000 onward but then dips down again from 2010, reinforcing instead the use of the term instruction (Figs 13, 14). It is interesting that it decreases in use and the term instruction prevails, given that in 2017 the ACRL board revised the 2007 ACRL Standards for

---

46 University of Toronto Act (1971), as amended in 1978. See sections 1 (aa), 1 (m), " 'teaching staff' means the employees of the University, University College, the constituent colleges and the arts and science faculties of the federated universities who hold the academic rank of professor, associate professor, assistant professor, full-time lecturer or part-time lecturer, unless such part-time lecturer is registered as a student, or who hold any other rank created by the Governing Council and designated by it as an academic rank for the purposes of this clause." University of Toronto Act, 1971. http://www.governingcouncil.utoronto.ca/Assets/Governing+Council+Digital+Assets/Policies/PDF/ppdec151978.pdf.

47 For decades librarians' pedagogical work has been defined as instruction rather than teaching. See *Information Literacy Instruction, Objectives for: A Model Statement for Academic Librarians* (Jan. 2001) https://www.ala.org/acrl/standards/objectivesinformation April 7, 2023; *Framework for Information Literacy*, ACRL, https://www.ala.org/acrl/sites/ala.org.acrl/files/content/issues/infolit/framework1.pdf ; *Guides Lines for Instruction Programs in Academic Libraries* (2011)

48 ALA, SPEC Kits, provide examples of job postings and terminology used, as in the case of instruction, see Association of Research Libraries, https://publications-arl-org.myaccess.library.utoronto.ca/SPEC_Kits.

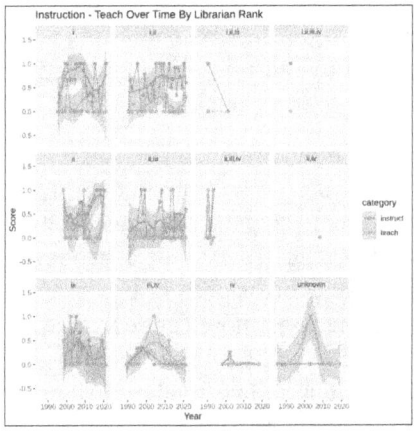

Figure 14 The 'Teaching' and 'Instruction' Terms Over Time by Rank. Copyright authors.

Proficiencies for Instruction Librarians and Coordinators to emphasize the role of teaching in librarianship.[49] This suggests that at the institutional-level the historical inequities and stratification continue to be played out between faculty and a predominantly female profession, librarianship, in the recruitment of new professionals at U of T in the lower ranks, librarians I and II (Figs 13, 14).

Limitations and Future Directions

There were several limitations to this study. Documents and reports published by professional associations, such as the Association of Research Libraries (ARL) and the Association of College and Research Libraries (ACRL), were not included in the study. The analysis of these numerous documents was outside the parameters of the current study but should be considered in future research. As is noted in the *ACRL Proficiencies for Assessment Librarians and Coordinators* (2017), "proficiencies may be used to write job descriptions that define duties of... librarians, assess performance and guide evaluation, and design professional development programs" (para. 6). Comparing the language used in these documents to the job advertisements in a more comprehensive methodology will help researchers explore the role that professional organizations play in perpetuating gendered language in the profession. Furthermore, it can enable researchers to examine

---

49   ACRL, "Roles and Strengths of Teaching Librarians," American Library Association, May 15, 2017. http://www.ala.org/acrl/standards/teachinglibrarians

the relationship between professional organizations and hiring institutions and how these entities contribute and reinforce gendered inequality in the profession of academic librarianship.

Another direction for future research is a nuanced comparison of professional proficiency documentation of stereotypically female-dominated professions such as nursing to male-dominated ones such as engineering. This would be followed by the creation of a gendered language continuum between these two professions—in terms of expectations—on which librarianship, as well as more "gender neutral" professions such as law or architecture, could be fitted. Job ads and professional expectations, as flushed out in professional proficiencies and codes of conduct, could then be used to map the profession onto the non-gendered profession continuum.

Conclusion

In this neoliberal era, managerialism, an ideology put into practice, has contributed to the UTL hierarchy, a perpetuation of gendered biases and a shift of the decision-making authority to a few rather than the expertise of the librarians who work in the specific areas—all justified by the need for efficiency.[50] The results of this study were initially surprising. The researchers had expected the results of the analysis to expose primarily historical and internal developments related to the workplace and professional changes, such as retirement packages offered by Administration (1985-86, 1991-93, 1994-96, 2011-2018), the increased enrolment at the University and the evolving role of technology in the profession. The most striking changes to the UTL postings, however, have occurred since 2010 under the leadership of CL2, with the growth of an increased corporate structure in the UTL system. The year 2010-2011 appears to be the decisive turning point for many of the changes noted. To some degree the last retirement package offered in 2011 with an end-date of 2018 may have contributed to the need to replace librarians who were retiring. However, the increased use of feminized language exceeds previous periods, even when retirement packages were offered. In addition, the increase of contractual postings at the ranks of I and II correspond to the increased use of feminized

---

50 Vong, "More Critical, Less Managerial," 1-20. The UTL Library Council was disbanded and replaced by the Chief Librarian's Executive Council, https://onesearch.library.utoronto.ca/chief-librarians-executive-council-and-senior-administration-staff-list-st-george-campus.

language in the postings. Supporting this trend is the decrease in the number of postings at the rank of Librarian III, the main career path of established professionals. The increase in postings at the rank of I and II, combined with an increase in required experience, specialized knowledge and consistent expectation of managerial responsibilities at the lower ranks, conveys a different message than simply replacing retiring senior colleagues. Thus, the perpetuation of a feminized profession is reinforced at the most vulnerable level of the profession, when colleagues are in precarious employment. Furthermore, it should be stressed that the increase in teaching responsibilities is noteworthy. This, combined with the subtle rise in managerial responsibilities in the postings, the emphasis on recruiting at the lower levels, and the sharp increased use of using superlatives to request levels of expertise, serves to devalue librarians' expertise at the lower levels and perpetuates gender inequities.

Bibliography

Agostino, Carolie and Melanie Cassidy. "Failure to Launch: Feelings of Failure in Early Career Librarians." *Partnership* 14 no. 2 (2019): 1-7. https://doi.org/10.21083/partnership.v14i1.5224.

Association of College & Research Libraries (ACRL). "Roles and Strengths of Teaching Librarians." American Library Association, May 15, 2017. http://www.ala.org/acrl/standards/teachinglibrarians.

Association of College & Research Libraries (ACRL). SPEC Kits. https://publications-arl-org.myaccess.library.utoronto.ca/SPEC_Kits.

Association of College & Research Libraries (ACRL). *Information Literacy Instruction, Objectives for: A Model Statement for Academic Librarians* (Jan. 2001). https://www.ala.org/acrl/standards/objectivesinformation.

Association of College & Research Libraries (ACRL). *Framework for Information Literacy for Higher Education* (filed February 2015, approved January 2016). https://www.ala.org/acrl/standards/ilframework.

Association of College & Research Libraries (ACRL). *Guides Lines for Instruction Programs in Academic Libraries*. 2011, https://www.ala.org/acrl/standards/guidelinesinstruction.

Arceo-Gomez, Eva O., Raymundo M. Campos-Vazquez, Raquel Y. Badillo and Sergio Lopez-Araiza. "Gender Stereotypes in Job Advertisements: What do They Imply for the Gender Salary Gap?" *Journal of Labor Research* 43 (2022): 65–102.

Arinola, Adeola Adesoji and F. Oyewusi. "Gender Influence on Managerial Efficiency of Academic Librarians in Nigeria." *Gender and Behaviour* 7, no. 1 (2009): 2317-2329. doi:10.4314/gab.v7i1.45048.

Askehave, Inger and Karen Korning Zethsen. "Gendered Constructions of Leadership in Danish Job Advertisements." *Gender, Work and Organization* 21, No. 6 (November 2014): 531-545.

Beaudrie, Ronald and Robert Grunfeld. "Male Reference Librarians and the Gender Factor." *Reference Librarian* 33 (1991): 211-213.

Becksford, Lisa. "Teacher, Librarian, or Both? A Quantitative Investigation of Instruction Librarians' Teacher Identity." *College & Research Libraries* 83, no. 3 (2 May 2022).

Beile, Penny M. and Megan M. Adams. "Other duties as assigned: Emerging trends in the academic library job market." *College & Research Libraries* 61 (2000): 336–47.

Blackburn, Robert H. *Evolution of the Heart: A History of The University of Toronto Library up to 1981*. Toronto: University of Toronto Press, 1989.

Bosak, Janine and Sabine Sczesny. "Am I the Right Candidate? Self-Ascribed Fit of Women and Men to a Leadership Position." Sex Roles 58, Iss. 9-10 (2008): 682–688. https://doi.org/10.1007/s11199-007-9380-4.

Bruce, Lorne D. "Professionalization, Gender, and Librarianship in Ontario, 1920-75." Library & Information History 28, no. 2 (2012): 117-34.

Bruce, Lorne D. "From Library Work to Library Science: Forming Canadian Librarianship, 1920-1960." *Partnership: The Canadian Journal of Library and Information Practice and Research* 14, Iss. 1 (2019): 1-41. doi:10.21083/partnership.v14i1.4752.

Chervinko, James S. "Temporary Employees in Academic and Research Libraries." *Journal of Academic Librarianship* Vol 12 No. 4 (1986): 217-20.

Clark, Joe C. "What Employers Want: Entry-Level Qualifications for Music Librarians." *Notes* (2013): 472-493.

Consalvo, Annamary, Gina M. Doepker, Vandy Dubre and Joanna Neel. "Librarian-Faculty Collaboration for Literacy Courses: Promoting Better Learning for Preservice Teachers." *Language and Literacy* 24, Iss. 3 (2022): 107-130.

Deeken, J. and D. Thomas. "Technical Services job ads: Changes since 1995." *College & Research Libraries* 67 (2001): 136-145.

Deem, Rosemary. "New Managerialism' and Higher Education: The Management of Performance and Cultures in Universities in the United Kingdom." *International Studies in Sociology of Education* 8, Iss. 1 (1998): 47-70. https://doi.org/10.1080/0962021980020014.

Dewey, Melvil. "The Profession." *American Library Journal* I (1876): 5-6.

Duffy, B. E. and B. Schwartz. "Digital "Women's Work?": Job Recruitment ads and the Feminization of Social Media Employment." *New Media & Society* 20, no. 8 (2018): 2972-2989. https://doi.org/10.1177/1461444817738237.

Eva, Nicole and Mê-Linh Lê, John Sheriff. "Less Money, Less Children, and Less Prestige: Differences between Male and Female Academic Librarians." *Journal of Academic Librarianship* 47 (2021), 1-11 (p. 5). https://doi.org/10.1016/j.acalib.2021.102392.

Gaucher, Danielle, Justin Friesen, and Aarun C. Kay. "Evidence that Gendered Wording in job Advertisements Exists and Sustains Gender Inequality." *Journal of Personality and Social Psychology* 101, no. 1 (2011): 109-128.

Grigoriadou, Sofia Pr. "Artificial Intelligence Law and Management for E-Libraries." *Journal of Internet Law* 25 Iss. 10 (2022):1, 3-9

Henricks, Susan A. and Genevieve M. Henricks-Lepp. "Desired Characteristics of Management and Leadership for Public Library Directors as Expressed in Job Advertisements." *Journal of Library Administration* 54, no. 4 (2014): 277-290, doi: 10.1080/01930826.2014.924310.

Henry, Geneva. "Research Librarians as Guides and Navigators for AI Policies at Universities." *Research Library* Iss. no. 299 (2019): 47-66.

Hervieux, Sandy and Amanda Wheatley. *The Rise of AI: Implications and Applications of Artificial Intelligence in Academic Libraries.* ACRL Publications in Librarianship Ser., 78. Association of Colleges and Research Libraries, 2022.

Hervieux, Sandy and Amanda Wheatley. "Perceptions of artificial intelligence: A survey of academic librarians in Canada and the United States." *Journal of Academic Librarianship* 47 (2021): 1-11.

Horvath, Lisa Kristina and Sabine Sczesny. "Reducing Women's Lack of fit with Leadership Positions? Effects of the Wording of job Advertisements."*European Journal of Work and Organizational Psychology* 25, no. 2 (2016): 316-328.

Kay, Aaron C., Szymon Czaplinski and John T. Jost. "Left-Right Ideological Differences in System Justification following Exposure to Complementary Versus Noncomplementary Stereotype Exemplars." *European Journal of Social Psychology* 39 (2009): 290-298. doi:10.1002/ejsp.500

Kervyn, Nicolas, Vincent Y. Yzerbyt, Charles M. Judd and Ana Nunes. "A Question of Compensation: The Social Life of the Fundamental Dimensions of Social Perception." *Journal of Personality and Social Psychology* 96, no. 4 (2009): 828-842.

Kovacs, Ildiko and Kornelia Vamosi Zarandne. "Digital Marketing Employability Skills in Job Advertisements—Must Have Soft Skills for Entry-Level Workers: A Content Analysis." *Economics & Sociology* 15, Iss. 1 (2022): 178-192.

Lindstrom, Joyce and Diana D. Shonrock. "Faculty-Librarian Collaboration to Achieve Integration of Information Literacy." *Reference and User Services Quarterly* 46, no. 1 (2006): 18-23.

Lupton, Ben. "Explaining Men's Entry into Female-Concentrated Occupations: Issues of Masculinity and Social Class." *Gender, Work, and Organization* 13, no. 2 (2006): 103-128.

McNiff, Lindsay and Nicole Carter. "Contract Academic Librarians in Canada: Stories from a Nation-Wide Survey." *Canadian Journal of Academic Librarianship* 8 (2022); 1-31 (p. 3). https://doi.org/10/33137/cjal-rc-bu.v8.38451.

Mian, Anam. ARL annual salary survey 2021, Association of Research Libraries, https://doi-org.myaccess.library.utoronto.ca/10.29242/salary.2021.

Passet, Joanne E. "Men in a Feminized Profession: The Male Librarian, 1887-1921." *Libraries & Culture* 28, no. 4 (1993): 385-402, 386.

Papadopoulos, John. "New UofT Chief Librarian." *Slaw: Canada's Online Legal Magazine*, August 3, 2011. https://www.slaw.ca/2011/08/03/new-uoft-chief-librarian/.

Peele, David. "Librarians as Teachers: Some Reality, Mostly Myth." *Journal of Academic Librarianship* 10, no. 5 (1984): 267–71.

Reeves, Robert K. and Trudi Bellardo Hahn. "Job Advertisements for Recent Graduates: Advising, Curriculum, and Job-seeking Implications." *Journal of Education for Library and Information Science* 51, Iss. 2 (2010): 103-119.

Reitz, Tilman. "Academic Hierarchies in Neo-Feudal Capitalism: How Status Competition Processes Trust and Facilitates the Appropriation of Knowledge." *Higher Education; Dordrecht* 73, Iss. 6 (2017): 871-886. doi:10.1007/s10734-017-0115-3.

Schwartz, Meredith. "Women's Work: What If No One Wants To Work (Here) Anymore?." *Library Journal* 147, Iss. 10 (2022): 6.

Sloniowski, Lisa. "Affective Labor, Resistance, and the Academic Librarian." *Library Trends* 64, no. 6 (2016): 645-666.

Smalley, Topsy N. "Bibliographic Instruction in Academic Libraries: Questioning Some Assumptions." *Journal of Academic Librarianship* 3, no. 5 (1977): 280–83.

Sonne de Torrens, Harriet. "Academic Librarianship: The Quest for Rights and Recognition at the University of Toronto." In *In Solidarity: Academic Librarian Labour Activism and Union Participation in Canada*, edited by Jennifer Dekker and Mary Kandiuk, 81-102, 314-324. Sacramento, CA: Library Juice Press, 2013.

Sproles, Claudene and David Ratledge. "An Analysis of Entry-Level Librarian ads Published in American Libraries, 1982-2002." *Electronic Journal of Academic and Special Librarianship* 5, nos 2-3 (2004): 1-25.

Sproles, Claudene and David Ratledge. "An Analysis of the Changing Role of Systems Librarians." *Library Hi Tech; Bradford* 35, Iss. 2 (2017): 303-311.

Tang, Shiliang. "Understanding Unconscious Bias by Large-scale Data Analysis." PhD diss., University of California, 2019.

Tewell, E. C. "Employment Opportunities for new Academic Librarians: Assessing the Availability of Entry Level Jobs." *Portal: Libraries and the Academy* 12 no. 4 (2012): 407-23.

Thornton, Margaret, "The Changing Gender Regime in the Neoliberal Legal Academy." *Zeischrift für Rechtssoziologie (The German Journal of Law and Society)* 33, no. 2 (2014): 235-251.

Tokarz, Rayla E. "Creative, Innovative and Collaborative Librarians Wanted: The Use of Personality Traits in Librarian Job Advertisements." *Library Philosophy and Practice* (2019): 1-21.

Tokarz, Rayla E. and Tati Mesfin. "Stereotyping Ourselves: Gendered Language Use in Management and Instruction Library Job Advertisements." *Journal of Library Administration* 61, no. 3 (2021), 301-311 (p. 301).

University of Toronto. *Facts & Figures*. 2010 to 2021. https://data.utoronto.ca/facts-and-figures/.

University of Toronto Library. Chief Librarian's Executive Council. https://onesearch.library.utoronto.ca/chief-librarians-executive-council-and-senior-administration-staff-list-st-george-campus.

University of Toronto, Policies for Librarians, http://www.governingcouncil.utoronto.ca/policies/lpolicy.htm.

University of Toronto Governing Council, University of Toronto Act (1971), http://www.governingcouncil.utoronto.ca/Assets/Governing+Council+Digital+Assets/Policies/PDF/ppdec151978.pdf.

Vong, Silvia. "More Critical, Less Managerial: Addressing the Managerialist Ideology in Academic Libraries." *Partnership* 16, no. 2 (2021): 1-20.

Watson, Cate. "Narratives of Practice and the Construction of Identity in Teaching." *Teachers and Teaching* 12, no. 5 (2006): 509–26, https://doi.org/10.1080/13540600600832213.

Wilson, Pauline. "Librarians as Teachers: The Study of an Organization Fiction." *Library Quarterly* 49, no. 2 (1979): 146-62.

Yadav, Akhilesh K.S. "Key skills and competencies of LIS professionals in the digital library environment: a content analysis of job advertisements." *Library Management; Bradford* 43, Iss. ½ (2022): 50-65.

Zai, Robert. "Neither Fish nor Fowl: A Role Theory Approach to Librarians Teaching." *Journal of Library Administration* 55, no. 1 (2015): 1–23. https://doi.org/10.1080/01930826.2014.978680.

Table 1 Masculine and Feminine Terms in Gender-Decoder by Danielle Gaucher, Justin Friesen, and Aaron C. Kay.

Feminine

agree-, affectionate-, child-, cheer-, collab-, commit-, communal-, compassion-, connect-, considerate-, cooperat-, co-operat-, depend-, emotiona-, empath-, feel-, flatterable-, gentle-, honest-, interpersonal-, interdependen-, interpersona-, inter-personal-, inter-dependen, inter-persona-, kind-, kinship-, loyal-, modesty-, nag-, nurtur-, pleasant-, polite-, quiet-, respon-, sensitiv-, submissive-, support-, sympath-, tender-, together-, trust-, understand-, warm-, whin-, enthusias-, inclusive-, yield-, share-, sharin-

Masculine

active-, adventurous-, aggress-, ambitio-, analy-, assert-, athlet-, autonom-, battle-, boast-, challeng-, champion-, compet-, confident-, courag-, decid-, decision-, decisive-, defend-, determin-, domina-, dominant-, driven-, fearless-, fight-, force-, greedy-, head-strong-, headstrong-, hierarch-, hostil-, impulsive-, independen-, individual-, intellect-, lead-, logic-, objective-, opinion-, outspoken-, persist-, principle-, reckless-, self-confiden-, self-relian-, self-sufficien-, selfconfiden-, selfrelian-, selfsufficien-, stubborn-, superior-, unreasonab-

Table 2 Subset of Words from S. Tang Lexicon Identified in Gender Analysis of Librarian Postings (words overlapping the master list identified in the LinkedIn Gendered Data Analysis from "Understanding Unconscious Bias by Large-scale Data Analysis" by Shiliang Tang, 2019)

Neutral

experience, reference, academic, excellent, responsible, develop, use, relevant, effective, acceptable, essential, part, participate, graduate, sound, outstanding, individual, key, central, record, maintain, plan, adapt, collaborate, coordinate, report, associate, advanced, engage, approach, subject, possess, close, specific, create, significant, facilitate, assume, search, apply, identify, hold, full, foreign, term, limited, experienced, original, perform, integrate, set, improve, busy, post, study, end, efficient, critical, join, offer, keep, different, ideal, complete, transition, act, make, seek, point, think, exceptional, select, preserve, explain, produce, further, intellectual, fill, regard, articulate, respect, contact, free, grow, clear, bring, advise, solve, show, exhibit, fluent, place, thorough, present, document, reach, sustain, private, determine, describe, copy, comfortable, administer, screen, back, great, run, state, suitable, author, keen, credit, consistent, display, define, cover, convey, survey, add, reliable, compile, broadcast, accomplished, early, popular, medical, face, merge, link, mobile, lecture, backup, instruct, see, gather, form, find, play, return, update, transform, smart, interpret, restore, inform, bind, capable, consult, eager, easy, edit, emerge, envision, approachable, favourable, feature, inject, renew, integral, intelligent, layout, live, manipulate, match, missing, note, old, alternate, persuade, useful

Feminine

support, appropriate, include, desirable, design, diverse, creative, good, assist, necessary, ensure, special, content, flexible, book, serve, complex, rare, meet, enthusiastic, change, communicate, positive, enhance, interact, accessible, help, small, ask, teach, cooperative, familiar, organize, unique, cultivate, object, prepare, inclusive, understand, modern, committed, detailed, responsive, kind, encourage, inspire, involve, open, short, organized, engaged, partner, clean, model, expect, view, date, enable, formal, respond, exchange, need, shape, purchase, learn, deep, dedicated, share, care, natural, exciting, social, enjoy, relate, trust, mature, supportive, sophisticated, love, contemporary, list, continue, imaginative, religious, ill, perfect, stay, thoughtful, request, sensitive, welcome, attached, minor, express, benefit, fine, barren, fragile, mix, call, supplement, attend, arrange, correspond, trustworthy, appeal, age, unite, advocate, visit, want, concerned, embrace, dream, photograph, equal, file, follow, generous, give, remain, green, guest, host, like, proper, progressive, little, accept

Masculine

research, strong, successful, incumbent, team, provide, head, professional, master, innovative, print, access, manage, high, chief, major, technical, dynamic, build, implement, energetic, focus, contribute, large, promote, international, lead, scholarly, control, deliver, oversee, senior, demonstrate, practice, physical, achieve, knowledgeable, supervise, assess, focused, important, conduct, finance, train, solid, institute, traditional, order, superior, excel, leading, take, scientific, direct, principal, review, trade, active, undertake, skilled, outside, represent, command, challenge, chair, standard, expert, main, deal, initiate, secure, carry, explore, loan, film, establish, certain, track, adept, productive, strengthen, qualified, practical, investigate, transfer, require, aboriginal, do, fast, hire, cross, negotiate, robust, risk, function, representative, historic, guide, bilingual, expand, rich, address, acquire, accurate, sexual, mentor, recommend, move, shift, common, check, gain, board, advance, travel, employed, capture, resolve, arm, repair, regular, utilize, own, official, operate, extend, interview, issue, grant, pilot, start, forge, competitive, consolidate, constructive, objective, test, succeed, urban, incorporate, independent, devise, pay, accomplish, title, supply, begin, upload, sufficient, suited, become, award, turn, tie, account, authoritative, target, handle, leave, total, agnostic, cold, load, station, exercise, premier, employ, die, determined, prompt, prove, demand, pursue, decisive, patent, indigenous, crucial, overseas, experiment, criminal, retrieve, cool, measure, mark, march, execute, foremost, informed

Table 3   Terminology used in Postings for Level of Qualifications (NER)

adept, competency, comprehensive, deep knowledge, deliver, demonstrate, demonstrated, depth, detailed, effective, effectively, emphasize, essential, evidence, evidence of, excellence, excellent, exceptional, exemplary, experience, experience, experience in, experienced, familiar, familiarity, high, highly, indepth, in-depth, knowledge, knowledge of, knowledgeable, necessary, outstanding, positive, prove, proven, relevant, skill, solid, sound, strong, strongly, substantial, success, successful, superior, thorough

Table 4 Managerial Responsibilities: Terminology (NER)

access management, accountability, accurately, administer, administration, administrative, administrative team, advice, advise, advocacy, analytical, analyze, analyze financial, apply policies, approach, aptitude, assess, assign, assurance, audit, budget, budgetary management, budgeting, build, building, building awareness, business, challenging situations, change management, change policies, changing need, coach, coaching, collaborative, collective agreement, collective agreements, communicate decisions, community building, compiles, conduct, consistent approaches, consultation, consultative, contractual, coordinate, coordinating, coordination, create, creates learned, cultivate, daily operations, day operations, day-to-day services, deadline, deadlines successfully, decision, definite asset, deliver, delivery circulation, departmental, departmental council, departmental policies, departmental procedures, deputize, design, detail-oriented, develop, developing assessment, developing management, developing policies, developing processes, developing program, developing, development, developmental plans, diplomacy, diplomatic, direct, direct management, director, discussion, document workflows, draft, effective operations, efficient, efficiently, engagement, enhance, enhance awareness, ensuring plan, establish, establish mechanisms, establish metadata, establish standing orders, established policies, establishing priorities, evaluate, evaluating, evening supervisor, event coordination, execute, execution, executive, excellent project management, facilitate, facilitation, facilities administrator, facility, financial, financial control, financial functions, financial management, financial resources, flows, forge, forge relationships, form, foster, function, functional operations, fundraising, funnel, goal, government, guidance, help aids, help develop, help train, hire, hiring, identifies fund-, identifies opportunities, identify, identifying objective, implement, implementate, implementation, implementing change, implementing plan, implementing policies, implements policies, improve, improve processes, increase awareness, independently, infrastructure, initiate, instruct, integrated workflow, intercultural, interpersonal, investigates systemic, judgement, judgment, lead, lead change, lead training, leader, leadership, leading, leading-, leading project, leverage, liaise, librarian policies, library management, library operations, library policies, library policy, library workflows, love of learning, maintain, maintain awareness, maintaining awareness, make collections, make recommendations, make resources, make scholarly, manage, management, management policies, management projects, management team, management workflows, manager, managerial, managing, managing change, manipulate, marketing, meeting deadline, meeting objectives, mentor, mentoring, microdat-, monitor, monitoring, negotiate, negotiation, nvivo, of hest, operation, operationalize, optimize, ordering, -ordinator, organisational, organizational, organization, organizational, organizational change, organize, organizing, overall, overall assessment, overall coordination, overall development, overall management, overall operation, overall operations, overall planning, overall responsibility, overall supervision, overall vision, oversee, oversees recruitment, oversight, perform, performance management, personal development, personnel, personnel management, persuade, planning, plan, planning, planning team, play a, play an, policies, policy, policy discussions, policy interpretation, policy issues, policy matters, policy formulation, premises, prepares monthly, prepares report, principal responsibilities, prioritize, priority, problem resolution, problem solving, problem solving, problem report, problem-solving, procedure, procedure oversight, productive, productive relationships, programmatic goals, project-, project aims, project coordinator, project development, project director, project life-cycle management, project management, project opportunities, project partners, project plan, project planning, project prioritization, project skills, project team, promote, promote awareness, promoting awareness, promotion, promotional skills, propose, provide advice, provide expertise, provide guidance, provide leadership, provision, public relations, public services, publicity, publicize, realistic plans, recommendation, recruiting, recruitment, relation, relationship, relationship building, remediate, renew, report, represent, resolution. Resolve, resolve integration, resolve issues, resolve service, responsibilities, responsible, responsible for, responsible management, responsibility, restore, retention, review, revise, schedule, schedule content, screen design, scripting, self-directed, self-motivated, senior level, senior management, serials, student services, service planning, set priorities, setting policy, setting priorities, several administrative, shift priorities, show leadership, smooth operation, solution, solve, spearhead, staff recruitment, staff supervision, staff training, staffed, staffing, staying abreast, stewardship, track, strategic, strategic guidance, strategic leadership, strategic marketing, strategic operations, strategic plan, strategic planning, strategic plans, strategic program, strategically assess, strategically develop, strategy, strengthen, supervise, supervision, supervisor, supervisory,

supervisory duties, supervisory responsibilities, supervisory, support, sustain, sustain resources, synthesis, systematic, tactic, tailor, taking responsibility, team building, team leadership, team orientation, team responsible, team skills, teambuilding, team-building, teamwork, to evaluate, to initiate, to manage, to plan, to supervise, track, train, training, troubleshoot, under supervision, unionized, valuate, visioning, work flows, workflow, workflow guidance

Table 5   Pedagogical Responsibilities (NER)

aid, aids, classroom learning, concise, course, courseware, creating content, ctsi, curricula, curricular, curriculum, datacite, deliver, deliver workshops, delivery, demonstration, design, educate, evaluation, experimentation, expert, expertise, guide, information literacy, ingest, instruct, instruction, instructional, instructor, interpretive, learn, learning, learning materials, lecture, libguide, libguides, literacy, online guides, online instruction, pedagogical, pedagogically, pedagogy, presentation, presenting, reading, research guides, seminar, specialist, standardized, student learning, subject guides, teach, teaching, teamwork, train, training, tutorial, video, wiki, workshop, workshops

Information Literacy is not Scalable
A Call to Re-envision IL Teaching in the Academy

Esther Atkinson and Sheril Hook

Introduction

In 2016, *Guardian* columnist George Monbiot wrote, "The ideology that dominates our lives has, for most of us, no name."[1] This is because the term 'neoliberal' or 'neoliberalism' is largely unknown to the average citizen and very difficult to define. Even though this philosophy of our current political economy remains somewhat opaque, Monbiot says that everything from the climate crisis, to financial meltdowns, to the current mental health emergency can be traced back to the policies of neoliberalism. His article remains essential reading because it is no secret that for the past half a century, Europe and North America have been participants in the neoliberal agenda that has created a system of social, political, and economic inequality.[2] The economic foundation upon which neoliberal policies are built relies on the free-market to encourage competition that is supposed to lead to innovation,

---

1 George Monbiot, "Neoliberalism—The Ideology at the Root of All Our Problems," *The Guardian*, April 15, 2016, https://www.theguardian.com/books/2016/apr/15/neoliberalism-ideology-problem-george-monbiot.

2 See, for example, Hubert Buch-Hansen and Angela Wigger, "Revisiting 50 Years of Market-Making: The Neoliberal Transformation of European Competition Policy," *Review of International Political Economy* 17, no. 1 (2010): 20-44, doi: 10.1080/09692290903014927.

efficiency, and profitability.³ While some may argue these ideals have been achieved, as in all things, their pursuit has had unintended consequences in many sectors of society, including higher education.⁴

Few operating within higher education, including students, faculty, or staff are immune to the pressures imposed by the neoliberal-informed policies adopted by university administrations. The impact of these policies on the budgets of colleges and universities has resulted in reduced staffing, increased competition among departments for funding, the implementation of metrics to justify that funding in order to survive, and planning that resembles a corporate model.⁵ This shift towards a corporate model by institutions of higher education has led to fewer tenured faculty and librarians, an overreliance on the precarious labour of contract instructors, and treating students like customers, all of which undermines the importance of acquiring a university education.⁶ Students pursuing higher education are no longer being educated to become "civic individuals" with the ability to identify and address societal issues; instead they are being trained for jobs as knowledge workers.⁷ When Universities Canada states that 80% of the best paying jobs require a university degree, it reinforces the idea that higher education leads directly to higher earnings and distorts the traditional meaning of an education.⁸

---

3   Buch-Hansen and Wigger, "Revisiting"; Monbiot, "Neoliberalism."

4   Jason Coleman and Lis Pankl, "Rethinking the Neoliberal University: Critical Library Pedagogy in an Age of Transition," *Communications in Information Literacy* 14, no. 1 (2020): 66-74, doi: 10.15760/comminfolit.2020.14.1.15; John Marenbon, "Our Research Funding System is Shortchanging the Humanities," *The Guardian*, December 5, 2018, https://www.theguardian.com/education/2018/dec/05/our-research-funding-system-is-shortchanging-the-humanities.

5   Henry A. Giroux, "Bare Pedagogy and the Scourge of Neoliberalism: Rethinking Higher Education as a Democratic Public Sphere," *The Educational Forum* 74, no. 3 (2010): 184-196, doi: 10.1080/00131725.2010.483897; Monbiot, "Neoliberalism"; Karen P. Nicholson, " 'Being in Time': New Public Management, Academic Librarians, and the Temporal Labor of Pink-Collar Public Service Work," *Library Trends* 68, no. 2 (2019): 130-152, doi: 10.1353/lib.2019.0034.

6   John M. Budd, "A Critique of Customer and Commodity," *College & Research Libraries* 58, no. 4 (1997): 310-321, doi: 10.5860/crl.58.4.309; Giroux, "Bare Pedagogy"; Karen P. Nicholson, "The McDonaldization of Academic Libraries and the Values of Transformational Change," *College & Research Libraries* 76, no. 3 (2015): 328-338, doi: 10.5860/crl.76.3.328.

7   Giroux, "Bare Pedagogy," 186; Henry A. Giroux, "Authoritarianism and the Challenge of Higher Education in the Age of Trump," *Action, Criticism, & Theory for Music Education* 18, no. 1 (2019): 6-25, 16, doi: 10.22176/act18.1.6; Nicholson, "The McDonaldization", 330.

8   Universities Canada, "Stats," accessed March 27, 2023, https://www.univcan.ca/facts-and-stats/stats/80-top-jobs-require-university-degree/.

As the corporate mode of management takes over the administration of universities, the libraries within these institutions of higher education find themselves in a position of needing to demonstrate their relevance in order to continue to receive funding. Despite the fact that libraries are non-revenue generating departments that have traditionally been considered a public good, they are now positioned as an unpaid service provider to the broader institution.[9] Scholars have argued that when libraries employ a customer service model this creates a context where individuals feel they are qualified to provide accurate feedback on their experiences.[10] When libraries adopt changes based on this feedback they shift their role from being a public good to being a service provider that is driven by customer choice.[11] In doing so, libraries become beholden to the needs and wants of external stakeholders who are given the power to influence the library's future, rather than positioning these knowledge organizations as an essential faculty partner in students' intellectual development.

As librarians shifted their work and approach to educating students over the past several decades to meet the demands of the broader socio-political environment, they turned to information literacy (IL) in the late 1980s, a term that superseded bibliographic instruction, as the way forward.[12] Although the U.S. American Library Association (ALA) was the first to publish IL standards, many other countries followed suit.[13] It is no surprise that the language used to describe information literacy in these instruction documents mirrored that in neoliberal discourse; they included standards, learning outcomes, and assessment measures, namely the Association of College and

---

9   Scholars note that much of the work of libraries and librarians is invisible and thus unacknowledged and unrewarded. Since women dominate the profession, this feminized labour is largely undervalued: see Karen P. Nicholson, "Spatial Thinking, Gender and Immaterial Affective Labour in the Post-Fordist Academic Library," *Journal of Documentation* 78, no. 1 (2022): 96-112, doi: 10.1108/JD-11-2020-0194; Lisa Sloniowski, "Affective Labor, Resistance, and the Academic Librarian," *Library Trends* 64, no. 4 (2016): 645-666, doi: 10.1353/lib.2016.0013.

10 Budd, "A Critique," see especially page 311; Nicholson, "The McDonaldization," see especially page 331.

11 Budd, "A Critique," see especially page 315; Nicholson, "The McDonaldization," see especially page 331.

12 "Presidential Committee on Information Literacy: Final Report," Washington, DC: American Library Associaion, 1989.

13 Sandra Campbell, "Defining Information Literacy in the 21st Century," in *Information Literacy: International Perspectives*, ed. Jesús Lau (München: IFLA publications, 2008): 17-26; Estela Morales Campos, Bur"Information Literacy, Universities, and the Access to Information," in *Information Literacy: International Perspectives*, ed. Jesús Lau (München: IFLA publications, 2008): 89-100.

Research Library (ACRL) *Information Literacy Competency Standards for Higher Education*.[14] Members of the ACRL, a division of ALA, began to create IL standards across disciplines, which aligned with a subject liaison model already deeply entrenched in academic libraries.[15] It also sparked an interest in creating assessment tools to measure learning outcomes and, therefore, the effectiveness of library instruction.[16] While there was significant enthusiasm for this model, there were those who resisted this approach to IL instruction.[17] Their challenge, supported by others, resulted in the *Standards* being replaced by a *Framework*: ACRL's *Framework for Information Literacy for Higher Education* in 2015.[18]

The *Standards* were an effective skills-based approach to educating students because a check-list was an easy fit for the neoliberal model of assessment through metrics. The *Framework* is an attempt to override this method and to allow for more critical pedagogies to be developed. Nevertheless, the problem remains: how can librarians who have specialized knowledge of information production, distribution, and organization participate in ensuring students become information literate with the limited resources they have for teaching? The answer, for many library professionals, was to create scalable instruction programs that addressed information literacy learning outcomes, largely based on skill development rather than deep learning, designed to reach the maximum number of students, and required minimal

---

14 Association of College and Research Libraries, *Information Literacy Competency Standards for Higher Education* (Chicago: Association of College & Research Libraries, 2000).

15 The value of the subject liaison model itself has been questioned since it relies on faculty buy-in in order to integrate library instruction into their classes. Additionally, over the past decade the liaison model, where it did exist, has been slowly curtailed or eliminated altogether in favour of functional teams that have been created to meet the needs of the university in areas such as data management, scholarly communications, and digital humanities.

16 Irvin R. Katz, "ETS Research Finds College Students Fall Short in Demonstrating ICT Literacy: National Policy Council to Create National Standards," *College and Research Libraries News* 68, no. 1 (2007): 35-37, doi:10.5860/crln.68.1.7737; Megan Oakleaf, Carolyn Radcliff, and Michelle VanHoeck, *So What? The Results and Impact of a Decade of IMLS-Funded Information Literacy Assessments*, Paper presented at Library Assessment Conference, Seattle, United States, 2014.

17 James Elmborg, "Critical Information Literacy: Implications for Instructional Practice," *Journal of Academic Librarianship* 32, no. 2 (2006): 192-199, doi:10.1016/j.acalib.2005.12.004; Christine Pawley, "Information Literacy: A Contradictory Coupling," *Library Quarterly* 73, no. 4 (2003): 422-452, doi: 10.1086/603440; Eamon Twell, "A Decade of Critical Information Literacy: A Review of the Literature," *Communications in Information Literacy* 9, no. 1 (2015): 24-43, doi:10.15760/commin-folit.2015.9.1.174.

18 Association of College and Research Libraries, *Framework for Information Literacy for Higher Education*, Chicago: Association of College & Research Libraries, 2015.

investment. Essentially, efficient and effective education from librarians that could be measured, and could therefore potentially ensure that their role in the academy would be viewed as important to student success.[19] Trying to be efficient in reaching as many students as possible led to the creation of stand-alone and multi-purposed online tutorials or instructional videos that could be incorporated into existing credit courses through learning management systems or offered as links on the library web site. While there certainly is a place for these learning objects in library instruction, the heavy reliance on this approach elides what is essential in student learning: critical thinking.

This chapter examines some of the literature that reflects the neoliberal policy of efficiency in teaching information literacy vis-à-vis a scalable instructional model to demonstrate that this approach reinforces the shift from educating students to develop a civic outlook to training students to achieve measureable skills. It argues that while there is a place for skill building in information literacy and research in order to enhance learning and that this can be done effectively through online modules, videos, tutorials, or even one-shot library instruction, these should not be favoured over other modes of instruction that are better suited to helping students become information literate critical thinkers. Critical thinking is an essential attribute of college and university graduates and is the very thing for which they need support. Librarians can become part of this process by teaching credit courses, but those courses need to move beyond skill development related to information and instead teach critical engagement with information. We argue here that they also need to move beyond generic IL credit courses into a discipline-focused model that teaches information competency and knowledge that is complementary to disciplines in order to facilitate transfer.[20] We are not advocating for similarity across disciplines but rather an approach to teaching information literacy that is responsive to broad disciplines and based in a credit course model.

---

19 Nicholson, "The McDonaldization."

20 Dana Lynn Driscoll and Wenq Cui, "Visible and Invisible Transfer: A Longitudinal Investigation of Learning to Write and Transfer across Five Years," *College Composition and Communication* 73, no. 2 (2021): 229- 260.

Neoliberalism and the Academic Library: The Problem of Scalable Instruction

As the academic library becomes increasingly beholden to the principles of neoliberalism, their leaders have adapted to the ebb and flow of the market economy. The library and its employees are now subject to what some consider to be an oppressive regime of performance measurements and standards in order to receive the funding available in a given year.[21] Many authors cite this as the impetus for finding innovative ways to provide IL instruction and as a means to adjust to the varied challenges that arise from shrinking library budgets. Thus, it is not surprising to see that many library professionals have searched for innovative ways to meet the new language of standards in order to demonstrate their value to administrators in charge of the purse strings. As Karen Nicholson points out, when higher education adopts the corporate organizational model, the goal is to produce graduates that are prepared to become workers in the knowledge economy and that means being information literate.[22] Part of the corporate model is to find a way to scale production while decreasing costs in areas such as labour and materials. The following discussion shows that this model has seeped into library instruction and there are consequences for student learning: scalable instruction limits our efforts to engage students in critical thinking about information.

According to Bruce Keisling, the terms "scalability" or "scalable" within the library profession are relatively new. As a concept, scalable refers to the ability for something to change in size while maintaining its ability to perform at an optimal level. He goes on to say that it originated in the 1970s with computer networking and architecture but was later adopted in organizational theory as a way to help organizations become bigger, better, and move more rapidly.[23] It is not surprising that with the shift to an online environment, the concept of scalability in teaching had the potential to solve many of the issues academic libraries faced in trying to maintain their "service" quality,

---

21   Monbiot, "Neoliberalism"; Nicholson, "Spatial Thinking," see especially page 100.

22   Nicholson, "Spatial Thinking," 101. See also Karen P. Nicholson, Nicle Pagowsky, and Maura Seale, "Just-in-Time or Just-in-Case? Time, Learning Analytics, and the Academic Library," *Library Trends* 68, no. 1 (2019): 54-75, doi:10.1353/lib.2019.0030.

23   Bruce Kiesling, "Blended Learning: Scaling Library Services and Instruction to Support Changing Educational Landscapes," *Library Management* 39, no. 3-4 (2018): 207-215, doi: 10.1108/LM-08-2017-0080.

including growing their IL programming with fewer staff and financial resources, while also trying to prove their teaching relevance to the academy.[24] Many library professionals have embraced this approach to education. However, an examination of how some authors frame their discussions shows the influence of neoliberal policies that reward efficiency, effectiveness, and innovation rather than foster students' intellectual growth.

Kim G. Read and Maureen Joyous Morasch argue that the use of performance support in a course's learning management system is an option "to provide a scalable solution to information literacy needs of online students" because it meets them at their point of need and as a result, librarians can be more "efficient."[25] Efficiency is also a theme in Susan Mikkelsen and Sara Davidson's article in which they describe their success in using pre-programmed asynchronous library tours on iPods as a way to deal with the limited budget and staffing at the University of California's new Merced campus. The financial and workload issues combined with the increasing student population made face-to-face library instruction untenable.[26] This is not unique to the University of California system. More students are opting to attend institutions with online learning options and this can be a challenge for libraries that do not see an increase in funding or staff support. At the University of Houston, for example, Ashley Lierman and Ariana Santiago report that the creation of online asynchronous learning modules were used to replace or supplement in-person teaching as a way "to address both online course growth and limited instructional capacity."[27] Based on their findings, when instructors adopted these learning objects, "they have proven to provide flexible and scalable options for online IL instruction."[28] At Washington State University, the library's instruction

---

24 At the time of Keisling's publication, he notes that the library literature did not talk about scaling the library organizationally. Keisling, "Blended Learning," 209.

25 Kim G. Read and Maureen J. Morasch, "Research Performance Support: Connecting Online Graduate Students from the LMS to the Library," *Internet Reference Services Quarterly* 21, no. 3-4 (2016):101-113, 101-102, doi: 10.1080/10875301.2016.1240736. See also Sarah Lemire, "Scaling Instruction to Needs: Updating an Online Information Literacy Course," *Reference & User Services Quarterly* 56, no. 1 (2016): 17-22, doi: 10.5860/rusq.56n1.17.

26 Susan Mikkelsen and Sara Davidson, "Inside the iPod, Outside the Classroom," *Reference Services Review* 39, no. 1 (2011): 66-80, doi: 10.1108/00907321111108123.

27 Ashley Lierman and Ariana Santiago, "Developing Online Instruction According to Best Practices," *Journal of Information Literacy* 13, no. 2 (2019): 206-221, 206, doi: 10.11645/13.2.2649.

28 Lierman and Santiago, 218.

team designed an online IL project that was scalable and customizable, both of which were intended to address the ongoing problem of staff shortages.[29]

When presenting their strategies for scalable IL instruction, several authors offer the rationale that this option is an effective way to maintain their roles as educators and therefore ensuring they remain essential to the functioning of the academy. Seth Allen offers readers "a manual that can help the academic library articulate a scalable, sustainable, plan for embedded librarianship in online courses" and ways to help measure "the effectiveness" of the plan.[30] The results from the data from assessments can then be provided to the accrediting agencies as evidence of the effectiveness of the program. Similarly, Laura Gariepy and colleagues used rubrics to assess learning outcomes after IL sessions that can be presented to approving bodies to show the value of the library and these rubrics are adaptable and scalable for use in one-shot sessions, credit courses, and embedded IL programming.[31]

What these authors illustrate is that the library's reaction to an administration's pressure to demonstrate importance within the academy is by submitting to and reinforcing neoliberal policies of efficiency and scalability. As Keisling put it: "We need to deploy capacity, expand reach, preserve quality, and control costs" by using online modules that can replace successful in-person instruction.[32] The question whether online modules can indeed be substituted for live encounters with librarians does not have a straightforward answer. Certainly, some aspects of IL instruction can be done using online tutorials or modules as stand-alone or embedded in a course site. In doing so, librarians can assess lower order thinking (i.e., skills) and this is an important part of learning. However, higher order thinking is not achievable through a one-shot model or online training that focuses on skill

---

29 Steve Borrelli, Corey M. Johnson, and Lara Cummings, "The ILE Project: A Scalable Option for Customized Information Literacy Instruction and Assessment," *Communications in Information Literacy* 3, no. 2 (2009): 128-141, doi: 10.15760/comminfolit.2010.3.2.76.

30 Seth Allen, "Mapping Uncharted Territory: Launching an Online Embedded Librarian Program," *Journal of Library and Information Services in Distance Learning* 11, no. 1-2 (2017): 251-261, 251, 257, doi: 10.1080/1533290X.2016.1193416.

31 Laura W. Gariepy, Jennifer A. Stout, and Megan L. Hodge, "Using Rubrics to Assess Learning in Course-Integrated Library Instruction," *Portal: Libraries and the Academy* 16, no. 3 (2016): 491-509, doi: 10.1353/pla.2016.0043.

32 Keisling, "Blended Learning," 211.

development. If librarians only focus on teaching lower order thinking, then they will continue to undermine their expertise and role in teaching. We posit that teaching lower order, skills-based information literacy does not require the expertise of librarians and that such teaching, when warranted, could easily be offered through other means.

The success of online modules may depend on the nature of a particular audience and how they are targeted. Graduate students, for example, may be more inclined than undergraduate students to pursue links for more information or watch videos on how to accomplish a specific task for an assignment.[33] Undergraduate students, on the other hand, may be more likely to use their own devices to access modules that appeal to their experiences as part of the social media generation when learning about what the library has to offer.[34] Thus, there is a role for online IL modules under certain circumstances. But to suggest this approach to ensuring students graduate with the necessary IL education (i.e., beyond skills) is a scalable, time saving, and cost-efficient solution is not only an overstatement, but it also undermines our ability to partner with faculty on curriculum development and step away from a service ethos when it comes to teaching.

Research has shown that the development of online or e-learning modules can be time consuming and expensive if those involved in their creation do not possess the necessary expertise. In their examination of the actual costs for developing online courses in health education, Edward Meinert and colleagues found that there was considerable variance in budgetary needs. In two of the cases reported, the time needed to record lectures and make edits based on content changes was underestimated as was the price for software and hardware. As such the extra time staff devoted to the work was not properly compensated.[35] In only one case discussed in their study did the production of online lectures come within budget and this was a result of the fact that staff involved with the project had previous experience doing this type of work.[36] These authors conclude that good proj-

---

33 Read and Morasch, "Research Performance," see especially 109-111.

34 This is the point that Mikkelsen and Davidson made with their use of the iPod: "Inside the iPod," 67.

35 Edward Meinert et al., "Examining Cost Measurements in Production and Delivery of Three Case Studies Using E-Learning for Applied Health Sciences: Cross-Case Synthesis," *Journal of Medical Internet Research* 21, no. 6 (2019): e13574, 7, doi: 10.2196/13574.

36 Meinert et al., 7.

ect management and better budgeting to compensate for unexpected contingencies are needed in order to better deliver e-learning courses.[37] This conclusion suggests that libraries that want to participate in the production of online modules need to procure additional staff with the expertise, or develop it themselves, in order to make learning objects a reality. But with shrinking budgets, the rapid pace of technological obsolescence, and hiring freezes, this approach appears neither efficient nor cost-effective, as often claimed.

In addition to not being a cost-effective option, adopting online modules for IL instruction exacerbates the problem of the changing temporal rhythm of the library as a workplace.[38] As Karen Nicholson has argued, the shift to online work has increased the speed at which libraries are expected to operate in order to meet the needs of a 24/7 society. Librarian workloads have increased; they are burdened by the feeling of not keeping up, and find their work is often devalued.[39] Teaching IL has not remained immune to this pressure; librarians create one-shot sessions that are targeted and tailored for students who require immediate answers or can apply the training immediately to a course project; but their teaching approach often depicts research as quick, easy, and efficient.[40] In this model, IL classes become repetitive one-offs and lead to librarian burnout.[41] This issue is confounded by the fact that we are not entirely sure one-shot IL sessions are effective in achieving their stated learning outcomes. In a systematic review of the research on the effectiveness of one-shot instruction, Dani Cook found that the poor study design of these studies makes it difficult to draw any firm conclusions. The results of Cook's meta-analysis show there may be some positive effect on learning for the short-term and for targeted skills, but the lack of sufficient data makes it difficult to say more.[42]

Information literacy instruction, therefore, runs counter to what faculty expect of students in their classrooms when it is reduced to a

---

37   Meinert et al., 10.
38   Nicholson, "Being in Time,"; Nicholson, "Spatial Thinking."
39   See Nicholson, "Being in Time," 137-138, 142-143.
40   Nicholson, 144.
41   Nicholson, 140.
42   Dani Brecher Cook, "Is the Library One-Shot Efective? A Meta-Analytic Study," *College & Research Libraries* 83, no. 5 (2022): 739-750, doi: 10.5860/crl.83.5.739.

skills based approach rather than building or developing students' intellectual curiosity.[43] As Sophie Bury has shown, faculty expect students to acquire the ability to access the information needed for their coursework and, most importantly, learn to engage with that information critically.[44] But students often do not acquire the ability to think critically by the time of their graduation.[45] One possible reason for this is that the process by which one becomes a critical thinker is neither efficient nor scalable. Learning is a slow, gradual process that requires time to read, reflect, engage with information, and practice writing. None of these can be adequately developed in a one-shot, skills-based IL session.

There are convincing discussions of how an IL credit course that is part of a student's course curriculum contributes to their ability to think critically. Compared to one-shot IL instruction, students who complete credit courses specifically designed to enhance information literacy and overall student learning have better academic outcomes.[46] This is because such courses provide an opportunity to slow down the process of learning how to find research, engage thoughtfully with that material, and then write about it critically.[47] One-shot instruction, on the other hand, is skills based and while such teaching has its place in helping students become independent and proficient in doing research, it can be interpreted as reductive and a way of "dumbing down" the process.[48] Although the benefits of IL credit courses to student intellectual growth have been acknowledged, these courses are not widely adopted by institutions of higher education.

---

43 Nicholson, "Spatial Thinking," 100-101.

44 Sophie Bury, "Learning From Faculty Voices on Information Literacy: Opportunities and Challenges for Undergraduate Information Literacy Education," *Reference Services Review* 44, no. 3 (2016): 237-252, 241, doi: 10.1108/RSR-11-2015-0047.

45 Boglarka S. Huddleston et al., "Faculty Perspectives on Undergraduate Research Skills: Nine Core Skills for Research Success," *Reference & User Services Quarterly* 59, no. 2 (2019): 118-130, 119, doi: 10.5860/rusq.59.2.7277.

46 Yvonne Mery, Jill Newby and Ke Peng, "Why One-Shot Information Literacy Sessions Are Not the Future of Instruction: A Case for Online Credit Courses," *College & Research Libraries* 73, no. 4 (2012): 366-377, 375, doi: 10.5860/crl-271.

47 Margaret Artman, Erica Frisicaro-Pawlowski, and Robert Monge, "Not Just One Show: Extending the Dialogue About Information Literacy in Composition Classes," *Composition Studies* 38, no. 2 (2010): 93-110.

48 Nicholson, "The McDonaldization."

Slow Teaching: The Benefits and Barriers to IL Credit Courses

Academic libraries that successfully developed and offered a credit course report, for the most part, being successful in teaching students both IL and critical thinking ability.[49] What this suggests is that these courses contribute to the overall education of students at a deeper level than a one-shot session can provide. However, despite the interest in and benefits of such programming, a recent survey discovered that less than 20% of universities in the United States have adopted credit courses in IL.[50] This does not vary significantly from research reports published as early as the 1970s.[51] The reasons for such a low uptake on including an IL course in the university curriculum should come as no surprise; many of the barriers to implementing classes offered by libraries can be linked to the restrictive neoliberal agenda, as well as traditional views about the role of academic librarians in teaching. Implementing successful IL courses depends on funding, sufficient staffing, administrative support, teaching expertise, appropriate academic credentials, and time, all of which are subject to the pressures imposed by the academy's adoption of a framework of competition. We suggest that within an information economy that requires educated civic individuals that meet the needs of the modern democratic society, academic librarians' teaching roles need to shift toward a more comprehensive credit course model. This, however, requires navigating around specific barriers to be successful.

The lack of published guidelines on how to embed an IL course into a university's curriculum is one of the reasons Raven and Rodrigues cite as the motivation for publishing a report outlining their experiences of the process.[52] In response, they document their success at creating

---

49   Jean Marie Cook, "A Library Credit Course and Student Success Rates: A Longitudinal Study," *College & Research Libraries* 75, no. 3 (2014): 272-283, doi: 10.5860/crl12-424; Meg Raven and Denyse Rodrigues, "A Course of Our Own: Taking an Information Literacy Credit Course from Inception to Reality," *Partnership: The Canadian Journal of Library and Information Practice and Research* 12, no. 1 (2017): 1-20, doi: 10.21083/partnership.v12i1.3907.

50   Nadine Cohen, et al., "A Survey of Information Literacy Credit Courses in US Academic Libraries," *Reference Services Review* 44, no. 4 (2016): 564-282, 567, doi: 10.1108/RSR-03-2016-0021; Spencer Jardine, Sandra Shropshire, Regina Koury, "Credit-Bearing Information Literacy Courses in Academic Libraries: Comparing Peers," *College & Research Libraries* 79, no. 6 (2018): 768-784, 769, doi: 10.5860/crl.79.6.768; Raven and Rodrigues, "A Course of Our Own," 2.

51   Cohen et al., "A Survey."

52   Raven and Rodrigues, "A Course of Our Own," 4. For another case report, see Ellen Daugman, Leslie McCall, and Kaeley McMahan, "Designing and Implementing an Information Literacy Course in the Humanities," *Communications in Information Literacy* 5, no. 2 (2012): 127-143, doi: 10.15760/comminfolit.2012.5.2.108.

and delivering a second year IL credit course that became a popular choice for students. However, they do note that one of the reasons for their success lies in the strong support of the University Librarian advocating on the library's behalf to get the course approved, scheduled, and delivered.[53] Not all institutions report having similar support when trying to put forward a proposal for a course. Often there is resistance from administrators who do not see an IL credit course as an efficient or scalable option; sometimes administrators expect the course to be easy for students.[54] Additionally, faculty perceptions concerning who is responsible for teaching IL can impede successful inclusion of a library credit course.[55] Librarians report that acquiring faculty buy-in for an IL course is difficult and most still only want the one-shot class session.[56]

Successful implementation of an IL credit course does not mean librarians would no longer experience workload challenges.[57] As discussed above, with the increasing pace of work in the online world, librarians are experiencing an increase in their workloads, expectations about the speed at which the work is to be completed, and feelings of not keeping up.[58] When making the decision to implement an IL credit course, one would expect librarians to be in a position to make decisions on how to manage the scope of their work. Deciding to deliver a credit course should include discussion about what other library work must be abandoned to make room for this project. However, this may not be possible or comfortable for all librarians. Some librarians reported that teaching an IL course did not reduce the number of requests for one-shot in-class library instruction and one can imagine there might be a reluctance to say no to teaching that in some small way supports student IL development.[59] Communicating with faculty and others about new approaches to teaching that no longer include one-shot sessions is imperative and should be done as part of transition plan to a new model of IL teaching.

---

53 Raven and Rodrigues, "A Course of Our Own," 17.
54 Cohen et al., "A Survey," 575; Jardine, Shropshire, and Koury, "Credit-Bearing," 775.
55 Huddleston et al., "Faculty Perspectives," 124.
56 Cohen et al., "A Survey," 573.
57 Raven and Rodrigues, "A Course of Our Own," 16.
58 Nicholson, "Being in Time."
59 Jardine, Shropshire, and Koury, "Credit-Bearing," 772.

Planning for new work without an increase in the staffing complement should include a strategy for abandoning other work. When libraries are already experiencing reduced staffing, meeting the expectations of faculty becomes increasingly difficult. In some instances when librarians agree to teach an IL course, they should not be expected to do so in addition to their other work. Many libraries reported that teaching a course was classified as overload and in some cases, they were not financially compensated for their time.[60] In other cases, libraries were left with having to fund the library course from their own budgets even when such courses were designed to support the curriculum of a specific discipline.[61] Budget cuts, hiring freezes, and the fact that libraries are not revenue generating departments within an institution make it exceptionally challenging to advocate for the introduction of an IL course.

In addition to the financial and staffing restrictions, the other impediment to introducing an IL course identified by librarians is their lack of training to teach a credit course. Some have indicated they were ill prepared by their library school education to take on teaching an undergraduate course; others have pointed out that they do not have the relevant subject knowledge to become a course instructor. Nevertheless, librarians with a deep understanding of a particular subject area report great success in keeping students engaged, which translates into meeting the learning outcomes.[62] Librarians' acknowledgement of their own deficiencies in teaching qualifications complements the perception faculty have about who should teach aspects of IL to students. For the most part, faculty believe it is their role to ensure students become good critical thinkers and are able to find and evaluate information relevant to the subjects they teach. In our experience many faculty do not engage with a librarian to incorporate IL into their curriculum. This is often because they are unwilling to surrender limited class time. What confounds this situation is this: faculty say students need to graduate with the necessary critical thinking skills and

---

60 Cohen et al., "A Survey," 571.

61 Margaret G. Burke, "Academic Libraries and the Credit-Bearing Class: A Practical Approach," *Communications in Information Literacy* 5, no. 2 (2012): 156-173, 169, doi: 10.15760/comminfolit.2012.5.2.110.

62 Jeanne Armstrong, "Designing a Writing Intensive Course with Information Literacy and Critical Thinking Learning Outcomes," *Reference Services Review* 38, no. 3 (2010): 445-457, doi: 10.1108/00907321011070928.

say they are responsible for helping them achieve this. If this is the case, then why are students failing to meet this goal? What is getting in the way?

We suggest that the speed at which the world is operating—what Karen Nicholson says is the 24/7 cycle—is one source of the problem. Students of the Gen X or millennial generation have been conditioned to expect their needs to be met instantaneously.[63] They may place a similar expectation on finding, reading, and using information. Researching a topic, learning the specific discourse of a subject area, and reading widely to gain the fundamental knowledge necessary to operate as a critical thinker takes time. It is not something that can be accomplished in a matter of a few hours and it certainly cannot be taught in 50 minutes.[64] It takes time, patience, and resilience on the part of the learner to expend the effort to study and understand a subject deeply. Reading, concentrating, and reflecting are habits that are essential to a university or college education. Separating critical thinking development from information literacy serves only to reduce the latter to a set of skills rather than teach students to make connections between complex ideas.[65] Unless we acknowledge this separation as one source of the problem, we will not solve the issue of IL and critical thinking. Relying solely on one-shot sessions, online chat, and other "time-saving" initiatives for students may only exacerbate the problem. These approaches continue to give students the impression that finding, reading, evaluating, and using information is fast and easy.[66]

Despite the barriers to implementing an IL credit course identified by authors in the literature, these courses are popular and students recognize the value and applicability of what they learn.[67] This is because such courses are another context in which students have an

---

63   Nicholson, "Being in Time."

64   Artman, Frisicaro-Pawlowski, and Monge, "Not Just One Shot."

65   Lori Arp and Craig Gibson, "Library Literacy," *RQ* 35, no. 1 (1995): 27-35, https://www.jstor.org/stable/20862812; Shannon L. Reed and Kirilka Stavreva, "Layering Knowledge: Information Literacy as Critical Thinking in the Literature Classroom," *Pedagogy: Critical Approaches to Teaching Literature, Language, Culture, and Composition* 6, no. 3 (2006): 435-452, doi: 10.1215/15314200-2006-004.

66   Nicholson, "Being in Time."

67   Cook, "A Library Credit Course,"; Julie Biando Edwards, "Added Value or Essential Instruction?: Librarians in the Twenty-First-Century Classroom," *Reference & User Services Quarterly*, 57, no. 4 (2018): 285-293, doi: 10.5860/rusq.57.4.6706; Mery, Newby, and Peng, "Why One-Shot,"; Raven and Rodrigues, "A Course of Our Own."

opportunity to develop their critical thinking skills. Over the course of a semester, instructors can provide pedagogically sound approaches to teaching students how to thoughtfully engage with the literature they are reading and develop their ability to reason through the writing process. Transfer, inquiry based learning, problem based learning, opportunities for discussion and reflection are not conducive to the one-shot 50 minute session.[68] Furthermore, students learn best when they receive constructive feedback from instructors and an opportunity to repeat the process as a form of practice and this is best achieved in a credit course.[69] Learning to be a good critical thinker, therefore, requires time to read and time to practice writing.[70] Since these are the very attributes faculty identify as both necessary and lacking in students at the time of graduation, then one wonders why there is such resistance to a library's information literacy program being embedded in key areas of the university curriculum.

In agreement with Owusu-Ansah's statement on the relevance of bibliographic instruction in an IL program, we are not suggesting the abandonment of online learning modules, in-class sessions, drop-in workshops, or reference services.[71] Instead, we acknowledge there is a need for each of these somewhere along a student's learning pathway and each should be planned in a thoughtful and deliberate way. But if university and colleges are supposed to create graduates with an understanding of their civic responsibility to protect fellow citizen's rights while solving their society's problems, then it is imperative that faculty also take responsibility for embedding research and writing into their classes and not rely on the library to solve what is ostensibly a larger educational problem brought on by the academy's adoption of neoliberal policies.[72] In fact, this is the very point made by authors of the ACRL *Framework*: "Teaching faculty have a greater

---

68 Mandi Goodsett, "Best Practices for Teaching and Assessing Critical Thinking in Information Literacy Online Learning Objects," *Journal of Academic Librarianship* 46, no. 5 (2020): 102163, doi: 10.1016/j.acalib.2020.102163.

69 Mandi Goodsett and Hanna Schmillen, "Fostering Critical Thinking in First-Year Students Through Information Literacy Instruction," *College & Research Libraries* 83, no. 1 (2022): 91-110, doi: 10.5860/crl.83.1.91.

70 Arp and Gibson, "Library Literacy."

71 Edward K. Owusu-Ansah, "Information Literacy and Higher Education: Placing the Academic Library in the Center of a Comprehensive Solution," *The Journal of Academic Librarianship* 30, no. 1 (2004): 3-16, 10, doi: 10.1016/j.jal.2003.11.002.

72 Armstrong, "Designing a Writing Intensive Course"; Giroux, "Bare Pedagogy."

responsibility in designing curricula and assignments that foster enhanced engagement with the core ideas about information and scholarship within their disciplines."[73] However, they also note: "Librarians have a greater responsibility in identifying core ideas within their own knowledge domain that can extend learning for students, in creating a new cohesive curriculum for information literacy, and in collaborating more extensively with faculty."[74] We believe this latter statement is a good opportunity to revisit the role of the credit course in a holistic IL program. As others have pointed out it is important for libraries to have credit courses and other methods of sustained reinforcement of IL for students so they emerge from their college experience ready to face global challenges.[75] Credit courses can help students understand information resources both within their disciplines and the academic environment more broadly if those courses are designed to develop critical thinking.[76] One way this can happen is to shift academic librarian teaching to a scholar-librarian model. [77] In this model the librarian teaches a credit course that focuses on the role of information in a discipline as opposed to standalone instruction in information retrieval. Scholar-librarians that would teach this type of credit course would engage in research to help develop an effective pedagogical model that is anchored to IL as a discipline[78].

---

73 ACRL, *Framework*, 7.

74 ACRL, 7.

75 Rebecca S. Albitz, "The What and Who of Information Literacy and Critical Thinking in Higher Education," *Portal: Libraries and the Academy* 7, no. 1 (2007): 97-109, 103, doi: 10.1353/pla.2007.0000; Owusu-Ansah, "Information Literacy," 10.

76 See for example Artman, Frisicaro-Pawlowski, and Monge, "Not Just One Shot"; Reed and Stavreva, "Layering Knowledge"; Brenda Refaei, Rita Kumar, and Stephena Harmony, "Working Collaboratively to Improve Students' Application of Critical Thinking to Information Literacy Skills," *Writing & Pedagogy* 7, no. 1 (2015): 117-137, doi: 10.1558/wap.v7il.l7232.

77 We thank Scott McLaren, Associate Librarian York University Libraries for sharing the idea of the scholar librarian with us.

78 For more on information literacy as a discipline, see 1) William Badke, "A rationale for information literacy as a credit-bearing discipline," *Journal of Information Literacy*, 2 no. 1 (2008): 1-22. https://doi.org/10.11645/2.1.42 and 2) Clarence Maybee, Karen Kaufmann, Virgina Tucker and John Budd, "Recognizing information literacy as a discipline: Reflections on an ACRL 2023 panel discussion," *College & Research Libraries News*, 84 no. 10 (2023): 363. https://doi.org/10.5860/crln.84.10.363.

Continuing to Struggle Against the Neoliberal Influence on Education

The academy's adoption of neoliberal policies has created a system of education that produces graduates with the skills to enter the workforce rather than critical thinkers ready to take on important social issues.[79] Since critical thinking is antithetical to the neoliberal agenda, the roles of faculty and librarians are at odds with the very institutions that employ them. That said, it is essential that both groups continue to struggle against the continuation of a curriculum that privileges skill development over intellectual development. Decisions made by librarians to teach—in whatever context—must be made based on a different set of factors. Instead of considering how to demonstrate the library's relevance to the academy or to student learning, it might be best to emphasize the desired intellectual development for students. If we are committed to developing critical thinkers, then it is imperative that libraries resist the pressure to "fill in" for faculty while they attend a conference, cater to the whims of a 24/7 information cycle, or engage in the reductive approach of teaching "library skills".

As we emerge from a pandemic that required education to pivot from in-person to online instruction, there is a feeling of urgency in doing what is necessary to maintain the integrity of education's role in preparing people to participate in society. COVID-19 offers governments the perfect crisis opportunity to legislate changes to how education is delivered that conform to a neoliberal appetite for efficiency, cost-effectiveness, and scalability.[80] The successes experienced by colleges and universities in shifting to teaching online under these unusual conditions is the sort of evidence conservative governments need to justify making these changes permanent, or at least an option. But as this crisis has shown, not all students thrive in an online environment.[81] Under the pandemic faculty were encouraged to demonstrate compassion towards students by relaxing standards, but for some

---

79 Giroux, "Bare Pedagogy"; "Authoritarianism."

80 Naomi Klein, *The Shock Doctrine: The Rise of Disaster Capitalism* (Toronto: Vintage Canada, 2008); Philip Mirowski, *Never Let a Serious Crisis Go to Waste: How Neoliberalism Survived the Financial Meltdown* (London: Verso, 2013).

81 Jonathan Malesic, "My College Students Are Not OK," *New York Times*, May 13, 2022, https://www.nytimes.com/2022/05/13/opinion/college-university-remote-pandemic-html?smid=url-share.

this created a culture of disinterestedness and underperformance.[82] If this continues, instructors will not be able to foster critical thinking and engagement with course materials.

Librarians need to struggle against scalable IL teaching in higher education and advocate for a robust pedagogical approach that ensures students' success in developing critical thinking. By shedding light on the problems experienced by librarians implementing IL programs that tend toward bolstering a neoliberal agenda, we believe it is time for a monumental shift in how librarians approach IL teaching in the academy.

Bibliography

Albitz, Rebecca S. "The What and Who of Information Literacy and Critical Thinking in Higher Education." *Portal: Libraries and the Academy* 7, no. 1 (2007): 97-109. doi: 10.1353/pla.2007.0000.

Allen, Seth. "Mapping Uncharted Territory: Launching an Online Embedded Librarian Program." *Journal of Library and Information Services in Distance Learning* 11, no. 1-2 (2017): 251-261. doi: 10.1080/1533290X.2016.1193416.

American Library Association. "Presidential Committee on Information Literacy: Final Report." Washington, DC: American Library Association, 1989.

Armstrong, Jeanne. "Designing a Writing Intensive Course with Information Literacy and Critical Thinking Learning Outcomes." *Reference Services Review* 38, no. 3 (2010): 445-457. doi: 10.1108/00907321011070928.

Arp, Lori and Craig Gibson. "Library Literacy." *RQ* 35, no. 1 (1995): 27-35. https://www.jstor.org/stable/20862812.

Artman, Margaret, Erica Frisicaro-Pawlowski and Robert Monge. "Not Just One Shot: Extending the Dialogue about Information Literacy in Composition Classes." *Composition Studies* 38, no. 2 (2010): 93-110.

Association of College and Research Libraries. *Information Literacy Competency Standards for Higher Education*. Chicago: Association of College & Research Libraries, 2000.

Association of College and Research Libraries. *Framework for Information Literacy for Higher Education*. Chicago: Association of College & Research Libraries, 2015.

---

82 Malesic, "My College Students."

Badke, William. "A rationale for information literacy as a credit-bearing discipline," *Journal of Information Literacy*, 2 no. 1 (2008): 1-22. https://doi.org/10.11645/2.1.42.

Borrelli, Steve, Corey M. Johnson and Lara Cummings. "The ILE Project: a Scalable Option for Customized Information Literacy Instruction and Assessment." *Communications in Information Literacy* 3, no. 2 (2009): 128-141. doi: 10.15760/comminfolit.2010.3.2.76.

Buch-Hansen, Hubert and Angela Wigger. "Revisiting 50 years of Market-Making: The Neoliberal Transformation of European Competition Policy." *Review of International Political Economy* 17, no. 1 (2010): 20-44. doi: 10.1080/09692290903014927.

Budd, John M. "A Critique of Customer and Commodity." *College & Research Libraries* 58, no. 4 (1997): 310-321. doi: 10.5860/crl.58.4.309.

Burke, Margaret G. "Academic Libraries and the Credit-Bearing Class: A Practical Approach." *Communications in Information Literacy* 5, no. 2 (2012): 156-173. doi: 10.15760/comminfolit.2012.5.2.110.

Bury, Sophie. "Learning From Faculty Voices on Information Literacy: Opportunities and Challenges for Undergraduate Information Literacy Education." *Reference Services Review* 44, no. 3 (2016): 237-252. doi: 10.1108/RSR-11-2015-0047.

Campbell, Sandy. "Defining Information Literacy in the 21st Century." In *Information Literacy: International Perspectives*, Vol. 131, 17-26. Edited by ed. Jesús Lau. München: IFLA Publications, 2008.

Campos, Estela Morales. "Information Literacy, Universities, and the Access to Information." In *Information Literacy: International Perspectives*, Vol. 131, 89-100. Edited by ed. Jesús Lau. München: IFLA Publications, 2008.

Cohen, Nadine, Liz Holdsworth, John M. Prechtel, Jill Newby, Yvonne Mery, Jeanne Pfander and Laurie Eagleson. "A Survey of Information Literacy Credit Courses in US Academic Libraries." *Reference Services Review* 44, no. 4 (2016): 564-582. doi: 10.1108/RSR-03-2016-0021.

Coleman, Jason and Lis Pankl. "Rethinking the Neoliberal University: Critical Library Pedagogy in an Age of Transition." *Communications in Information Literacy* 14, no. 1 (2020): 66-74. doi: 10.15760/comminfolit.2020.14.1.15.

Cook, Dani Brecher. "Is the Library One-Shot Effective? A Meta-Analytic Study." *College & Research Libraries* 83, no. 5 (2022): 739-750. doi: 10.5860/crl.83.5.739.

Cook, Jean Marie. "A Library Credit Course and Student Success Rates: A Longitudinal Study." *College & Research Libraries* 75, no. 3 (2014): 272-283. doi: 10.5860/crl12-424.

Daugman, Ellen, Leslie McCall and Kaeley McMahan. "Designing and Implementing an Information Literacy Course in the Humanities." *Communications in Information Literacy* 5, no. 2 (2012): 127-143. doi: 10.15760/comminfolit.2012.5.2.108.

Driscoll, Dana Lynn and Wenqi Cui, "Visible and Invisible Transfer: A Longitudinal Investigation of Learning to Write and Transfer across Five Years." *College Composition and Communication* 73, no. 2 (2021): 229- 260.

Edwards, Julie Biando. "Added Value or Essential Instruction?: Librarians in the Twenty-First-Century Classroom." *Reference & User Services Quarterly* 57, no. 4 (2018): 285-293. doi: 10.5860/rusq.57.4.6706.

Elmborg, James. "Critical Information Literacy: Implications for Instructional Practice." *Journal of Academic Librarianship* 32, no. 2 (2006): 192-199. doi: 10.1016/j.acalib.2005.12.004.

Gariepy, Laura W., Jennifer A. Stout and Megan L. Hodge. "Using Rubrics to Assess Learning in Course-Integrated Library Instruction." *Portal: Libraries and the Academy* 16, no. 3 (2016): 491-509. doi: 10.1353/pla.2016.0043.

Giroux, Henry A. "Bare Pedagogy and the Scourge of Neoliberalism: Rethinking Higher Education as a Democratic Public Sphere." *The Educational Forum* 74, no. 3 (2010): 184-196. doi: 10.1080/00131725.2010.483897.

Giroux, Henry A. "Authoritarianism and the Challenge of Higher Education in the Age of Trump." *Action, Criticism, & Theory for Music Education* 18, no. 1 (2019): 6-25. doi: 10.22176/act18.1.6.

Goodsett, Mandi. "Best practices for teaching and assessing critical thinking in information literacy online learning objects." *Journal of Academic Librarianship* 46, no. 5 (2020): 102163. doi: 10.1016/j.acalib.2020.102163.

Goodsett, Mandi and Hanna Schmillen. "Fostering Critical Thinking in First-Year Students through Information Literacy Instruction." *College & Research Libraries* 83, no. 1 (2022): 91-110. doi: 10.5860/crl.83.1.91.

Huddleston, Boglarka, Jeffrey D. Bond, Linda L. Chenoweth and Tracy L. Hull. "Faculty Perspectives on Undergraduate Research Skills: Nine Core Skills for Research Success." *Reference & User Services Quarterly* 59, no. 2 (2019): 118-130. doi: 10.5860/rusq.59.2.7277>.

Jardine, Spencer, Sandra Shropshire and Regina Koury. "Credit-Bearing Information Literacy Courses in Academic Libraries: Comparing Peers." *College & Research Libraries* 79, no. 6 (2018): 768-784. doi: 10.5860/crl.79.6.768.

Katz, Irvin R. "ETS Research Finds College Students Fall Short in Demonstrating ICT Literacy: National Policy Council to Create National Standards." *College & Research Libraries* 68, no. 1 (2007): 35-37. doi: 10.5860/crln.68.1.7737.

Keisling, Bruce. "Blended Learning: Scaling Library Services and Instruction to Support Changing Educational Landscapes." *Library Management* 39, no 3-4 (2018): 207-215. doi: 10.1108/LM-08-2017-0080.

Klein, Naomi. *The Shock Doctrine: The Rise of Disaster Capitalism*. Toronto: Vintage Canada, 2008.

Lemire, Sarah."Scaling Instruction to Needs: Updating an Online Information Literacy Course." *Reference & User Services Quarterly* 56, no. 1 (2016): 17-22. doi: 10.5860/rusq.56n1.17.

Lierman, Ashley and Ariana Santiago. "Developing Online Instruction According to Best Practices." *Journal of Information Literacy* 13, no. 2 (2019): 206-221. doi: 10.11645/13.2.2649.

Malesic, Jonathan. "My College Students Are Not OK." *New York Times*. May 13, 2022. https://www.nytimes.com/2022/05/13/opinion/college-university-remote-pandemic-html?smid=url-share.

Marenbon, John. "Our Research Funding System is Shortchanging the Humanities." *The Guardian*. December 5, 2018. https://www.theguardian.com/education/2018/dec/05/our-research-funding-system-is-shortchanging-the-humanities.

Maybee, Clarence, Karen Kaufmann, Virgina Tucker and John Budd. "Recognizing information literacy as a discipline: Reflections on an ACRL 2023 panel discussion." *College & Research Libraries News* 84, no. 10 (2023): 363. https://doi.org/10.5860/crln.84.10.563.

Meinert, Edward, Abrar Alturkistani, Kimberley A. Foley, David Brindley and Josip Car. "Examining Cost Measurements in Production and Delivery of Three Case Studies Using E-Learning for Applied Health Sciences: Cross-Case Synthesis." *Journal of Medical Internet Research* 21, no. 6 (2019): e13574. doi: 10.2196/13574.

Mery, Yvonne, Jill Newby and Ke Peng. "Why One-shot Information Literacy Sessions Are Not the Future of Instruction: A Case for Online Credit Courses." *College & Research Libraries* 73, no. 4 (2012): 366-377. doi: 10.5860/crl-271.

Mikkelsen, Susan and Sara Davidson. "Inside the iPod, Outside the Classroom." *Reference Services Review* 39, no. 1 (2011): 66-80. doi: 10.1108/00907321111108123.

Mirowski, Philip. *Never Let a Serious Crisis Go to Waste: How Neoliberalism Survived the Financial Meltdown*. London: Verso, 2013.

Monbiot, George. "Neoliberalism—The Ideology at the Root of All Our Problems." *The Guardian*. April 15, 2016. http://www.theguardian.com/books/2016/apr/15/neoliberalism-ideology-problem-george-monbiot.

Nicholson, Karen P. "The McDonaldization of Academic Libraries and the Values of Transformational Change." *College & Research Libraries* 76, no. 3 (2015): 328-338. doi: 10.5860/crl.76.3.328.

Nicholson, Karen P. " 'Being in Time': New Public Management, Academic Librarians, and the Temporal Labor of Pink-Collar Public Service Work." *Library Trends* 68, no. 2 (2019): 130-152. doi: 10.1353/lib.2019.0034.

Nicholson, Karen P. "Spatial Thinking, Gender and Immaterial Affective Labour in the Post-Fordist Academic Library." *Journal of Documentation* 78, no. 1 (2022): 96-112. doi: 10.1108/JD-11-2020-0194.

Nicholson, Karen P., Nicole Pagowsky and Maura Seale. "Just-in-Time or Just-in-Case? Time, Learning Analytics, and the Academic Library." *Library Trends* 68, no. 1 (2019): 54-75. doi: 10.1353/lib.2019.0030.

Oakleaf, Megan, Carolyn Radcliff and Michele Van Hoeck. "What? The Results & Impact of a Decade of IMLS-Funded Information Literacy Assessments." Paper presented at the Library Assessment Conference: Seattle, United States, 2014.

Owusu-Ansah, Edward K. "Information Literacy and Higher Education: Placing the Academic Library in the Center of a Comprehensive Solution." *The Journal of academic Librarianship* 30, no. 1 (2004): 3-16. doi: 10.1016/j.jal.2003.11.002.

Pawley, Christine. "Information Literacy: A Contradictory Coupling." *Library Quarterly* 73, no. 4 (2003): 422-452. doi: 10.1086/603440.

Raven, Meg and Denyes Rodrigues. "A Course of Our Own: Taking an Information Literacy Credit Course from Inception to Reality." *Partnership: the Canadian Journal of Library and Information Practice and Research* 12, no. 1 (2017): 1-20. doi: 10.21083/partnership.v12i1.3907.

Read, Kim G. and Maureen Joyous Morasch. "Research Performance Support: Connecting Online Graduate Students from the LMS to the Library." *Internet Reference Services Quarterly* 21, no. 3-4 (2016): 101-113. doi: 10.1080/10875301.2016.1240736

Reed, Shannon L., and Kirilka Stavreva. "Layering Knowledge: Information Literacy as Critical Thinking in the Literature Classroom." *Pedagogy: Critical Approaches to Teaching Literature, Language, Culture, and Composition* 6, no. 3 (2006): 435-452. doi: 10.1215/15314200-2006-004.

Refaei, Brenda, Rita Kumar and Stephena Harmony. "Working Collaboratively to Improve Students' Application of Critical Thinking to Information Literacy Skills." *Writing & Pedagogy* 7, no. 1 (2015): 117-137. doi: 10.1558/wap.v7i1.17232.

Sloniowski, Lisa. "Affective Labor, Resistance, and the Academic Librarian." *Library Trends* 64, no. 4 (2016): 645-666. doi: 10.1353/lib.2016.0013.

Tewell, Eamon. "A Decade of Critical Information Literacy: A Review of the Literature." *Communications in Information Literacy* 9, no. 1 (2015): 24-43. doi:10.15760/comminfolit.2015.9.1.174.

Universities Canada. "Stats." Accessed March 27, 2023, https://www.univcan.ca/facts-and-stats/stats/80-top-jobs-require-university-degree/.

Tits, Texts, and Talk
The Neoliberal Shaping of Academic Librarians' Work

Eva Revitt

The Coronavirus pandemic accomplished what decades of collective bargaining and policy development could not: it unchained librarians from the library. By April 2020 some 3.9 billion people, or half the world's population, were under some form of lockdown including stay-at-home orders, curfews, and quarantines.[1] In Canada, over 2000 academic librarians began working from home. The impact of the lockdown on academic libraries has been described as seismic; however, what librarians actually do changed little. The pandemic offered the opportunity to demonstrate what experientially librarians know to be true: our work is overwhelmingly accomplished in front of a computer. However, this is not how the work of librarians is typically viewed. Social consciousness constructs librarians' work as work done by women, task-oriented, regularized, and place based. The conceptualization of the librarian as female is empirically rooted. According to the Canadian Association of Professional Academic Librarians' (CAPAL) census, 74% identified as women.[2] However, the typically associated imagery of the librarian surrounded by books is more the figment of a historicized and dated imagination. The breadth and depth

---

1 Alasdair Sandford, "Coronavirus: Half of Humanity Now on Lockdown as 90 Countries Call for Confinement", *Euronews*, April 3, 2020, https://www.euronews.com/2020/04/02/coronavirus-in-europe-spain-s-death-toll-hits-10-000-after-record-950-new-deaths-in-24-hou.

2 Eva Revitt et. al., *2018 Census of Canadian Academic Librarians User Guide and Results Summary* (Toronto: Canadian Association of Professional Academic Librarians, 2019), doi: 10.7939/DVN/JRDEPL.

of the profession was underscored by the same census that revealed the rich plethora—413 in total—of job titles held by academic librarians including that of Clinical Outreach Librarian, Data and Geographic Information Systems (GIS) Librarian, Digital Repositories Librarian, eLearning Librarian, User Experience Librarian, and Community Services Librarian to name a few. The exploration and analysis of the social and economic devaluation of work that is perceived as work that is typically done by women is beyond the scope of this chapter. However, it is understood that socially and historically rooted notions of gendered work, roles, skill sets, and abilities persist and shape present-day perceptions.

The International Labour Organization identifies a number of benefits to working from home including "the reduction in commuting times; greater autonomy and flexibility in the organization of work; a better work-life balance; increased motivation and reduced turnover; and enhanced productivity and efficiency."[3] Working from home full time may not be possible or even desirable; however, I assert that the flexibility to do so as professional and personal circumstances permit is important to most, if not all, academic librarians. However, when society shifted to a post-pandemic reality, within the profession, there was no tendency to have this flexibility quantified and codified in some working-from-home guidelines. For example: in late fall of 2021 as universities were anticipating a return to more in-person teaching. York University, one of Canada's largest academic library systems, informed full-time librarians and archivists that in January of 2022 they are expected to be on campus at least four days per week.[4] After pushback from librarians, archivists, and the faculty association, York rescinded the guideline. This chapter is not about the applicability of work-from-home guidelines or York University. Instead, I'm interested in examining how it is that a perceived need for such guidelines comes about in the first place? Canada's vast geography, provincial/territorial jurisdiction for education, regionalism, and lack of a national system for post-secondary education means that Canadian universities are independent and autonomous creatures of statutes.[5] Yet,

---

3   Internal Labour Organization, *An Employer's Guide to Working from Home in Response to the Outbreak of COVID_19*, (ISBN 9789220322536, Geneva, 2020) 14.

4   CAUT Listserve, November 16, 2021.

5   Glen A. Jones, ed., *Higher Education in Canada: Different Systems, Different Perspectives* (New York: Routledge, 1997).

despite the specific context of each university, academic librarians, from coast to coast to coast, know that what we do and how we do it is understood in a particular way. I want to examine what happens at the macro level that shapes this common (mis)understanding of librarians' work, work that we as librarians experience quite differently.

It is true that documents such as work-from-home guidelines that articulate bright red lines provide a reassuring level of transparency and constancy; however, I will argue in this chapter that texts—policies, guidelines, information on websites, annual activity reports, documents of professional associations or accreditation bodies and so on—are purveyors of institutional power and as such they are deployed because they are organizationally relevant and not because they are meaningful in the lives of the individuals they address. I begin by discussing how ideological processes distort our understanding of everyday social phenomenon, such as the work of academic librarians, and particularly within a capitalist system. I then review how ideological ways of knowing are dispersed and transported via texts. I move on to examine the relationship between texts and readers, and how the process of reading organizes our consciousness. I conclude by discussing how objectification, the byproduct of ideologically infused discourse and text, works to advance neoliberal values. Texts have been around for centuries; however, in the twenty-first century our reliance on texts has reached unprecedented levels. The workings of our modern society, including the functions of corporate capitalism, would not be possible without texts. The goal of this chapter is to reframe how we understand the role of texts and raise awareness of their controlling and distorting capacities.

Ideology as a Process of Knowing Social Phenomenon

Webster's Encyclopedic Unabridged Dictionary of the English Language defines ideology as "the body of doctrine, myth, symbol, etc., of a social movement, institution, class, or large group."[6] In the social sciences ideology is typically understood as a system of shared beliefs that is relevant to society, though not necessarily true; thus, ideology as a term has negative connotations of being rigid, erroneous,

---

6 *Webster's Encyclopedic Unabridged Dictionary of the English Language* (New York: Gramercy Books, 1994), s.v. "Ideology."

or disconnected from daily life. Ideology is used here differently.[7] It is not a body of ideas but a process, a way of living and knowing the world. Ideology as a process of reasoning, of sense-making, that is embedded in our lived experience is rooted in Karl Marx. Marx articulated this conceptualization of ideology in the German Ideology, which he wrote with Friedrich Engels in 1845 and 1846. The German Ideology is a sustained critique of how the German ideologists, intellectuals, and philosophers of the time thought about society and reality. Marx and Engels criticized many of the German ideologists' conceptions as groundless, detached from the real world, dismissive of history, and ignorant of the importance of social connections.[8]

For Marx and Engels, reality and knowledge—everything about our being, what we know, and how we come to know it—is rooted in the activities of people.[9] History and society are nothing more than processes that reside in the activities of people. In the German Ideology, they lay the groundwork for "historical materialism", the argument that laws, religion, morality, indeed the mental, social, and material preoccupations of human societies are bound up with the "mode of material production" of any age.[10] The mode of material production is a phrase used by Marx and Engels to mean any activity, economic, technological, industrial, agrarian, domestic, and so on that is done to produce or accommodate for the necessities of life. Our social reality, that is how we talk, how we think, how we learn, and how we come to understand our social selves and others, is intertwined with history and the manner in which we provide for ourselves. Ideas and concepts cannot be separated from the experiences and actions of people, which in turn cannot be separated from our history and mode of material production. It is for this reason, for example, that a great thinker like Aristotle could not conceive of the cost of human labour as the basis for the value of commodities because Greece was a slave owning society. Aristotle's process of reasoning was bound by the historical and

---

7   For ideology in the social sciences, see Christoph Henning, "Ideology," in *The Blackwell Encyclopedia of Sociology*, ed. George Ritzer (Malden, MA: Blackwell, 2007).

8   Karl Marx and Friedrich Engels, *The German Ideology: Includes: These on Feuerbach and the Introduction to the Critique of Political Economy* (New York: Prometheus Books, 1998), 46-47.

9   Dorothy E. Smith, "Ideology, Science and Social Relations: A Reinterpretation of Marx's Epistemology," *European Journal of Social Theory* 7, no. 4 (2004): 445-462, doi: 10.1177/1368431004046702.

10 Jan Kandiyali, "Historical Materialism: Marx," in *A Companion to Nineteenth Century Philosophy*, ed. John Shand (Hoboken, NJ: Wiley Blackwell, 2019), 236-360.

economic context in which he lived.¹¹ Our way of knowing the world is given and ideologically predetermined by the material and historical conditions into which we are born. In this chapter, ideology is understood as a process of knowing and living and not as a belief system.

Our current mode of production is the capitalist system. And within such a system, I or you, the reader, we, could not live without the labour of thousands of people that we never see. This desk at which I am sitting, or this computer on which I am writing this chapter was manufactured, assembled, stored, transported, displayed, and shipped by working individuals located temporally and geographically away from me. This specialization and division of labour necessitates a profound level of human interdependence. However, we do not experience life in this interdependent way. Cocooned in our individual homes and condos, accompanied by a public discourse of rugged individualism, we, particularly in the west, pride ourselves on our independence and valorize one's ability to make it "on our own." This is ideology as process at work. The complex economic workings of our society, or as Marx would say of our material mode of production, of capitalism, obscures the linkages between individuals. As individuals, we know what is happening in our daily lives. We are the experts of our local context, how we live, and how we experience our daily particularities. However, when what we can observe and experience transcends our local context, we fill the gaps with ideological ways of knowing.¹² Marx argued that the distortions in our thinking about reality are rooted in the mode of production where components may appear as independent when in fact they are not. For Marx, everything about our social reality and how we provide for ourselves is interconnected.¹³

Dorothy Smith, the Canadian sociologist and social theorist, extends Marx and Engels' conceptualization of ideology as a process of knowing to mainstream sociology. Theories and concepts can be useful in helping us understand the activities and behaviors of people; however, Smith argues that these same theories and concepts also abstract and divorce people from their own experience and local context.

---

11   Jamie Arrosi, "Marx 101: Aristotle, Slavery, and the Equivalent Form of Value," *Political Theorist, Scholar, Educator* (blog), July 2, 2019, https://www.jamiearoosi.com/blog/2019/7/2/marx-101-aristotle-slavery-and-the-equivalent-form-of-value.

12   Smith, "Ideology."

13   Paula Allman, *On Marx: An Introduction to the Revolutionary Intellect of Karl Marx* (Rotterdam: Sense Publishers, 2007).

Smith points out that words and phrases like cultural capital, norms, or delinquency are examples of concepts that are assumed to exist outside of people. They are given agency and made real through how we talk and write about them, yet they are without referent. Smith refers to these stylistic devices as "blobontology."[14] Blobontologies are not grounded in the activities of people. In public and academic discourse, library services is a construct from which people have disappeared. Arguably, the library is an actual place and not a theoretical concept; however, we talk and write as if the building has the capacity to act and to provide independently of people an array of services that we associate with libraries. The "Research and Reference Services: Frequently Asked Questions" page on the Library of Congress website, the world's largest library, exemplifies the point made. The page provides answers to questions often asked by library patrons. I draw attention not to the information provided, but to the anthropomorphized framing of the questions:

- Does the Library offer any courses or training for researchers?
- Can I ask reference questions of the Library of Congress via email, letter, or telephone?
- What online databases and indexes does the Library make available to researchers on site?
- Can the Library of Congress tell me how much my book is worth?

In the above text, the library is training, answering, and providing. It has human characteristics and capacities. The problem is not that we talk this way, but rather that we do not problematize the erasure of people. As Smith and Marx argue, it is not the lexical devices and figures of speech that is the issue; language is not the problem, but rather the erroneous assumptions that we make about what lies underneath.[15] Theories, labels, and lexical expressions, such as the metonym discussed below, abstract, obscure, and mask what is really happening. Yet, these concepts, labels, categories, expressions, and so on are useful and necessary communication devices, and their use makes it possible for us to examine how ideological processes

---

14 Dorothy E. Smith, *Institutional Ethnography: A Sociology for People* (Toronto: Alta Mira Press, 2005), 56.

15 Dorothy E. Smith, *The Conceptual Practices of Power: A Feminist Sociology of Knowledge* (Toronto: University of Toronto Press, 1990), 31-57; Allman, *On Marx*.

manifest in our daily environment and shape our experiences. In short, they make ideological processes visible. Smith underscores that, in and of themselves, labels, theories, ideas, concepts and so on are not ideological; "they are ideological by virtue of being distinctive methods of reasoning and interpreting society."[16]

A metonym is a word or a phrase that is used as a substitute for something that it is closely associated with; for example, Bay Street is a metonym for the financial markets in Canada. Wall Street accomplishes the same within the US context. The metonymic slippage is particularly profound in the case of the library and the librarian.[17] The library stands in for the librarian in a way that a hospital or a school never does for the work of a nurse or a teacher. In everyday parlance, services are provided by the library, but patients are cared for in hospitals and students are taught in schools. The activities of people, of medical professionals, of teachers and educators, are more readily implicated in the latter because services are offered in the building and not by it. In the case of librarians, their work is assumed yet cannot be reduced to them. Lexical devices allow us to speak about library services without worrying about how those services come to be. From here the jump to objectification and an objectified knowing of librarians' work, discussed elsewhere in this chapter, is inevitable.

I argue that the expressions *in the building* versus *by the building* are more than mere semantics; but rather a reflection of how things are conceptually wired in our minds. Our way of speaking and writing is not incidental. Within social consciousness, the librarian, when she exists (and it is always a she) is a servant of the library doing library work, not academic work. Cut off from the disciplinary grounding of library and information science, her work is deintellectualized and confined to the building. This knowing of librarians' work is not rooted in the activities of what librarians actually do. It is a knowing that is ideologically constructed. The lexical devices used in this construction simultaneously reflect and reproduce this ideological way of knowing. They also mask the activities of real people and render the

---

16 Smith, The Conceptual, 36.

17 Deborah Hicks, "Person or Place: Rhetorical Construction of Librarian and Library by the Information Profession Community," *The Canadian Journal of Information and Library Science* 40, no. 4 (2016): 318-33, doi: 10.29173/cais949.

work invisible thus facilitating a process of knowing that leads to false assumptions about reality.

These ideological distortions are concretized in texts—policies, guidelines, information on websites, documents of professional associations or accreditation bodies— which in turn reinforce the very ideological processes out of which they arise. Texts are typically examined for what they say and how they say it. The focus of analysis is on the text. This is particularly true of scholarship that examines academic librarians' work, institutional role, and status.[18] In these instances, the texts are institutionally sanctioned. As dictates, they have authority and agency. I want to reframe how we think about the text and shift the focus away from the content, although this is where the discussion must necessarily begin, to examining how the text is active and activated in the reader. In short, I want to direct our gaze away from the information that texts provide and onto the macro discourses that texts carry and project.

The Text as Active and the Text-Reader Conversation

My analysis of texts follows an approach developed by Dorothy Smith.[19] Smith defines texts broadly as a "material form that enables replication (paper/print, film, electronic, and so on) or what is written,

---

18 See Jennifer Dekker and Mary Kandiuk, eds. *Solidarity: Academic Librarians Labour, Activism and Union Participation in Canada* (Sacramento: Library Juice Press, 2014); David Fox, "A Demographic and Career Profile of Canadian Research University Librarians," *Journal of Academic Librarianship* 33, no. 5 (2007): 540-550, doi: 10.1016/j.acalib.2007.05.006; Mary Kandiuk and Harriet M. Sonne de Torrens, "Librarians in a Litigious Age and the Attack on Academic Freedom," in *Current Issues in Libraries, Information Science and Related Fields*, edited by Anne Woodsworth and W. David Penniman. *Advances in Librarianship*, Volume 39 (Bingley: Emerald Group Publishing, 2015), 3-45, doi: 10.1108/S0065-283020150000039009; Gloria J. Leckie and Jim Brett, "Academic Status for Canadian University Librarians: An Examination of Key Terms and Conditions," *Canadian Journal of Information and Library Science* 20, no. 1 (1995): 1-28; Gloria J. Leckie and Jim Brett, "Job Satisfaction of Canadian University Librarians: A National Survey," *College & Research Libraries* 58, no. 4 (1997): 31-47, doi: 10.5860/crl.58.1.31; Laurie A. Prange, "A New Expectation for Post-Secondary Librarians: Faculty Status, Collective Agreements, and the Online Evidence of Teaching," (master's thesis, Memorial University, 2013), https://research.library.mun.ca/11287/; Eva Revitt and Sean Luyk, "The Role of Library Councils in Canadian Higher Education: An Exploratory Study," *Canadian Journal of Higher Education* 49, no. 1 (2019): 140-158, doi: 10.7202/1060828ar; Jennifer L. Soutter, "The Core Competencies for 21st Century CARL Librarians: Through a Neoliberal Lens," *Journal of Radical Librarianship* 2 (2016), 35-67, https//journal.radicallibrarianship.org/index.php/journal.

19 Dorothy E. Smith, *Texts, Facts and Femininity: Exploring the Relations of Ruling* (London: Routledge, 1993); *Writing the Social: Critique, Theory and Investigations* (Toronto: University of Toronto Press, 1999); *Institutional Ethnography*; Dorothy E. Smith and Susan M. Turner, eds., *Incorporating Texts into Institutional Ethnographies* (Toronto: University of Toronto Press, 2014).

drawn, or otherwise reproduced."[20] Texts are typically treated as independent sources of information, or when the text itself is the source of data or analysis the texts are often assumed to be "inert, dead, and out of context."[21] Texts are mostly treated as something that is given to us. These are texts that exist on their own and independently of people. The focus of analysis becomes the text as opposed to how the text is taken up. To contrast, Smith regards texts as active and implicit in regulating institutional discourses.

Discourse, in the most basic sense, is written or spoken communication. However, Smith argues that discourse is an activity that structures the practices of people in a particular place and time; infused with ideological ways of knowing "discourse constrains what they [people] can say and write and what they say or write reproduces and modifies discourse."[22] This is an understanding of discourse as active within us. Discourse is not something that is done to us. It is not something with agency and power over individuals. Institutional discourse does not prescribe action but rather provide "the terms under which what people do becomes institutionally accountable."[23] By paying attention to how we talk and how we write, we can actually see how discourse regulates and organizes institutional practices. Ideological ways of knowing operate within institutional discourses and institutional discourses are transported via texts.

To help us understand how discourse and text are active, Smith (2005) introduces the "text-reader conversation" (101-122). For Smith, texts are like a speaker. The act of reading "brings text into action in the readers who activate it ... and anchors the text in the local actualities in which people are at work."[24] Words and sentences are implicit in coordinating our consciousness and in imprinting themselves on our mind and thoughts: Labels, categories, and symbols in particular frame the reading for the reader. For example, many collective agreements, that is the document that outlines the rights and responsibilities of academic staff at universities across Canada, specify

---

20 Smith, *Institutional Ethnography*, 228.
21 Smith, *Texts*, 90.
22 Smith, *Institutional Ethnography*, 224.
23 Smith, *Institutional Ethnography*, 113.
24 Smith, *Institutional Ethnography*, 105.

work hours for academic librarians, typically thirty-five hours (35) per week.[25] I'm not interested in having a discussion about librarians' workload, rather I want to highlight how the text not only provides information, i.e. the number of hours librarians are expected to work per week, but also how the text is activated in the reader. The text projects onto the reader's consciousness and structures how to read what comes next. The thirty-five-hour work week sets up a frame, almost instructions, for reading what follows orientating the reader to picking out and reading in the regularized and the repetitive in librarians' professional practice.

The text-reader conversation is a process that replaces individual perspectives, subjectivities, and experiences and translates them into an objectified account of the institutional. The actual work experiences of academic librarians are irrelevant. Smith focuses on the performative character of texts, the imprinting and the activating that happens in the reader when they read.[26] This is text and discourse as active, as projecting onto our mind and orienting our consciousness to librarians' work as the type of work that fits within a thirty-five-hour work box, as quantifiable, measurable, and regularized work would. The thirty-five-hour work week is concretized in texts that simultaneously reflect and reinforce an institutional discourse that structures librarians' work in a particular way.

Texts and the institutional discourses they carry may appear like they are bound or self- contained but they are not. Individual texts never stand alone. They are interlocked into textual chains and hierarchies at all levels of institutional activity and extend beyond into legal, professional, and governmental frameworks across the country and the globe with purpose and intentionality. Institutional discourses, such as the regularizing discourse of librarians' work, reproduce and replicate. And as they reproduce and replicate, they leave objectification in their wake. Objectification is an inherent byproduct of institutional discourses and integral to the actualization of neoliberal values.

---

25 Leckie and Brett, "Academic Status"; Marnie R. Harrington and Natasha Gerolami, "High and Lows: An Examination of Academic Librarians' Collective Agreements," in *In Solidarity: Academic Librarians Labour Activism and Union Participation in Canada*, edited by Jennifer Dekker and Mary Kandiuk (Sacramento, CA: Library Juice Press, 2014), 151-170.

26 Smith and Turner, *Incorporating Texts*.

Objectification: In Service of Neoliberalism

Neoliberalism is a messy term that has come to encompass a social, political, and economic perspective that at its core is about preferencing the interests of the financial markets over the needs of people in society. The Oxford Dictionary of Critical Theory asserts that neoliberalism is a "new phase in the development of the capitalist mode of production" which advances the belief that economic growth, supported by a free market, is the most efficient way to allocate resources and achieve human progress and potential.[27] Neoliberalism privileges competition, entrepreneurism, valorizes individual freedom of choice, and demonizes state intervention, professing instead that all goods and public services, including health care and education, should be priced and privatized. Neoliberalism is not new, its philosophical origins stretch back to the 19th century; however, since the 1980s it has enjoyed a level of resurgence particularly in the economic policies of Ronald Regan and Margaret Thatcher. An example of how neoliberal values have seeped into social consciousness is the notable shift in the last decades of the twentieth century from health care and education being considered a public good to it being considered a public expense. With the understanding that public services are an expense come expectations of accountability which in turn are drivers of an "audit explosion" where quantification, preoccupation with institutional performativity, internal control systems, and outcomes are considered paramount to, and sometimes at the expense of, the provision of health services and education.[28]

There is no shortage of scholarship exploring neoliberal values, thought, and approaches to managing the public and private sectors. However, scholarship connecting neoliberalism with objectification is less pronounced with most studies examining the relationship through a gender or sexualized lens.[29] Yet, objectification as an aspect of de-humanization is integral to the actualization of neoliberal values.

---

27 *The Oxford Dictionary of Critical Theory* (2nd edition), ed. Ian Buchanan (Oxford: Oxford University Press, 2018), s.v. "Neolibreralism."

28 Michael Power, *The Audit Society: Rituals of Verification* (Oxford: Oxford University Press, 1997).

29 Alexandra Rutherford, "Feminism, Psychology, and the Gendering of Neoliberal Subjectivity: From Critique to Disruption," *Theory & Psychology* 28, no. 5 (2018): 619-644, doi: 10.1177/0959354318797194; Elena Teran Tassinari and Shoba Arun, "Performing Beauty: Femininity Ideology, Neoliberalism and Aesthetic Labor Among Young Women in Mexico," *Revista de Estudios de Género: La Ventana* 6, no. 53: 441-484.

Processes of rationalization, a key determinant of neoliberal policy, are far easier to accomplish when people are eliminated from view.

Objectified knowledge is knowledge that is produced within established power structures. In *Writing the Social: Critique, Theory, and Investigation*, Smith discusses the rhetorical practices that are used within the professions, organizations, governments, the media, and other complexes that bring about objectification.[30] A nominal is something that exists in name only such as digitization, curation, and organization. It is actually the infinitive verb form of the nominal—to digitize, to curate, to organize,—that maintains the presence of people. Smith observed that nominals conveniently preserve the accomplishments of people while eliminating their presence and activities.[31] Phrases such as knowledge mobilization, collection management, digital preservation, and so on are ubiquitous in the discipline of library and information science. In these phrases the presence of the subject and their subjectivities is suspended, and agency is transferred from people to the concept. The expertise, development of processes, and coordination of complex activities that is required, for example, to effectively make millions of digital texts and objects accessible and discoverable is subsumed by the concept of collection management. Stripped of the action of people, collection management becomes the actor. Arguably, within librarianship, nominals are the laurels on which it rests. In our effort to endlessly innovate and demonstrate value, librarians employ nominals effortlessly, even aggressively, yet by doing so we facilitate the production of an objectified knowledge of our craft.

Grounding this discussion in my own work as an academic librarian I want to share an example of objectification. Objectification is typically defined as treating and/or seeing a person as if they were an object, a thing, or a commodity. This type of objectification is an important phenomenon and is the type of objectification that is readily exemplified when labels and categories stand in for people. At the institution where I work, librarians are labeled as Professional Resource Faculty (PRF) in the faculty association collective agreement. The PRF designation is not an account of our role but an institutional characterization

---

30 Smith, *Writing the Social*. See especially pages 52-62.

31 Smith, Dorothy E. "Texts and the Ontology of Organizations and Institutions," *Studies in Cultures, Organizations & Societies* 7, no. 2 (2001): 159-198, doi: 10.1080/10245280108523557

of it. I once arrived at a committee meeting and was presumed to be the minute-taking and administrative "resource" for the committee to do its work. This is a category and characterization that supports institutional purposes: the category is a nebulous catch-all phrase that allows for the netting of positions that do not neatly fit into the narrowly construed definition of academic staff. The PRF category is thus institutionally relevant because it facilitates a way for the faculty association to expand its membership while simultaneously underscoring the "otherness" of PRF faculty from instructional faculty. The otherness helps to justify differentiated salary scales. Texts via lexical devices such as categories and labels not only mask the real experiences of people, they bring objectification into existence.

Martha Nussbaum has identified seven features of objectification:

- *instrumentality*
  the treatment of a person as a tool for the objectifier's purposes;

- *denial of autonomy*
  the treatment of a person as lacking in autonomy and self-determination;

- *inertness*
  the treatment of a person as lacking in agency, and perhaps also in activity;

- *fungibility*
  the treatment of a person as interchangeable with other objects;

- *violability*
  the treatment of a person as lacking in boundary-integrity;

- *ownership*
  the treatment of a person as something that is owned by another (can be bought or sold);

- *denial of subjectivity*
  the treatment of a person as something whose experiences and feelings (if any) need not be taken into account.[32]

The metonymic conflation of the library and the librarian and the personification of the library building make fungibility and inertness

---

32 Martha C. Nussbaum, "Objectification" *Philosophy and Public Affairs* 24, no. 4 (1995), 257.

particularly acute forms of objectification in the working lives of librarians. The degree to which the library and librarian are treated as interchangeable is unique; it is difficult to think of another profession or group whose identity is similarly fused with another object. Lexical expressions invisibilize; but objectification goes further, deeper because it produces an objectified knowing. Objectified knowledge has nothing to do with impartiality or fairness. Objectified knowledge is knowledge that is constructed within established power structures. To know something objectively is to know it within the discourse, text, language, practices, and processes of the institution. Objectified knowledge subsumes the experiences and activities of the individual, their subjectivities, particularities, context, and circumstance. Practices of objectification advance neoliberal agendas because they nullify the relevance and situatedness of individuals making processes of rationalization, regulation, and reorganization appear sensical, achievable, and logical.

Conclusion

Academic librarians are engaged with the organization of knowledge. The practice of academic librarianship is rooted in the ethical, theoretical, and technical foundations of library and information science. It is a profession dedicated to making knowledge accessible. However, far from being recognized as integral to the university's core mission of teaching, learning, and knowledge creation, librarians' contribution is often narrowly defined. In this chapter I have presented why librarians' work is conceived in a particular way. Articulating Karl Marx's conceptualization of ideology, I have argued that our way of knowing and understanding the world is historically and materially predetermined by the world into which we are born. Ideology as a process of knowing and living is baked into how we speak, write, and communicate; and how we speak, write, and communicate is bracketed by the world we live in. The way we know and understand our world is concretized in texts. Texts are material, replicable, and iterative. They are ubiquitous and indispensable to the functions of modern society. These characteristics make texts the ideal go-between amongst individuals. Texts carry and reproduce institutional discourses which in turn are infused with ideological ways knowing.

Discourse, although variously theorized, is written or spoken communication. Text and discourse are typically regarded as external to the individual—as information that we happen upon. The goal of this chapter was to disrupt this understanding and bring to the forefront the operative, controlling, and activating capacities of text and discourse. Highlighting the work of the Canadian social theorist Dorothy Smith, I have argued that texts and discourses permeate our consciousness and allow for interpretive practices that rise out of and reflect ideological ways of knowing social reality—such as the regularized, task-oriented, and place-based conception of librarians' work. Smith draws our attention to the role of texts and the discourses they carry as active because these are the means by which institutions exercise power. Texts and institutionalized discourses objectify because they "shift from the perspectives of individuals to a view from nowhere."[33] When the subjectivities and experiences of people are eliminated from view, processes of rationalization, quantification, subsumption—of neoliberalism—are easier to achieve. Once born, discourses become self-replicating. Structuring and shaping as they travel along, they create an institutionalized and objectified understanding of what is really happening. At this macro level discourses are immensely powerful because they are "invisible as power."[34] However, text and discourse cannot exist outside of people. We are all implicated in reproducing discourses and texts that contribute to our own subjugation. Labels, categories, and other lexical devices make institutional discourses visible. By becoming attuned to the way we talk, write, and otherwise communicate, we can take meaningful steps to advance an understanding of our work that is grounded in the actualities of that work.

Bibliography

Allman, Paula. *On Marx: An Introduction to the Revolutionary Intellect of Karl Marx*. Rotterdam: Sense Publishers, 2007.

Aroosi, Jamie. "Marx 101: Aristotle, Slavery, and the Equivalent Form of Value." *Political Theorist, Scholar, Educator* (blog), July 2, 2019. https://www.jamiearoosi.com/blog/2019/7/2/marx-101-aristotle-slavery-and-the-equivalent-form-of-value.

---

33 Smith, *Institutional Ethnography*, 120.
34 Smith, Writing the Social, 174.

Dekker, Jennifer, and Mary Kandiuk, eds. *In Solidarity: Academic Librarians Labour, Activism and Union Participation in Canada*. Sacramento: Library Juice Press, 2014.

Fox, David. "A Demographic and Career Profile of Canadian Research University Librarians." *Journals of Academic Librarianship* 33, no. 5 (2007): 540-550. doi: 10.1016/j.acalib.2007.0.006.

Harrington, Marnie R. and Natasha Gerolami. "High and Lows: An Examination of Academic Librarians' Collective Agreements." In *In Solidarity: Academic Librarians Labour Activism and Union Participation in Canada*, edited by Jennifer Dekker and Mary Kandiuk, 151-70. Sacramento, CA: Library Juice Press, 2014.

Henning, Christoph. 2007. "Ideology." In *The Blackwell Encyclopedia of Sociology*, edited by George Ritzer. Malden. MA: Blackwell, 2007. doi: 10.1002/9781405165518.wbeosi009.

Hicks, Deborah. "Person or Place: Rhetorical Construction of Librarian and Library by the Information Profession Community." *The Canadian Journal of Information and Library Science* 40, no. 4 (2016): 318-33. doi: 10.29173/cais949.

ILO (International Labour Organization). 2020. *An Employer's Guide to Working from Home in Response to the Outbreak of COVID-19*. ISBN 9789220322536. Geneva: ILO. https://www.ilo.org/wcmsp5/groups/public/—-ed_dia-logue/—-act_emp/documents/publication/wcms_745024.pdf

Jones, Glen A. Editor. *Higher Education in Canada: Different Systems, Different Perspectives*. New York: Routledge, 1997.

Kandiuk, Mary, and Harriet M. Sonne de Torrens. "Librarians in a Litigious Age and the Attack on Academic Freedom." In *Current Issues in Libraries, Information Science and Related Fields*, edited by Anne Woodsworth and W. David Penniman, 3-45. Advances in Librarianship, Volume 39. Bingley: Emerald Group Publishing, 2015. doi: 10.1108/S0065-283020150000039009.

Kandiyali, Jan. "Historical Materialism: Marx" In *A Companion to Nineteenth Century Philosophy*, edited by John Shand, 236-360. Hoboken, NJ: Wiley Blackwell, 2019.

Leckie, Gloria J., and Jim Brett. "Academic status for Canadian university librarians: An examination of key terms and conditions." *Canadian Journal of Information and Library Science* 20, no. 1 (1995): 1–28. http://www.utpjournals.com/canadian-journal-of-information-and-library- science.html.

Leckie, Gloria J., and Jim Brett. "Job Satisfaction of Canadian University Librarians: A National Survey." *College & Research Libraries* 58, no. 1 (1997): 31-47. doi: 10.5860/crl.58.1.31.

Marx, Karl, and Friedrich Engels. *The German Ideology: Includes: Theses on Feuerbach and the Introduction to the Critique of Political Economy*. New York, Prometheus Books, 1998. First published 1932.

McCoy, Liz. "Activating the Photographic Text." In *Knowledge, Experience and Ruling Relations: Essays in the Social Organization of Knowledge*, edited by Marie Campbell and Ann Manicom, 181-92. Toronto: University of Toronto Press, 1995.

Nussbaum, Martha, C. "Objectification." *Philosophy and Public Affairs* 24, no. 4 (1995): 249-291.

Power, Michael. *The Audit Society: Rituals of Verification*. Oxford: Oxford University Press, 1997.

Prange, Laurie A. "A New Expectation for Post-secondary Librarians: Faculty Status, Collective Agreements, and the Online Evidence of Teaching." Master thesis, Memorial University, 2013. https://research.library.mun.ca/11287/.

Revitt, Eva, and Sean Luyk. "The Role of Library Councils in Canadian Higher Education: An Exploratory Study." *Canadian Journal of Higher Education* 49, no. 1 (2019): 140-158. doi: 10.7202/1060828ar.

Revitt, Eva, Ebony Magnus, John Wright, and Alvin Schrader. *2018 Census of Canadian Academic Librarians User Guide and Results Summary*. Toronto: Canadian Association of Professional Academic Librarians, 2019. doi: 10.7939/DVN/JRDEPL.

Rutherford, Alexandra. "Feminism, Psychology, and the Gendering of Neoliberal Subjectivity: From Critique to Disruption." *Theory & Psychology* 28, no. 5 (2018): 619-644. doi: 10.1177/0959354318797194.

Sandford, Alasdair. 2020. "Coronavirus: Half of Humanity Now on Lockdown as 90 Countries Call for Confinement." *Euronews*, April 3, 2020. https://www.euronews.com/2020/04/02/coronavirus-in-europe-spain-s-death-toll-hits-10-000-after-record-950-new-deaths-in-24-hou.

Smith, Dorothy E. *The Conceptual Practices of Power: A Feminist Sociology of Knowledge* Toronto: University of Toronto Press, 1990.

Smith, Dorothy E. *Texts, Facts, and Femininity: Exploring the Relations of Ruling*. London, England: Routledge, 1993.

Smith, Dorothy E. *Writing the Social: Critique, Theory and Investigations*. Toronto: University of Toronto Press, 1999.

Smith, Dorothy E. "Texts and the Ontology of Organizations and Institutions." *Studies Cultures, Organizations & Societies* 7, no. 2 (2001): 159-198. doi: 10.1080/10245280108523557

Smith, Dorothy E. "Ideology, Science and Social Relations: A Reinterpretation of Marx's Epistemology." *European Journal of Social Theory* 7, no. 4 (2004): 445-462. doi: 10.1177/136843100404670.

Smith, Dorothy E. *Institutional Ethnography: A Sociology for People*. Toronto: Alta Mira Press, 2005.

Smith, Dorothy E., and Susan M. Turner, eds. *Incorporating Texts into Institutional Ethnographies*. Toronto: University of Toronto Press, 2014.

Soutter, Jennifer L. "The Core Competencies for 21st Century CARL Librarians: Through a Neoliberal Lens." *Journal of Radical Librarianship* 2 (2016): 35-67. https://journal.radicallibrarianship.org/index.php/journal

Teran Tassinari, Elena and Shoba Arun. "Performing Beauty: Femininity Ideology, Neoliberalism and Aesthetic Labor Among Young Women in Mexico." *La Ventana. Revista de Estudios de Género* 6, no. 53 (2021): 441-484.

Webster's Encyclopedic Unabridged Dictionary of the English Language, s.v. "Ideology." New York: Gramercy Books, 1994.

The Proletarianization of Academic Librarianship

Sam Popowich

> "It must be remembered that the white group of laborers, while they received a low wage, were compensated in part by a sort of public and psychological wage. They were given public deference and titles of courtesy because they were white."[1]

Introduction

In "The Library of Babel" (1941), Jorge Luis Borges offers a striking image of the library under the shadow of human extinction: "I suspect that the human species—the unique species—is about to be extinguished, but the Library will endure: illuminated, solitary, perfectly motionless, equipped with precious volumes, useless, incorruptible, secret."[2] In the current context of impending climate catastrophe, we are indeed living under the shadow Borges predicted, but the academic library—like the social, political, and economic world at large—continues to develop at a rapid pace. Indeed, the library is far from "perfectly motionless", but rather is constantly undergoing complex and accelerating change. And while Borges' 20th century saw wholesale upheaval punctuated by wars, revolutions, and economic crises, the

---

1 W. E. B. Du Bois, *Black Reconstruction: An Essay Toward a History of the Part which Black Folk Played in the Attempt to Reconstruct Democracy in America, 1860-1880: Chapter 16: Back Toward Slavery* (New York, NY: Russell & Russell, 1935), 688, https://search.alexanderstreet.com/view/work/bibliographic_entity%7Cdocument%7C4386940.

2 Jorge Luis Borges, "The Library of Babel," in *Labyrinths: Selected Stories and Other Writings*, eds. Donald A. Yates and James E. Irby (London: Penguin, 1970), 85.

21st century gives no indication that such transformations are likely to cease.

Academic librarianship has perforce responded to all these upheavals and transitions, and the structure and orientation of the profession can be mapped to various inflections or mutations in the capitalist mode of production. The transition from the welfare state to neoliberalism is the most important of these inflections, as we are still living with its effects. The postwar period of improved living standards and generalized prosperity saw the rise to dominance of the military-industrial complex and of high-tech scientific knowledge and procedures with academic libraries as full participants in this process.[3] The prominence given in library education to a figure like Vannevar Bush, who headed the US Office of Scientific Research and Development during World War Two and was instrumental in the Manhattan Project, can stand here for librarianship's exaltation of its military-industrial complicity.[4]

The neoliberal "war on higher education" that began in the 1970s had similar effects on the profession as the postwar transition, which had less to do with "information science" specifically and more to do with political economy at large.[5] These effects were slower to reach the academy and academic librarianship as universities retained a certain immunity to capitalist economic restructuring. This immunity arose from the fact that universities were what Rosa Luxemburg called "parasites of surplus value" that is, receiving shares from capitalist profits rather than being directly involved in surplus-value production.[6] Despite its slow start, since the 1990s neoliberal processes of globalization, outsourcing/deprofessionalization, the corporatization of higher education, austerity, and deregulation have expanded into academia

---

3 For development in the postwar period, see Allan Luke and Kapitzke Cushla, "Literacies and Libraries: Archives and Cybraries," *Pedagogy, Culture & Society* 7, no. 3 (1999): 467-91, https://doi.org/10.1080/14681369900200066. For the roles of libraries in these processes, see Sam Popowich, *Confronting the Democratic Discourse of Librarianship: A Marxist Approach* (Sacramento: Library Juice Press, 2019).

4 Wayne Wiegand, "Tunnel Vision and Blind Spots: What the Past Tells Us About the Present: Reflections of the Twentieth-Century History of American Librarianship," *The Library Quarterly* 69, no. 1 (1999): 1-32, http://jstor.org/stable/4309267.

5 For the "war on education," see Henry A. Giroux, *Neoliberalism's War on Higher Education* (Chicago: Hawmarket, 2014); Jamie Brownlee, *Academia Inc: How Corporatization is Transforming Canadian Universities* (Black Point, NS: Fernwood Publishing, 2015), 55.

6 Rosa Luxemburg, "Malthus," in *The Accumulation of Capital* (Abingdon: Routledge, 2009), 194-99.

from their original home in the private sector, imposing the commodity logic of that sector on publicly-funded organizations ostensibly still concerned with the public good rather than private profit.[7][8]

The exacerbation of these changes on the profession in recent years has made academic librarianship begin to pay serious attention to the political economy of library work. Questions of precarity, working conditions, equity, diversity, and inclusion, and the widespread shift to immaterial or cognitive labour in the capitalist centres are increasingly fraught as academic libraries find themselves at the forefront of deprofessionalization and the privatization of higher education itself. These questions play out especially vehemently over issues of equity, inclusion, social justice, and intellectual freedom. The heatedness and "polarization" of these controversies are due in large part to what David Roediger, drawing on the pioneering work of W.E.B. Du Bois, noted with respect to the construction of whiteness in industrializing America. "Whiteness," Roediger writes, "was a way in which white workers responded to a fear of dependency on wage labor and to the necessities of capitalist work discipline."[9] Resistance to social justice and EDI initiatives and the continuation of racism within the profession as a whole indicate that academic librarians, faced with the same concerns as white blue-collar workers in the early 20th century, have tended to respond in the same way, adding to whiteness a sense of their own professional and class superiority as ways – they think – of staving off proletarianization.

---

7 For globalization, see Karen P. Nicholson, "On the Space/Time of Information Literacy, Higher Education, and the Global Knowledge Economy," *Journal of Critical Library and Information Studies* 2, no. 1 (2019): 1-31, https://doi.org/10.24242/jclis.v2i1.86. For outsourcing/deprofessionalization, see Robert Renaud, "Learning to Compete: Competition, Outsourcing, and Academic Libraries," *Journal of Academic Librarianship* 23, no. 2 (1997): 85-90, https://doi.org/10.1016/S0099-1333(97)90003-3; Katherine A. Libby and Dana M. Caudle, "A Survey on the Outsourcing of Cataloging in Academic Libraries," *College & Research Libraries* 58, no. 6 (1997): 550-60, https://doi.org/10.5860/crl.58.6.550; Claire Lise Bénaud and Sever Bordeianu, *Outsourcing Library Operations in Academic Libraries: An Overview of Issues and Outcomes* (Westport, CT: Libraries Unlimited, 1998). For the corporatization of higher education, see Ronald Cox, "The Corporatization of Higher Education," *Class, Race and Corporate Power* 1, no. 1 (2013), Article 8, doi: 10.25148/CRCP.1.1.6092151. For austerity, see Karen P. Nicholson, "The McDonaldization of Academic Libraries and the Values of Transformational Change," *College and Research Libraries* 76, no. 3 (2015): 328-38, https://doi.org/10.5860/crl.76.3.328.

8 Frederic Jameson, *Postmodernism, or, The Cultural Logic of Late Capitalism* (Durham, NC: Duke University Press, 1991).

9 David Roediger, *The Wages of Whiteness: Race and the Making of the American Working-Class* (New York: Verso, 1999), 13.

Seale and Mirza have looked at the relationship between prestige and library labour and at the characterization of library workers as "essential" in the context of the global pandemic.[10] The *Precarity in Libraries* research group is doing important work in understanding precarity within the profession.[11] Recent research by Zvyagintseva and Noûs has demonstrated the ways librarianship has moved from being the work of the "parasites of surplus value" to being fully integrated in a generalized process of surplus-value production and the transfer of public money into private hands.[12]

In their description of precarious labour, Henninger et al. note that neoliberalism's "focus on deregulated free-market economies, individual empowerment, and 'labour flexibility'... prioritizes economic efficiencies for employers and produces an individualistic market of disposable and commodified labour, in part by stripping workers of social protections and relationships.[13] In this chapter, I want to dig deeper into the figure of the "disposable worker" identified by the *Precarity in Libraries* group. Drawing on accounts of Autonomist Marxists in particular, I will situate academic libraries in what they call the "social factory"—the post-Fordist neoliberal labour regime—which began in the 1970s and which by the 1990s had succeeded in dismantling the welfare state in the name of austerity, labour discipline, and the free market.

Labour and The Neoliberal Turn

In the crisis of profitability and labour unrest that provoked the transition to neoliberalism, welfare state protections (especially the Keynesian goal of full employment) were identified as obstacles to

---

10 Maura Seale and Rafia Mirza, "Empty Presence: Library Labor, Prestige, and the MLS," *Library Trends* 68, no. 2 (2019): 252-268, doi: 10.1353/lib.2019.0038; "The Coin of Love and Virtue: Academic Libraries and Value in a Global Pandemic," *Canadian Journal of Academic Librarianship* 6 (2020): 1-30, doi: 10.33137/cjal-rebu.v6.34457.

11 Henninger et al., "Perceptions and Experiences of Precarious Employment in Canadian Libraries: An Exploratory Study," *Partnership* 14, no. 2 (2019): 1-22, doi: 10.21083/partnershiv14i2.5169; "Factors Associated with the Prevalence of Precarious Positions in Canadian Libraries: Statistical Analysis of a National Job Board," *Evidence Based Library and Information Practice* 15, no. 3 (2020): 78-102, doi: 10.18438/eblip29783.

12 Lydia Zvyagintseva, "Articulating our Very Unfreedom: The Impossibility of Refusal in the Contemporary Academy," *Canadian Journal of Academic Librarianship* 7 (2021): 1-21, doi: 10.33137/cjalrcbu.v7.36367; Camille Macos Noûs, "Message from the Grassroots: Scholarly Communication, Crisis, and Contradictions," *Canadian Journal of Academic Librarianship* 7 (2021): 1-27, doi: 10.33137/cjalrcbu.v7.36448.

13 Henninger et al., "Perceptions and Experiences," 3.

restoring capital's discipline over labour.[14] Full employment and solid welfare protections meant that workers could afford to lose a position because it was easy enough to find another and social services could provide adequate support in the interim. Only by removing this safety net could capital reassert its dominance over workers; only if the world outside was hard and dangerous enough could "discipline [function] by threatening you with forced expulsion."[15] The threat of disposability was successful precisely because workers lost the social safety net that would allow them to leave jobs with poor working conditions, low wages, and no benefits. Low unemployment also meant less competition for jobs by what Marx and Engels called the "reserve army" of labour.

The dismantling of the welfare state was combined with the "subsumption" of intellectual and cognitive labour under capitalist logics of profit and exchange. The rapid developments in information and communications technologies (ICTs) in the postwar period enabled the storage of past intellectual labour in (radically cheapened) computerized technology. The idea of technology as stored-up human labour is one of the foundational insights of Marx's *Capital* and has remained important in Marxist political economy.[16] The rise of desktop and mobile computing since the 1980s has opened up previously untouched areas of labour to this ability to store and operationalize intellectual labour, allowing the capitalist logic of surplus value production to colonize cognitive work, with serious repercussions for academic librarianship.

One of the ways in which labour can be made disposable is to make all labour qualitatively the same; in this way, no individual worker brings anything different to their work, and so they can be easily replaced – in the language of mainstream economics, labour-power becomes a

---

14   The work of economist John Maynard Keynes (1883-1946) provided the blueprint for the postwar welfare state economies in Britain and North America. Keynesianism was primarily a response to the Great Depression, seeing economic stability as resulting not from the freedom of markets, but rather from stable aggregate demand, which entailed high public spending and low unemployment to "kick start" to keep the economy going. Neoliberalism was, in part, a rejection of the Keynesianism in favour that had led to thirty years of prosperity and relative economic stability, in favour of free-market fundamentalism. See Quinn Slobodian, *Globalists: The End of Empire and the Birth of Neoliberalism* (Cambridge, Mass.: Harvard University Press, 2018) 119, 164.

15   Grégoire Chamayou, *The Ungovernable Society: A Genealogy of Authoritarian Liberalism* (London: Polity Press, 2021), 24.

16   Karl Marx, *Capital: A Critique of Political Economy, Volume 1* (London: Penguin Books, 1973).

fungible good. Classical political economists noticed this phenomenon as it applied to physical labour.[17] What is new to the neoliberal period is the reduction of *intellectual* or *cognitive* labour to this level of interchangeability. The Italian Autonomist Franco Berardi writes that in the 21st century, "as a general tendency work is performed according to the same physical patterns: we all sit in front of a screen and move our fingers across a keyboard. We type."[18] In order for this process to work in the intellectual and cognitive sphere, intellectual labour must also be reduced to this fungible, qualitative homogeneity.

How did this process occur? In the late 1960s and early 1970s the combined powers of capital and the state pushed through a vast suite of radical reforms intended to restructure postwar capitalism to increase profits and to discipline a labour force that had become "ungovernable". The full extent of these changes only became apparent in the 1990s as computerization, financialization, downsizing, and globalization became dominant factors in contemporary life in the capitalist metropoles. The expansion of computerized services and the outsourcing of cataloguing and metadata work dating back to the 1990s marked a major transformation in academic librarianship, but the roots of this shift go back another twenty years.

In 1993, John Buschman called for a critical perspective on ICTs in librarianship while pointing out the ways in which technology has affected library labour conditions, eroding librarianship's "occupational distinctiveness."[19] In hindsight, Buschman's view now seems naïve. "If information technology is to live up to its promise for greater productivity," he wrote, "managers need to consider its consequences for human beings and the qualities of their work environments."[20]

The disparity in working conditions exposed by the COVID-19 pandemic (articulated along racial and gender lines and expressed in terms of "essential" – or hyperexploitable – workers), the exposure of inhumane working conditions in the surveillance economy exemplified by Amazon, and the callous seizing of the "opportunity" of the pandemic

---

17 Karl Marx, *The Poverty of Philosophy* (Moscow: Progress Publishers, 1955).

18 Franco Berardi, *The Soul at Work: From Alienation to Autonomy* (Cambridge, Mass.: MIT Press, 2009), 74.

19 John Buschman, *Critical Approaches to Information Technology in Librarianship: Foundations and Applications* (Westport, CT: Greenwood Press, 1993), 99.

20 Buschman, *Critical Approaches*, 100.

to pursue neoliberal restructuring (e.g. layoffs and the cutting of departments that don't maximize surplus value extraction) at Laurentian, University of Alberta, Ontario College of Art & Design University, and elsewhere, all indicate the scale of social crisis made possible by the advent of ICTs, capitalist "bottom line" logic, and fractional divisions in the working-class itself.

That this process is not an anomaly, but is simply the latest moment in a fundamental dynamic of capitalism itself, is shown by the fact that already in 1847, Marx could write that "machines are not wage-earners... In England, strikes have regularly given rise to the invention and application of new machines. Machines were, it may be said, the weapon employed by the capitalists to quell the revolt of specialized labour."[21]

Strikes can be understood as only one kind of crisis faced by capitalist profitability, but the lesson can be generalized to other forms of crisis (climate crisis, financial crisis, pandemic): capital's response to crisis is to increase automation to try to make itself less reliant on the "ungovernability" and individualism of human labour. The technological developments which, by the 1990s, were causing such a foundational shift in librarianship were not part of some autonomous, self-directing process particular to libraries. Rather, they were part of capital's response to a crisis of profitability, inflation, and slow economic growth that occurred in the 1970s.[22] The decline in labour protections, the disciplining of the ungovernable labour force, the homogenization of work, and the expansion of the "reserve army" of the unemployed or precarious, were the cost of this restoration of profitability.

As Grégoire Chamayou has noted, American capitalists recognized the profitability crisis by the late 1960s; they blamed it on rising labour costs due to increased labour militancy (which dovetailed with the civil rights, gay rights, and women's movements and anticolonial struggles of the 1960s).[23] Neoliberalism must be understood not merely as an economic response to financial slumps, but as a general solution to the pressure on profits arising from the increasing demands and ungovernability of labour made possible by full employment and the

---

21 Marx, *The Poverty of Philosophy*, 145-46.

22 Hadas Thier, *A People's Guide to Capitalism: An Introduction to Marxist Economics* (Chicago: Haymarket, 2020), 211.

23 Chamayou, *The Ungovernable Society*.

welfare state. Similarly, David Harvey contends that neoliberalism was not a spontaneous reaction to the economic crisis of the early 1970s but was in fact a long-planned response to the postwar settlement that created the welfare state in the first place.[24]

Chamayou and Harvey both, therefore, align with Autonomist Marxism's reversal of the dominant way of understanding the developments of capital, including technological development. Two prevalent views are, one, that "things just happen"—computers developed after World War Two simply because some researchers were interested in them and some capitalists then recognized their economic potential—or, two, that capital makes decisions (around automation, say) to which labour responds. For example, even many early Marxists thought that capital developed solely according to an internal logic of competition, technological innovation, and "neutral" efficiencies. While Engels, after the death of Marx, tried to challenge this "productive force determinism," it was "destined to be disastrously installed as the official version [of Marxism] in the Second International."[25] Autonomist Marxism, which developed in the 1960s and was forced to contend with the neoliberal turn, argued that on the contrary it was the unfolding of the life of the working-class (in all its "ungovernability") that forced capital to constantly revolutionize its methods. In this view, capital needs labour but labour (as the producer of real wealth) does not need capital; and so the compromise between capital and labour that made postwar reconstruction possible was always going to be short-lived, as capital sought a way to reassert its dominance over politics and the economy.

The compromise between labour and capital arose in the aftermath of World War Two in order to deradicalize workers (once the Soviet Union became the primary challenger to capitalist dominance) and to reconstruct the capitalist economy. In this compromise, capital gave up a share of profits to labour (mainly via the labour unions, which were to be brought into the capitalist administrative fold, and tax-funded social services) in order to increase consumption and improve living standards. The state used high taxes to fund welfare services like Medicare in Canada, first introduced in Saskatchewan in 1947, and the

---

24   David Harvey, *A Brief History of Neoliberalism* (Oxford: Oxford University Press, 2005), 15.

25   Paul Blackledge, *Reflections on the Marxist Theory of History* (Manchester: Manchester University Press, 2006), 53; Stuart Hall, "Rethinking the 'Base and Superstructure' Metaphor," in *Selected Writings on Marxism*, edited by Gregor McLennan, 62-90 (Durham, NC: Duke University Press, 2021), 72.

National Health Service in the UK the following year. This compromise led to the postwar boom in wages and consumption whose representative is the upwardly-mobile suburban family who own their own home, able to purchase a car every two years, and who became the privileged target of public library services and public education in the 1950s. Massive movement to the suburbs forced public libraries to rethink their service offerings and academic libraries expanded in order to serve the increasing university enrollment of the new postwar phenomenon, the teenager.[26]

The neoliberal turn was well underway by the late 1970s and the elections of Margaret Thatcher (1979) and Ronald Reagan (1980) represented the complete capture of state power by neoliberal ideology. One of the major characteristics of this capture was the full-scale assault on organized labour to strip away the last remaining protections of the welfare state working-class. Both Reagan and Thatcher showed their willingness to attack labour organizations, with Reagan breaking the air traffic controllers' strike in 1981 and Thatcher the miners' strike in 1984-5. The air-traffic controllers provide a signal example of the changes that had taken place in the politics and economies of the capitalist centres since the war.

In August of 1981, Reagan fired over 11,000 air traffic controllers who had violated a return-to-work order and remained on strike. The breaking of this strike is significant because, as Harvey points out, the air-traffic controllers union, "Professional Air Traffic Controllers Organization (PATCO)," "was more than an ordinary union: it was a white-collar union which had the character of a professional association. It was, therefore, an icon of middle-class rather than working-class unionism."[27] This made PATCO different from, say, the National Union of Mineworkers.

Over the course of the 1970s, then, the disciplining of labour expanded from blue collar labour to white collar workers, illustrated by the breaking of PATCO. How can we explain this expansion and what can it tell us about the political economy of academic librarianship? To

---

26 Christie M. Koontz, "A History of Location of US Public Libraries Within Community Place and Space: Evolving Implications for the Library's Mission of Equitable Service," *Public Library Quarterly* 26, no. 1-2 (2007): 75-100, doi: 10.1300/J118v26n01_05; Stuart Hall and Paddy Whannell, *The Popular Arts* (Durham, NC: Duke University Press, 2018), 19-20.

27 Harvey, *A Brief History of Neoliberalism*, 25.

understand this process we need to turn to the theoretical framework of Autonomist Marxism. Autonomism sees the expansion of the raw power of capital and the capitalist state as part of an ongoing cyclical process of capitalist development rather than merely a response to particular crises. Autonomism therefore normalizes class struggle, seeing it as a consequence of working-class life, rather than simply an acute reaction to the specific conditions of a particular crisis.

Autonomism and the Social Factory

Autonomist Marxism arose out of Italian workerism, a left-wing movement dating back to the 1950s which grew disillusioned with the traditional working-class political institutions, the Communist Party and trade-unions. An "extra-parliamentary" left movement, workerists saw working-class life not negatively, merely as a necessary product of capitalism, but as positive and valuable in its own right. Just as human labour pre-exists capital, so have workers always existed independently of capital. The fact that capital has had to discipline and govern workers in the name of profit is an infringement on the self-determining form-of-life of the working multitude and an indication of its power and agency within the labour-capital relationship. From this perspective, workers do not fight against an agenda set by capital, rather capital is always responding to the spontaneous creativity of working-class life. Capital, in this sense, is always on the back foot.[28]

The Fordist assembly-line was the epitome of labour-discipline in the postwar period: fast, efficient, isolating, mind-numbingly repetitive with little room for error, and most importantly, worked on by interchangeable labourers. The white, male, industrial worker was the paradigm of this period, though the "unskilled" labour of the assembly line lent itself to the replacement of men's labour by the cheaper labour of women. The inclusion of women on the assembly-lines helped give workerists (and especially Autonomist feminists) a key insight: that capitalist exploitation was not limited to those who worked in factories, that the exploitation of labour for surplus value included the exploitation of women's work in the home (leading to the "Wages for Housework"

---

28 Nick Dyer-Witheford, *Cyber-Marx: Cycles and Circuits of Struggle in High-Technology Capitalism* (Champaign, IL: University of Illinois Press, 1999); Steve Wright, *Storming Heaven: Class Composition and Struggle in Italian Autonomist Marxism* (London: Pluto Press, 2002).

movement in the 1970s).[29] Non-waged labour such as housework plays a key role in the reproduction of capitalist exploitation from generation to generation. (I use "non-waged" rather than "unpaid" in this context because in Marxist political economy, some portion of all wage-labour is always unpaid; this portion makes up surplus value).

Autonomist feminists like Silvia Federici analyzed the way women's work in the home served capital by maintaining and reproducing the physical bodies and moral orientations of industrial workers, and this insight led to an understanding of the ways capital's need to discipline and control workers' lives extends beyond the factory into civil society itself. Such discipline requires that workers not lead an independent existence even off the factory floor. All time becomes company time, even – or perhaps especially – women's time performing unpaid reproductive labour. This "unproductive" women's work became the clearest example of the "social factory", the unremunerated work of having children and instilling in them the discipline necessary to become the next generation of workers. In this way, labour costs were increasingly "externalized" and civil society itself increasingly structured by the logics and power dynamics of capitalist exploitation, increasingly reliant on non-waged, non-industrial work to maximize profit.

By the same token, consumption also becomes part of factory discipline, as the purchasing of consumer goods (increasingly built with planned obsolescence in mind) becomes a pillar of economic stability. This too derives from Ford, who paid his workers sufficient wages that they could afford to buy Ford automobiles.

However, workers will always find a way to resist and disrupt capital in order to steal back some agency, some space, some control over their own work and their own time. Capital's response to these working-class challenges (strikes, slowdowns, assembly-line disruptions, etc.) is not only to increase discipline and replace more workers with machines inside the factories, but to expand the scope of factory discipline outside the factory into civil society. A further deepening and expansion of labour exploitation – by stripping away *more* agency and by including *more* areas of non-waged work – is thus always on the horizon, as capital always deals with the unruliness of labour with the same tactics: automation, precarity, increased extraction of non-waged work.

---

29 Silvia Federici, *Revolution at Point Zero: Housework, Reproduction, and Feminist Struggle* (Toronto: Between the Lines, 2012).

The experience of the rapid expansion of Fordism after the war (for example in the Italian "economic miracle" of the 1950s) have given Autonomists deep insights into the neoliberal turn in the 1970s.

One of the effects of post-Fordism and the social factory, then, was to expand capitalist organization and discipline into sectors that had previously been immune (health care, higher education, etc.). This entailed the expansion of the category of "worker" into class fragments that traditionally had not been considered working-class: the liberal professions, professors, librarians, etc. These middle-class professions, jobs that were considered "white collar" or managerial, were brought into the fold of capitalist discipline and surplus-value extraction. Prior to this shift, doctors, lawyers, librarians, etc, were not paid wages but rather were given a share of the profits of capitalists in return for their services.[30] Eventually, however, the "professional-managerial class" as a class "between labour and capital" began to be treated in exactly the same way as industrial workers, subject to the same logic and discipline (competition, austerity, precarity, loss of benefits, etc.).[31] Neoliberalism, then, should be understood as the phase of capitalism in which many previously untouched sectors of labour found their work slowly restructured and made profitable. Suddenly, the surplus value produced by emotional, affective, socially reproductive, and cognitive labour became, for the first time, directly (not just indirectly) exploitable.

True to the patriarchal and racist nature of capitalism, women's reproductive work and the work of people of colour remain predominantly non-waged, while technological, creative cognitive work performed by white men has been incorporated into the "cash nexus" of wage labour. This process has been traced in the computer industry by Mar Hicks and has gradually been applied to academic librarianship.[32] It is

---

30   Luxemburg, *The Accumulation of Capital*, 198.

31   Barbara Ehrenreich and John Ehrenreich, "The Professional-Managerial Class," in *Between Labor and Capital*, ed. Pat Walker (Boston: South End Press, 1979), 5-45.

32   Mar Hicks, *Programmed Inequality: How Britain Discarded Women Technologists and Lost Its Edge in Computing* (Cambridge, Mass: MIT Press, 2017). For how the patriarchal and racist nature of capitalism has made its way into academic librarianship, see Lisa Sloniowski, "Affective Labor, Resistance, and the Academic Librarian," *Library Trends* 64, no. 4 (2016): 645-66, doi: 10.1353/lib.2016.0013; Sam Popowich, "The Power of Knowledge, Objectified: Immaterial Labour, Cognitive Capitalism, and Academic Librarianship," *Library Trends* 68, no. 2 (2019): 153-73, doi: 10.1353/lib.2019.0035; Karen P. Nicholson, "Spatial Thinking, Gender and Immaterial Affective Labour in the Post-Fordist Academic Library," *Journal of Documentation* 78, no. 1 (2022): 96-112.

in this sense that we must understand the novelty of Reagan's attack on the air traffic controllers: it was as if capital, having exhausted one natural resource (industrial workers) had discovered a rich seam of newly-exploitable value (the professional-managerial class).

There are two important consequences to this colonization of previously untouched sectors of work. The first is that these new workers are all having to confront – often for the first time – deskilling, deprofessionalization, and precarity; in other words, proletarianization. Class divisions have increasingly broken down and more and more people who would not have been considered working-class 20 or 30 years ago, have joined the ranks of the proletariat. Indeed, Nick Dyer-Witheford has argued that the term "proletarian" should be reintroduced as a way to encompass precisely those workers who do not belong to the "traditional" conception of working-class, either because they were white-collar professionals (now proletarianized) or because they are not actually "in work."[33] In other words, the group that Marx and Engels referred to as "the dangerous class" or the *lumpenproletariat*, the precariously employed, under-employed, or unemployed.[34]

The second consequence is ideological. People who have traditionally seen themselves as middle-class rather than working-class, professionals rather than labourers, or intellectuals rather than manual workers, continue to cling to these class identities long after they have been proletarianized. Ideological identification (what Althusser calls "interpellation") dies hard, especially amongst those most deeply entrenched in the intellectual and cultural work (and attendant privileges) necessary for the social reproduction of capitalism, like academics and librarians.[35] The difficulty academics and librarians typically have in seeing themselves as workers makes it hard, if not quite impossible, for them to protect themselves against the erosion of their working conditions, because they continue to rely on non-proletarian social relationships (collegial governance, academic freedom, faculty associations as opposed to unions, etc.). Academics and librarians tend to appeal to the "better nature" of capital and their traditions

---

[33] Nick Dyer-Witheford, *Cyber-Proletariat: Global Labor in the Digital Vortex* (Toronto: Between the Lines, 2015), 13, 137.

[34] See Clyde W. Barrow, *The Dangerous Class: The Concept of the Lumpenproletariat* (Ann Arbor: University of Michigan Press, 2020).

[35] Louis Althusser, *On the Reproduction of Capitalism: Ideology and Ideological State Apparatuses* (New York: Version, 2014), 190.

of participating in decision-making and professional privilege, when what is really needed is collective labour action in solidarity with other workers.[36]

While it is beyond the scope of this paper, it should be borne in mind that students have also been subject to a kind of proletarianization. Electronic exam proctoring is only one aspect of the application of factory surveillance and discipline to the student body; the creation of a reserve army of the academically unemployed–including in librarianship–through the graduation of more students than the academic professions can absorb is another important aspect. The pressure of unemployed academic graduates drives down academic wages and destabilizes collective agreements.

Subsumption and the Machine

In an unpublished draft of the sixth chapter of *Capital,* Marx (1973, 949-1048) argued that capitalist production begins when labour ceases to be simply a human activity and becomes instead a commodity, labour-power.[37] The labour of a serf under feudalism was not a commodity: the serf gave material goods to the lord in exchange for protection, but this exchange was not quantified through money: the serf's labour-power was not sold. Once labour-power becomes a commodity, the logic of capitalist efficiency in the name of surplus-value extraction begins to be applied to the conditions of labour itself.[38] The following analysis is presented sequentially for the sake of clarity, but should be understood as representing disjoint and overlapping processes in different social and economic formations.

The first moment, according to Marx, was the "formal subsumption" of labour under capital. Subsumption in this case means something like "inclusion and subordination" expressed in Hegelian terms.[39] Labour becomes subordinated to capitalist requirements for order, efficiency, and the elimination of risk. Under formal subsumption the capitalist

---

36 Sam Popowich, "Can Academics Strike?" *Culturico,* January 28, 2021, https://culturico.com/2021/01/28/can-academics-strike/.

37 Marx, *Capital,* 949-1048.

38 Antonio Negri, *Marx & Foucault* (Cambridge: Polity Press, 2017), 42-57.

39 Georg Wilhelm Friedrich Hegel, *The Science of Logic,* ed. George di Giovanni (Cambridge: Cambridge University Press, 2010), 555.

brings independent labourers together in a single place in order to benefit from economies of scale, unmediated communication, etc. A single shelter, a single supply of raw materials, a single source of decision and command, all brought together under a single authority allows the capitalist to decrease the costs associated with the labour process, ensure quality control, discipline workers, etc.

Formal subsumption makes possible an increased division of labour which leads to the next moment of subsumption, the *real* subsumption of labour under capital. Formally subsumed labour does not differ qualitatively from labour performed under pre-capitalist conditions, other than being centralized. The work of individual spinners or weavers does not change under conditions of formal subsumption. But under real subsumption the actual labour-process itself is taken apart, reduced to its simplest component actions, and built back up into a single efficient process in which each worker now only performs one small task among many. Adam Smith's famous pin factory is a classic example of the real subsumption of labour.[40]

For Marx, formal and real subsumption are associated with the production of absolute and relative surplus value. Absolute surplus value is the quantitative expansion of labour extracted from workers (e.g. through lengthening the working-day) while relative surplus value is its qualitative expansion (e.g. through increased productivity through division of labour or automation).[41] In *Capital*, Marx relates the two moments of subsumption and surplus-value as follows: in the first place "a merely formal subsumption of labour under capital suffices for the production of absolute surplus-value. It is enough, for example, that handicraftsmen who previously worked on their own account, or as apprentices of a master, should become wage-labourers under the direct control of a capitalist.[42] The production of *relative* surplus-value, on the other hand, proceeds "in so far as [capital] seizes upon industries previously only formally subordinate to capital, that is in so far as it continues to proselytize, and second, in so far as the industries

---

40 Adam Smith, *An Inquiry into the Nature and Causes of the Wealth of Nations*, ed. Andrew Skinner (London: Penguin Classics, 1982), 109-10.

41 Marx, *Capital*, 429-38.

42 Marx, 645.

already taken over continue to be revolutionized by changes in the methods of production."[43]

These two conditions—the conversion of sectors "previously only formally subordinate to capital"—and the revolutionization in methods of production—are precisely what academic librarianship has witnessed over the past twenty or thirty years. Universities, originally completely outside the logic and demands of capitalist profitability, were first brought formally under the control of capital, and now are finally being restructured and revolutionized in the process of real subsumption. Originally only "parasites of surplus value", academic workers of all stripes became, first, producers of absolute surplus value and now are being converted to producers of relative surplus value (through cheapening of labour, loss of benefits, automation, etc.). The result is the proletarianization of academic librarians (alongside other academics) as a result of the corporatization and privatization of academia itself.

The 2020-2021 COVID-19 pandemic, for example, provided an excuse for provincial governments in Canada to push ahead with the restructuring of universities in order to make them more profitable; preparation, I would suggest, to their privatization. This explains the massive budget cuts to University of Alberta (prompting a full-scale reorganization and undermining of collective agreements) and the bankruptcy of Laurentian University in Ontario, including massive layoffs of academics and staff and the forced adoption of new collective agreements. This is all part of the disciplining and cheapening of academic labour in order to make universities more attractive to private capital.

If the Fordist assembly-line is the mass-industrial version of Smith's pin factory, the robotic assembly-line may stand as the emblem of post-Fordist, neoliberal production. In his classic work, *Labour and Monopoly Capital*, Harry Braverman notes that "a single illustration, that of the first comprehensive assembly line, will have to suffice as an indication that the wrenching of the workers out of their prior conditions and their adjustment to the forms of work engineered by capital is a fundamental process."[44]

---

43   Marx, 646.

44   Harry Braverman, *Labor and Monopoly Capital: The Degradation of Work in the Twentieth Century, Second Edition* (New York: Monthly Review Press, 1998), 100.

Writing in 1978, Braverman offers a prescient example of what would happen when computerization was applied to non-industrial (i.e. white-collar) forms of labour. He quotes a remark made by Howard C. Carlson, a psychologist employed by General Motors, that "the computer may be to middle management what the assembly line is to the hourly worker."[45] Braverman also quotes from a 1973 Special Task Force report on "Work in America" to the effect that "the office today... is often a factory [...] computer keypunch operators and typing pools share much in common with the automobile assembly line."[46] As we have seen, the ongoing process of subsumption extends the most basic processes of labour dehumanization—assembly-line logic, drab repetition, lack of creativity, etc.—into areas of work which had previously been immune to them, such as academic librarianship. In *Capital*, Marx recognized the effect of automation on the production of relative surplus value. The machine, Marx writes, starts out as an extension of human tool-use, merely expanding the number of tools and their power beyond the natural limits of the human body.[47] Eventually, as less and less human activity is required to put the vast number of machines to use (i.e. the more "productive" labour becomes), the more precarious the situation of workers becomes (as workers become increasingly superfluous). Marx describes the eventual effects of this process in horrific terms. Machines "degrade [a worker] to the level of an appendage of a machine, they degrade his labour by turning it into a torment."[48]

Machinery—especially computerized machinery—not only replaces physical human labour, but also embodies scientific knowledge; the telescope and microscope, for example, embody all our scientific knowledge about optics. In a high-tech society, technology serves as the reification of the general stock of knowledge in the service of that society, embodying its values, opinions, ideologies, biases, and prejudices. The critique of such reification is a major ethical aspect of AI and algorithms today.

We can now understand, then, how technological development aids and supports the process of subsumption. The more technology

---

45 Braverman, *Labor and Monopoly Capital*, 234.
46 Braverman, 23.
47 Marx, *Capital*, 495.
48 Marx, 799.

embodies or objectifies scientific knowledge in addition to physical labour (the way a microscope embodies more scientific knowledge than a hammer), the more intellectual labour is brought under the control of capitalist economic logic: increased productivity, quantified efficiency, precarity, alienation. The development of technology and its role in the subsumption of new sectors of labour and the working-class – sectors that had previously been secure *outside* this process – has already had grave consequences for academic librarianship. Understanding subsumption and proletarianization in this way can help us better recognize the tensions and processes going on within the profession and in academia at large.

As the process of subsumption proceeds apace, academic librarians must come to terms with their proletarianization and prepare for class struggle alongside all other workers. This is in sharp contrast to the usual responses to crises within the profession: the adoption of new ideas or languages in the hope that they will be sufficient to get us through the crisis while protecting our professional-managerial status, or the insistence that the corporatization of librarianship is simply a mistake and that we ought to convince capital to allow us to retain our privileges and immunities. This second strategy is based on the idea that there was at one time a period of "good capitalism" to which we can and should return.[49]

However, the process of subsumption and the existence of the social factory demonstrate that the processes of corporatization and proletarianization are not accidental and that such a return is impossible. These two responses make academic librarianship doubly incapable of dealing adequately with political-economic changes to labour, working conditions, and the labour process. In Marxist language, the profession's response is overdetermined by idealism both in its philosophical sense ("we just need to think differently") and in the common sense which Fobazi Ettarh has called vocational awe: our calling must be immune to tawdry political-economic changes because librarianship serves a higher purpose, unsullied by sordid material considerations.[50]

---

[49] Popowich, *Confronting the Democratic Discourse of Librarianship*, 36-37.

[50] Fobazi Ettarh, "Vocational Awe and Librarianship: The Lies We Tell Ourselves," *In the Library With a Lead Pipe* (January 2018), accessed March 4, 2023, https://www.inthelibrarywiththeleadpipe.org/2018/vocational-awe/.

As both Noûs and Zvyagintseva have pointed out, however, ignoring questions of surplus-value extraction while trumpeting the socially beneficial narratives of librarianship—whether in the form of critical thinking, information literacy, openness, or pedagogy—simply leaves libraries unprepared to deal with the very real effects of capitalist development.[51] As a result, Noûs writes, "exclusion, inequity, and privilege are at the heart of many academic systems" including libraries.[52] The capacity to change academic libraries and their labour practices become increasingly difficult as subsumption proceeds. Zvyagintseva notes that "refusal [becomes] nearly impossible for academic librarians as workers."[53]

Under the welfare state, the power of discipline weakened, as the "ungovernable" workers could turn to welfare state protection and plenty of jobs to make the effects even of dismissal bearable. The purpose of the neoliberal turn was, in large part, to remove these welfare conditions in order to produce just the situation Zvyagintseva describes.

Indeed, as the *Precarity in Libraries* group has pointed out, while the costs of these changes in labour practice are borne by library workers, there is a net benefit to libraries as institutions and organizations.[54] For Noûs, "as much as we may have the urge to reform, it is important to remember that the system isn't broken, it was built this way."[55] Both Noûs and Zvyagintseva call for direct labour action in the face of the social factory and the reification of cognitive labour in new computing technologies. "Sabotage, slowdowns, degrowth, illegal strikes, mutual aid, and other forms of action must be explored by the dwindling community of academic workers."[56]

Conclusion

Prior to proletarianization, academic librarians played a dual role. On the one hand, they were "unproductive consumers" of commodities

---

51 Noûs, "Message from the Grassroots"; Zvyagintseva, "Articulating our Very Unfreedom."
52 Noûs, "Message from the Grassroots," 22.
53 Zvyagintseva, "Articulating our Very Unfreedom," 18.
54 Henninger et al., "Perceptions and Experiences," 14.
55 Noûs, "Message from the Grassroots," 22.
56 Zvyagintseva, "Articulating our Very Unfreedom," 18.

and providers of services paid for out of the profits of capital rather than as wages. On the other hand, their intellectual labour was vital for the reproduction of capitalist society. Antonio Gramsci described intellectuals as playing an important role in the maintenance of hegemony. The ideological prestige Du Bois saw attached to whiteness also applied to intellectual as opposed to manual labour, and this prestige itself was, in the industrial period, vital to the cultural reproduction of capitalist hierarchies. In this sense, the prestige attached to intellectual work indirectly supports capitalist reproduction.

But intellectual work also plays this role directly. Gramsci writes that "the state has and demands consent, but it also 'educates' this consent."[57] Over the course of the twentieth, and especially in the twenty-first century, capital has moved beyond the need either to support a class which does not contribute directly to profits but only—directly and indirectly—to social reproduction and the maintenance of consent. Intellectual workers and professionals, the "parasites of surplus labour", consumed commodities without producing; after John Ford, workers themselves became consumers as well as producers, making the "unproductive consumption" of the professional class redundant. Similarly, the culture industry took over the ideological role (the education of consent) and made that aspect of professional work unnecessary also.

From the capitalist perspective, once this dual move took place, the only remaining reason to retain a class of academics was to train "skilled" workers (i.e. to increase the exchange-value of some workers' labour-power) and to occupy the position of a labour aristocracy, to split the working-class and hold out the image of a privileged type of worker, a worker benefiting from the capitalist social order. The presence of a labour aristocracy gives the rest something to envy, covet, and aspire to, keeping them from focusing on the revolutionary overthrow of capitalist social relations altogether.

If, however, those are the only roles that academic librarians need to perform in capitalist society, then there is no reason to grant them privileges and immunities beyond what is required to perform that role: high wages, good benefits, job security. Once academic librarians become part of the logic of exchange-value, they become subject to cost-reduction as well. There remains no reason *not* to convert

---

57 Antonio Gramsci, *The Prison Notebooks, Volume 1*, ed. Joseph A. Buttigieg (New York: Columbia University Press, 1992), Q1, §47.

the labour aristocracy into direct producers of surplus-value, that is, into workers. This process occurs in parallel with the corporatization and privatization of higher education: once public good is taken out of the equation, there is no reason why private capital shouldn't extract profits and rents from universities.

But ideology always lags behind material reality, and so today many academic librarians do not see themselves as workers, but as a kind of hothouse-flower of enlightenment, teaching, and democracy. They maintain a rearguard action against identifying with other workers, erecting barriers of class and privilege against "non-academic staff". When the usual tactics applied by capital to reduce the privilege of a section of the working-class—precarity, austerity, downsizing, outsourcing, attacks on collective agreements—are turned on academic librarians, they find themselves at a loss. The category of tenure, like that of academic freedom, is a sop offered by capital to ensure that academics continue to see themselves as different from "ordinary" workers. As the case at Laurentian University demonstrated, however, tenure was never a protection against the unstoppable process of proletarianization.

Academic librarians cannot rely on either collegiality or vocational awe to halt this process. No amount of letter-writing, sidewalk chalking, or signage will "convince" the capitalist state to protect or save higher education as a public good. The state is not mistaken, it isn't missing the point or misunderstanding the library's value to a "democratic" society. The problem is not one of information or knowledge. Rather, the state is pursuing the logic of profit to the end, a logic which has no place for education at all beyond the tradeable investment in job skills for what Foucault calls the "entrepreneur of the self."[58] Real human education is impossible under capitalism, as it deforms human relationships to such an extent that all intellectual activity is corrupted by commodity exchange.

So what is to be done? Academic librarians have to figure out what they want. Going back to the old mode of unproductive consumption and its attendant privileges is impossible. I would suggest a future society not based on private property and the exploitation of labour would be a suitable goal. But no matter the goal, librarians who have now

---

58 Michel Foucault, *Birth of Biopolitics: Lectures at the Collège de France, 1978-79* (Basingstoke: Palgrave MacMillan, 2008), 226.

joined the ranks of the fully proletarianized must learn from proletarian labour tactics: the slowdown, the wildcat strike, sabotage. And we must abandon our privileged self-image and join with the other workers who are under attack by the same logic of subsumption and automation, such as teachers, health-care workers, and civil servants, as well as the even less privileged classes of workers: precarious workers, the service industry, migrant workers, and workers under the yoke of a settler-colonialist state, like the Palestinians. Deindustrialization means that we lost the large militant unions that produced waves of labour unrest a century ago, such as the Winnipeg General Strike of 1919; but this provides us with new opportunities for new forms of labour organization to take their place based on the post-Fordist labour regime of former parasites, precarious workers, illegal workers, sex workers, refugees, and all the other ungovernable and dangerous classes of the current moment of capitalist exploitation.

Bibliography

Althusser, Louis. *On the Reproduction of Capitalism: Ideology and Ideological State Apparatuses*. New York: Verso, 2014.

Barrow, Clyde W. *The Dangerous Class: The Concept of the Lumpenproletariat*. Ann Arbor: University of Michigan Press, 2020.

Bénaud, Claire-Lise and Sever Bordeianu. *Outsourcing Library Operations in Academic Libraries: An Overview of Issues and Outcomes*. Westport, CT: Libraries Unlimited, 1998.

Berardi, Franco. *The Soul at Work: From Alienation to Autonomy*. Cambridge, Mass: MIT Press, 2009.

Blackledge, Paul. *Reflections on the Marxist Theory of History*. Manchester: Manchester University Press, 2006.

Borges, Jorge Luis. "The Library of Babel." In *Labyrinths: Selected Stories and Other Writings*, edited by Donald A. Yates and James E. Irby, 78-86. London: Penguin, 1970.

Braverman, Harry. *Labor and Monopoly Capital: The Degradation of Work in the Twentieth Century, Second Edition*. New York: Monthly Review Press, 1998.

Brownlee, Jamie. *Academia, Inc: How Corporatization is Transforming Canadian Universities*. Black Point, NS: Fernwood Publishing, 2015.

Buschman, John. *Critical Approaches to Information Technology in Librarianship: Foundations and Applications*. Westport, CT: Greenwood Press, 1993.

Chamayou, Grégoire. *The Ungovernable Society: A Genealogy of Authoritarian Liberalism*. London: Polity Press, 2021.

Cox, Ronald W. "The Corporatization of Higher Education." *Class, Race and Corporate Power*, vol. 1, no. 1 (2013), Article 8. doiI: 10.25148/CRCP.1.1.6092151.

Du Bois, W. E. B. *Black Reconstruction: An Essay Toward a History of the Part which Black Folk Played in the Attempt to Reconstruct Democracy in America, 1860-1880: Chapter 16: Back Toward Slavery*, 659-698. New York, NY: Russell & Russell, 1935. https://search.alexanderstreet.com/view/work/bibliographic_entity%7Cdocument%7C4386940.

Dyer-Witheford, Nick. *Cyber-Marx: Cycles and Circuits of Struggle in High-Technology Capitalism*. Champaign, Il: University of Illinois Press, 1999.

Dyer-Witheford, Nick. *Cyber-Proletariat: Global Labor in the Digital Vortex*. Toronto: Between the Lines, 2015.

Ehrenreich, Barbara and John Ehrenreich. "The Professional-Managerial Class." In *Between Labor and Capital*, edited by Pat Walker, 5-45. Boston: South End Press, 1979.

Ettarh, Fobazi. "Vocational Awe and Librarianship: The Lies We Tell Ourselves." *In the Library With a Lead Pipe* (January 2018). Accessed March 4, 2023. https://www.inthelibrarywiththeleadpipe.org/2018/vocational-awe/.

Federici, Silvia. *Revolution at Point Zero: Housework, Reproduction, and Feminist Struggle*. Toronto: Between the Lines, 2012.

Foucault, Michel. *Birth of Biopolitics: Lectures at the Collège de France, 1978-79*. Basingstoke: Palgrave Macmillan, 2008.

Giroux, Henry A. *Neoliberalism's War on Higher Education*. Chicago: Haymarket, 2014.

Gramsci, Antonio. *The Prison Notebooks, Volume 1*. Edited by Joseph A. Buttigieg. New York: Columbia University Press, 1992.

Hall, Stuart and Paddy Whannell. *The Popular Arts*. Durham, NC: Duke University Press, 2018.

Hall, Stuart. "Rethinking the 'Base and Superstructure' Metaphor." In *Selected Writings on Marxism*, edited by Gregor McLennan, 62-90. NC: Duke University Press, 2021.

Harvey, David. *A Brief History of Neoliberalism*. Oxford: Oxford University Press, 2005.

Hegel, Georg Wilhelm Friedrich. *The Science of Logic*. Edited by George di Giovanni. Cambridge: Cambridge University Press, 2010.

Henninger, Ean, Adena Brons, Chloe Riley, and Crystal Yin. "Perceptions and Experiences of Precarious Employment in Canadian Libraries: An Exploratory Study." *Partnership* 14, no. 2 (2019): 1-22. DOI:10.21083/partnershiv14i2.5169.

Henninger, Ean, Adena Brons, Chloe Riley, and Crystal Yin. "Factors Associated with the Prevalence of Precarious Positions in Canadian Libraries: Statistical Analysis of a National Job Board." *Evidence Based Library and Information Practice* 15, no. 3 (2020): 78-102. doi: 10.18438/eblip29783.

Hicks, Mar. *Programmed Inequality: How Britain Discarded Women Technologists and Lost Its Edge in Computing*. Cambridge, Mass: MIT Press, 2017.

Jameson, Fredric. *Postmodernism, or, The Cultural Logic of Late Capitalism*. Durham, NC: Duke University Press, 1991.

Koontz, Christie M. "A History of Location of US Public Libraries Within Community Place and Space: Evolving Implications for the Library's Mission of Equitable Service." *Public Library Quarterly* 26, no. 1-2 (2007): 75-100. doi: 10.1300/J118v26n01_05.

Libby, Katherine A. and Dana M. Caudle. "A Survey on the Outsourcing of Cataloging in Academic Libraries." *College & Research Libraries* 58, n. 6 (1997): 550-560. doi: 10.5860/crl.58.6.550.

Luke, Allan and Cushla Kapitzke. "Literacies and Libraries: Archives and Cybraries." *Pedagogy, Culture & Society* 7, no. 3 (1999): 473-474. doi: 10.1080/14681369900200066.

Luxemburg, Rosa. *The Accumulation of Capital*. Abingdon: Routledge, 2009.

Marx, Karl. *The Poverty of Philosophy*. Moscow: Progress Publishers, 1955.

Marx, Karl. *Capital: A Critique of Political Economy, Volume 1*. London: Penguin Books, 1973.

Negri, Antonio. *Marx & Foucault*. Cambridge: Polity Press, 2017.

Nicholson, Karen P. "The McDonaldization of Academic Libraries and the Values of Transformational Change." *College & Research Libraries* 76, no. 3 (2015): 328-338. doi: 10.5860/crl.76.3.328.

Nicholson, Karen P. "On the Space/Time of Information Literacy, Higher Education, and the Global Knowledge Economy." *Journal of Critical Library and Information Studies* 2, no. 1 (2019): 1-31. DOI: 10.24242/jclis.v2i1.86.

Nicholson, Karen P. "Spatial Thinking, Gender and Immaterial Affective Labour in the Post-Fordist Academic Library." *Journal of Documentation* 78, no 1 (2022): 96-112. doi: 10.1108/JD-11-2020-0194.

Noûs, Camille Marcos. "Message from the Grassroots: Scholarly Communication, Crisis, and Contradictions." *Canadian Journal of Academic Librarianship* 7 (2021): 1-27. doi: 10.33137/cjalrcbu.v7.36448.

Popowich, Sam. *Confronting the Democratic Discourse of Librarianship: A Marxist Approach*. Sacramento: Library Juice Press, 2019.

Popowich, Sam. "The Power of Knowledge, Objectified: Immaterial Labour, Cognitive Capitalism, and Academic Librarianship." *Library Trends* 68, no. 2 (2019): 153-173. doi: 10.1353/lib.2019.0035.

Popowich, Sam. "Can Academics Strike?" *Culturico* (January 2021). https://culturico.com/2021/01/28/can-academics-strike/.

Renaud, Robert. "Learning to Compete: Competition, Outsourcing, and Academic Libraries." *The Journal of Academic Librarianship* 23, no. 2 (1997): 85-90. doi: 10.1016/S0099-1333(97)90003-3.

Roediger, David. *The Wages of Whiteness: Race and the Making of the American Working-class*. New York: Verso, 1999.

Seale, Maura and Rafia Mirza. "Empty Presence: Library Labor, Prestige, and the MLS." *Library Trends* 68, no. 2 (2019): 252-268. DOI: 10.1353/lib.2019.0038.

Seale, Maura and Rafia Mirza. "The Coin of Love and Virtue: Academic Libraries and Value in a Global Pandemic." *Canadian Journal of Academic Librarianship* 6 (2020): 1-30. doi: 10.33137/cjal-rcbu.v6.34457.

Slobodian, Quinn. *Globalists: The End of Empire and the Birth of Neoliberalism*. Cambridge, Mass: Harvard University Press, 2018.

Sloniowski, Lisa. "Affective Labor, Resistance, and the Academic Librarian." *Library Trends* 64, no. 4 (2016): 645-666. doiI: 10.1353/lib.2016.0013.

Smith, Adam. *An Inquiry into the Nature and Causes of the Wealth of Nations*. Edited by Andrew Skinner. London: Penguin Classics, 1982.

Thier, Hadas. *A People's Guide to Capitalism: An Introduction to Marxist Economics*. Chicago: Haymarket, 2020.

Wiegand, Wayne. "Tunnel Vision and Blind Spots: What the Past Tells Us about the Present: Reflections on the Twentieth-Century History of American Librarianship." *The Library Quarterly* 69, no. 1 (1999): 1-32. http://www.jstor.org/stable/4309267.

Wright, Steve. *Storming Heaven: Class Composition and Struggle in Italian Autonomist Marxism*. London: Pluto Press, 2002.

Zvyagintseva, Lydia. "Articulating our Very Unfreedom: The Impossibility of Refusal in the Contemporary Academy." *Canadian Journal of Academic Librarianship* 7 (2021): 1-24. doi: 10.33137/cjalrcbu.v7.36367.

Restructuring an Academic Library without Due Process at the Ontario College of Art and Design University

James Forrester & OCAD U Colleagues

Introduction

On May 5, 2021, four senior academic librarians, members of the Ontario Public Service Employees Union (OPSEU), were issued lay-off slips from the Dorothy H. Hoover Library at the Ontario College of Art & Design University (OCAD U). Without due acknowledgement for their years of dedicated service to the community the four academic professionals were laid-off during the global COVID-19 pandemic under the leadership of University Librarian Tony White.[1] The abrupt and poorly handled affair sent shock waves through the OCAD U community and within the profession of academic librarianship across Canada.[2] Compounding the situation was the absence of consideration for the professionals' years of dedicated service to OCAD U in the transformation of a college to a university. The administration's disrespect for academic professionals had not been seen since the termination of senior academic librarians at McMaster University Library in 2011 under

---

1 Tony White joined OCAD U on September 28, 2020, from The Metropolitan Museum of Art in New York City, as the Florence and Herbert Irving Associate Chief Librarian.

2 The Canadian Association of University Teachers (CAUT) President Brenda Austin-Smith, and Executive Director David Robinson wrote a letter on May 14, 2021 to OCAD University President and Vice Chancellor Ana Serrano expressing their concerns and dismay, see OCADFA Blog.

the University Librarian Jeffrey Trzeciak.³ OCAD U was a renowned historical art institution that celebrated its one-hundred-year anniversary in 1976.⁴ In 2002 it acquired degree-granting status as a university. How could this have happened? What went wrong at OCAD U?

The dismissal of the four senior librarians at OCAD U was tethered to the turbulent growing-pains of the Ontario School of Art's transition from a studio-based art college in the nineteenth century to a degree-granting university for undergraduates and graduate students in the twenty-first century and to the development of an academic library. OCAD U's change was part of a growing trend that witnessed several Canadian colleges transitioning to universities as well as the struggle in balancing student needs for creative expression as well as academic achievement.⁵ In the case of OCAD U, the administration's rhetoric about the role of the library during this transformative period (2008-2021) when obtaining government support found no basis in what actually transpired. The public rhetoric that ensured the growth of an academic library for degree programs and secured the confidence of government councils and funding to obtain accreditation as a post-secondary educational institute was regrettably not reflected in the internal management decisions.

From the late 1990s through to 2021 the cavalier attitudes expressed by administrators at OCAD and OCAD U concerning the need for an academic library and the role of professional librarians gradually exposed the increased creep of corporatization into the academy and a blatant lack of understanding about academic resources required by students at a degree granting institution. To fully understand the foundational chaos that led to the dismissal of the four senior librarians, it is important to understand the recent history of the library within the academic framework of OCA transitioning to OCAD University. This article provides a brief overview of the transition of a studio-based art school to a university and outlines the historical decisions concerning the building of an OCAD U library and the historical

---

3   Jim Turk, CAUT, "Academic Freedom for Librarians: What is it, and Why Does it Matter?" (August 25, 2010), 1–12.

4   Paul Fleck, "Art and Business: Ontario College of Art: A Hundred Years of Turbulence and Creativity," *Business Quarterly* 42, no.2 (1977), 79-81.

5   Natalie Samson, "Across Canada, More Colleges are Transitioning to Universities," *University Affairs*, June 2018, https://universityaffairs.ca/news/news-article/across-canada-more-colleges-are-transitioning-to-universities/.

status of professional librarianship at OCAD U that led to the precipitous events of May 2021.

The Evolution of the Ontario College of Art (1876—1996)

The early seeds of OCAD U's turbulent and at times tumultuous origins is virtually unknown outside the artistic community. OCAD U is situated in the downtown Toronto neighbourhood called The Ward. Historically, it was a mix of immigrants and refugees, reflecting a contemporary profile of Toronto rather than the traditional "Toronto the Good" WASP (White Anglo-Saxon Protestant) stereotype of the nineteenth century.[6] OCAD U was originally called the Ontario School of Art, founded by the Ontario Society of Artists, with a $1,000 grant from the Ontario Department of Education in 1876. At that time the population of the city of Toronto was only 60,000.[7] From the beginning there were administrative problems, exacerbated by tensions between the artists and members in the government council who wished to manage the curriculum and the enrollment. As these battles ebbed and flowed the name, location and affiliation of the school kept evolving, as it bounced back and forth between the Ontario Society of Artists and the Ontario Department of Education.

It was initially meant to be a hands-on, industrial training school, affiliated with The Mechanics Institute and the early Toronto Free Library movements.[8] That's the basis upon which the Ontario College of Art, known initially as the Ontario School of Art, originated. The Ontario School of Art began with the "South Kensington School" UK curriculum (now the Royal College of Art), which was an industrial arts school, as its model in 1876. By 1886, a different model attracted a group of Toronto artists who were inspired by the establishment of The Art Students League of New York in 1875 based on the Parisian atelier with master artisans. The New York school, the oldest in North America, is still operational today under its original name and continues to thrive

---

6 The description "Toronto the Good" stems from a study by C.S. Clark, *Of Toronto the Good : A Social Study : The Queen City of Canada as it is* (Montreal: Toronto Pub., 1898).

7 "History," OCAD University About, accessed March 12, 2023, https://www.ocadu.ca/about/history.

8 For information on the free books movement in Toronto and the Toronto Mechanics Institute, see Lorne Bruce, "Common School and Mechanics' Institute Libraries," in *Free Books for All: The Public Library Movement in Ontario 1850-1930* (Toronto & Oxford: Dundurn Press, 1994), 3-30; Daniel Payne, *A Mirror of Curriculum: Art Libraries and Studio-Based Education: The OCAD University Experience* (1876-2016) (self-pub., 2020), 91.

as a non-degree granting, hands-on, studio based, independent art school. This alternative art school became The Art Students' League of Toronto, which continued classes until 1906 when it disbanded.[9] By 1910, there were two rival schools in Toronto, The Toronto School of Art, and the Central Ontario School of Art, both housed on the upper floors of the Grange Building in Grange Park. In 1912 the Ontario Government, tired of this uncivil war decided to combine them into the Ontario College of Art (OCA), with an annual grant of $3,000, and George A. Reid as the new Principal. The Globe newspaper reported that a deputation committee met with the minister, and stated that "Ontario had fallen far behind in the teaching and the fostering of both fine and industrial art."[10] One result was that manufacturers were finding it difficult to secure capable designers. The endowment of a school that would teach industrial art as well as what are generally known as the 'fine arts,' would mean a great deal to the industrial advancement of the Province.[11] Despite the school's rocky origins, this 1912 deputation to the Ontario minister delivered the right political message, which would eventually provide capital for OCA to settle in a new location by 1920. The Art Gallery of Toronto (AGO) allowed OCA to build in Grange Park, with the construction funded by grants from both levels of government. In the case of the federal government, the money was specifically earmarked for "technical education" in the post WWI era when there were many returning veterans ready for training. Thursday, July 15th, 1920, saw the ground-breaking ceremony for the OCA Grange building, which would cost $120,000 and was one of the first purpose-built art education buildings in Canada.

1919 was a significant year. The OCA Act was amended, and George Reid appointed Arthur Lismer as Vice-Principal. Lismer had spent the three previous years as administrator of the Victoria School of Art (now Nova Scotia College of Art and Design) in Halifax. It was not long

---

9 There are also overlaps in terms of participants who founded two other art related groups, The Art Students League of Toronto (1886–1906) and the Arts & Letters Club of Toronto launched in 1908, which is still in operation on Elm Street. It celebrated a hundredth anniversary in 2008 with a published history, which noted that it was a men's club until 1985 when women were allowed to join. This segregation prompted the formation of The Toronto Heliconian Club for women in 1909, which is housed in an 1875 Yorkville designated church building. It continues to provide art studio and gallery space.

10 The Globe, "Government Support for School of Art: Deputation Tells Ministers that Ontario Lags Behind in Fostering Art," February 7, 1912, F 1140-12, Box 1. Ontario Society of Artists fonds, Archives of Ontario, Toronto, Ontario. See Payne, "A Mirror of Curriculum," 106.

11 The Globe, "Government Support," 9.

before there were conflicts between Lismer and the more conservative Reid. The same year saw the formation of The Group of Seven, who were responding publicly to the traditional artistic approach represented by Reid and his OCA teachers. The OCA curriculum reflected these different values, resulting in the 1927 resignation of Lismer and the more progressive students who were led by the Kitchener artist Edna Breithaupt.

George Reid retired the following year and was replaced by J. E. H. MacDonald, another member of the Group of Seven and a former pupil of Reid who was also an active member of the original Art Students League of Toronto. The OCA practice of hiring its own accredited OCA diploma graduates to be the next generation of instructors became a fixed pattern over the next forty years. Upon MacDonald's death in 1932, teacher Fred Haines became the Principal. Haines encouraged OCA teachers to study with exiled members of the Bauhaus movement while they were living in the United States during the 1930s and '40s. His daughter Dorothy H. Hoover (for whom the school's library was eventually named) describes his influence on the direction of the curriculum at the school:

> Well, if Reid introduced the first stage of the arts and crafts movement, my Dad [F. S. Haines] was responsible for the vastly different second stage, newly modernized by Walter Gropius. When the Bauhaus was forced to flee Nazi Germany, some of the refugees set up a school in Chicago. Father sent several of the staff there and Harley Parker to Black Mountain College, NC to study under Josef Albers.[12]

As in the case of many educational programs and institutions, the end of WWII in 1945 saw an influx of returning war veterans which introduced further changes to the Ontario College of Art. A Design Department opened in a remote Nassau Street location. Then in 1955 Sydney Watson was appointed Principal and an ambitious expansion of the campus was undertaken initially with a 1957 addition to the original Grange Wing, followed by a 1962 expansion which included a cafeteria and auditorium and, in 1967, a third extension at 100 McCaul Street.

---

12 Dorothy H. Hoover, "My Years at OCA," type written manuscript of interview conducted by Library Director Jill Patrick, OCAD U Archives, Dorothy Hoover fonds, n.d: from Payne, *A Mirror of Curriculum*, 55.

Labour, Conflicting Ideologies and Politics

Morris Wolfe in *OCA 1967-1972: Five Turbulent Years* (2001) describes the atmosphere of the school after 85 years of operation:

> In 1960, BELLS RANG to indicate the beginning and end of classes at the Ontario College of Art. Nude male models wore jock straps. Students and teachers had little or no say in the running of the College. OCA's sleepy governing body, Council, met twice a year to rubber stamp decisions made by the Principal Sydney Watson. In a 1962 interview, Watson was asked if there were a lot of rebels at OCA. 'No,' he replied, a 'student can't rebel, or he isn't going to graduate.' 'Is that a good thing,' he was asked. 'It's good for us,' said Watson. 'It makes it easier … to run the College.' In its various incarnations, OCA had been run that way since its founding in 1876.[13]

By the mid 1960s, often referred to as the Rebellious Era, the labour situation at OCA unfolded differently and in a "unique way." The phrase "we are unique" was often repeated to explain or exonerate the institution, in fact, the phrase unici sumus should have been the school's Latin motto.[14] It was not a high school, a college nor a university—it was a studio-based, hands-on art school. Many of the faculty had never attended university, but a core group of conservative figurative painters teaching in the Painting and Drawing Department felt threatened by change during this period. As a result Dennis Burton and Robert Hedrick, both abstractionists, formed The New School of Art, which followed the approach of The Art Students League of Toronto with no entrance or attendance requirements, no grades, no marks, and no diploma.[15] However, in the fall of 1965 the faculty at OCA banded together to organize a faculty association as a job security maneuver.[16]

While the history of OCA up to its Centennial Year in 1967 was relatively quiet on the public front, nothing prepared it for the upheaval over

---

13 Morris Wolfe, *OCA 1967-1972: Five Turbulent Years* (Toronto: Grub Street Books, 2001), 9.

14 OCAD University, OCAD University Strategic Mandate Agreement Proposal, May 1, 2014, http://www.ocadu.ca/Assets/document/sma-2014.pdf. The word "unique" is used a total of 14 times to describe the school.

15 Among the New School's instructors were Graham Coughtry, Arthur Handy, Ross Mendes, Gordon Rayner, Robert Markle, and Paul Young; see Wolfe, OCA 1967-1972, 14.

16 Payne, "A Mirror of Curriculum," p. 97.

the next five years. The school's enrollment reached 1,000 by 1968. At that time, the students went on strike to protest the firing of two conservative instructors.[17] The students and instructors battled with the autocratic Principal Sydney Watson when he attempted to modernize the curriculum. This controversy required the Education Minister Bill Davis to step in and he simply reinstated the instructors. Davis took the opportunity to hire Douglas T. Wright, a professor of civil engineering at the University of Waterloo (and later President of the University of Waterloo), to review the function of OCA. The Wright Report weighing in at 23 pages recommended a unicameral Council rather than adopting the university bicameral model. The 1968 report observed:

> The uniqueness of the College is a source both of strength and of weakness. Its relative isolation from the rest of the academic and educational world has tended to protect the College from influences which have led to important evolutionary changes in other post-secondary institutions.[18]

Wright also recommended that the hiring of former students as instructors be discontinued, as it tended to reinforce a traditional approach to both art and design. The revisions to the 1969 OCA Act which resulted from this upheaval was based largely on Wright's recommendations including the representation on Council by students and instructors for the first time. The Principal became the President in a gradual move toward becoming a University. By 1970 the context within which OCA functioned had changed dramatically with other colleges and some universities offering similar courses and programs. What the institution did was no longer unique.

The following year the newly formed Council decided to look further afield for a President who would shake things up—their choice was Roy Ascott, a young British art school academic with little administrative experience, who was hired in 1971. Ascott immediately picked up the mantle of former Principal Sydney Watson. He began by making serious modifications to curriculum and the school administration without consulting the OCA community or the Council which hired him. All

---

17 Wolfe, OCA 1967-1972, Appendix Two, 85.

18 Douglas T. Wright, *Report on the Ontario College of Art: Report on the Organizational Structure and Administration of the Ontario College of Art, Toronto* (to the Minister of University Affairs) (Toronto: s.n., 1968) 10.

departments and formal classes were abolished to make way for a 1960s free school. Many part-time instructors were replaced with new appointees, in what was described as an administrative breakdown.[19] Plaster models of classic figures were smashed, and the school calendar was printed on Tarot cards. He lasted less than one year and resigned in 1972.[20] In 1976 OCA and the AGO celebrated the 100th anniversary of the college with a travelling exhibition illustrating the artistic talent of both instructors and students. The exhibition catalogue aptly summarized what happened during Ascott's brief tenure as President:

> A tumultuous year followed. Faculty and students were divided in their support or rejection of his innovative programmes and autocratic methods. By the spring of 1972, when it became apparent that Ascott's term of office would be ended, a group of faculty and students split off from the College to form their own 'free school,' known as 'Z' ... 'Z' faded away.[21]

Following Ascott's return to England he was replaced as President by Clifford Pitt from 1972 to 1975; Pitt, who had no art background at all, but was an educational psychologist. With three presidents in four years, the OCA community sought stability. The conservative forces re-established departments and the curriculum largely reverted to what it had been before the revolution. Presumably Pitt's professional expertise assisted in efforts to restore balance to the college and unite the warring factions within.[22] Morris Wolfe quotes Pitt's declaration that entering OCA was "like entering a mad house. The place was in a complete state of anarchy. It was as if the lunatics had taken over the asylum ...".[23]

---

19 Wolfe, OCA 1967-1972, 68.

20 Michael Keating, "OCA Head is Forced to Resign," *Globe and Mail* (Toronto, Ontario), June 27, 1968, Canadian Newstream.

21 Ontario College of Art and Art Gallery of Ontario, 100 Years: Evolution of the Ontario College of Art (Toronto: Art Gallery of Ontario: Ontario College of Art, 1976), 20.

22 "New Head Finds Problems Exciting: Psychologist Takes on the OCA," *Globe and Mail* (Toronto, Ontario), August 26, 1972, Canadian Newstream.

23 Wolfe, OCA 1967-1972, 70.

OPSEU and Academic Librarianship

Internal labour issues continued within OCA. In 1981 the Ontario Labour Relations Board recognized OPSEU Local 576 for staff and at the same time issued a temporary certificate for a faculty unit, which OPSEU was simultaneously seeking to organize. Librarians working in the OCAD library had the necessary undergraduate degrees in information science, which were required when they were hired, but not the later mandated MLS/MLIS master's degree which were introduced in Canada in the 1970s. For this reason, OPSEU argued in 1981 that the librarians in 1981 were staff as opposed to faculty. They were denied academic status, despite the fact that in 1975-77 the Canadian Association of University Teachers (CAUT) and the Canadian Association of College and University Libraries (CACUL) officially recognized the concept of academic status for Canadian academic librarians.[24] The librarians' lack of masters degrees was not considered an issue for the OCA administration nor for the faculty who, because OCA was a studio-based art school, were not required to have a graduate level education. The Director of the OCA library in 1981, for example, had a Bachelor of Library Science, which was the original requirement, but as of that year it was no longer recognized by the ALA accreditation board. Therefore, less emphasis had been placed on the librarian staff acquiring the relatively new master's degree. The masters and doctoral programs for librarianship were new developments that began in the 1960s and were established in the 1970s in Canada.[25] At other universities and institutions during this transitional period, terms were negotiated to apply the new requirements for newly hired librarians, whilst recognizing the earlier requirements and years of experience of current employees. OPSEU, however, did not adopt this view. Due to this series of circumstances, and events, despite repeated attempts to alter the situation, librarians became permanently excluded from the faculty association and members of Local 576, which never fully recognized librarianship as an academic profession. This was the

---

24 Leona Jacobs, "Academic Status for Canadian Academic Librarians: A Brief History," in *In Solidarity: Academic Librarian Labour, Activism and Union Participation in Canada*, eds. Jennifer Dekker and Mary Kandiuk (Sacramento, CA: Library Juice Press, 2014), 9-38.

25 For an analysis of the newly established master degrees requirements for professional librarians in Ontario, see Harriet Sonne de Torrens, "Academic Librarianship: The Quest for Rights and Recognition at the University of Toronto," in *In Solidarity: Academic Librarian Labour, Activism and Union Participation in Canada*, eds. Jennifer Dekker and Mary Kandiuk (Sacramento, CA: Library Juice Press, 2014), 81-106; Bruce Lorne, "Professionalization, Gender, and Librarianship in Ontario, 1920-75," *Library & Information History* 28, no. 2 (2012): 117-134.

unfortunate, yet typical of the labour confusion that arises when new requirements for professionals are introduced.[26]

In 1999, the college (which had changed its name to the Ontario College of Art & Design in 1996), proposed a *Memorandum of Agreement* for the faculty association which included librarians as per the university model for the composition of faculty. The resistance came not from the librarians nor the faculty but from representatives within the OPSEU organization who rejected this proposal. If librarians had been included with the faculty, their professional academic status would have been recognized and, hence, protected under academic policies and benefits (e. g. academic freedom, research leaves and collegial terms of employment). Instead, OPSEU insisted that the librarians continue to be treated as support staff in the 2001 MOA, despite the fact that OPSEU represented CAAT-Academic staff at all Ontario community colleges where librarians were faculty members. As a result it became increasingly difficult to fill vacant librarian positions at OCAD due to the lack of professional recognition that was offered at other Canadian universities. In the two rounds of bargaining that took place in 2002 and 2005, librarians' insistence that they be granted academic status was ignored and rebuffed. Librarians emphasized that as OCAD shifted from a studio-based college program to a degree granting university the librarians without exception possessed the required academic qualifications. During the OPSEU 576 bargaining Peter Caldwell, Vice-President of Administration proposed once again that "academic librarians" be included in OCADFA. OPSEU once again rejected this offer and instead created an Appendix A to Unit 1 as a temporary measure designed to identify the roles and responsibilities of librarians in the university. This, however, was ignored by OCAD administration.

Although successive negotiations allotted academic librarians a separate appendix in the collective agreement—which addressed wage parity and tentatively recognized a modicum of the academic duties of librarians in a university environment—the administration ignored the precedent set by almost every other university in Canada as supported by the CAUT statement that "librarians at academic institutions

---

26 "Librarianship in Ontario, 1920-75," 125-129.

are entitled to academic status."[27] At other Canadian universities the OCAD U librarians would be members of a faculty association with tenure equivalency, research leaves and the ability to engage in peer review protected by academic freedom.

Equity and Governance

Tim Porteous, who was previously a speech writer for Pierre Elliot Trudeau and head of the Canada Council and CCA in Montreal, was appointed President from 1988 until he retired in 1995. Porteous was a well-known figure. Shortly after his arrival, the issue of employment equity erupted because 87% of the classes were taught by men, while 60% of the student body were women. In Spring 1989 a research report called "Equity 2000" was released with an optimistic projection that the number of classes taught by women would increase to 38% by the year 2000.[28] The policy change was effective and the number of women instructors reached 39.7%. Morris Wolfe wrote a detailed essay in Saturday Night magazine entitled "The Struggle for Equity at OCA" describing the conflict for and against equity in hiring at OCA, as well as sexual abuses, which turned into another fractious public battle between the forces of change and the status quo. Once again Wolfe underlines the on-going inner tensions at the school:

> Even at the best of times, OCA is a fractious place. You can't bring together that many creative people—262 faculty and approximately 2,800 full and part-time students, without having sparks fly. Frequently the sparks are the results of the never-ending war between the college's traditionalists and avant-gardists and their constant fears that if they relax their guard the other side will gain the upper hand.[29]

During the remainder of the President's term, financial issues escalated resulting in the accumulated debt of the college reaching $1.5

---

27 CAUT, Collective Agreement and Academic Status and Governance for Librarians, November 2018, section 1.1. https://www.caut.ca/about-us/caut-policy/lists/caut-policy-statements/policy-statement-on-academic-status-and-governance-for-librarians-at-canadian-universities-and-colleges.

28 Morris Wolfe, "The Struggle for Equity at OCA," *Saturday Night*, December 1990, https://www.grubstreetbooks.ca/essays/oca.html.

29 Wolfe, "The Struggle."

million. Porteous had to appeal to the Ministry of Colleges and Universities (MCU) for some form of relief. Richard Allen, the new Minister of Colleges and Universities was not particularly sympathetic to his appeal and blamed the financial situation on OCA's poor administration. The following year, Allen called for an external review of OCA's mission, programs, and operations. In 1991-92, the Task Force to Review the Ontario College of Art was appointed by the Ontario Council on University Affairs (OCUA) and their report recommended that a restructuring team be assembled to make major changes to the governance of the college by the 1994-1995 school year.

The restructuring team was led by Paul Nowack, who was the Dean of Applied Arts at Ryerson Polytechnic (now known as Toronto Metropolitan University). The team's efforts included establishing a bicameral governing model, rejecting the previous unicameral system, and replacing Department Heads, who were given an honorarium for their administrative duties, with Deans. The MCU Deputy Minister floated the idea that OCA should be merged with York University, a model which was already taking place with the University of Toronto absorbing the Ontario Institute for Studies of Education.

The Imaginary Library (1996—2022)

At the roots of the May 2021 developments were the on-going plans to expand the library to meet the needs of a degree granting institution—little of which came to fruition. In July 1996, OCA officially changed its name to the Ontario College of Art & Design (OCAD). President Alan Barkley (formerly president of Emily Carr College) arranged for a partnership with Open University in British Columbia which allowed OCAD students to pursue a Bachelor level degree.[30] In the mid-1980s the library collection had been relocated to the main floor of the Grange Wing. However, as the programs developed it became necessary to expand the library space. A proposal was put forward to devote all three floors of the Grange Wing to the library, which ultimately was considered too costly by the administration. Instead, on April 1st 1999, OCAD purchased a four-story office building at 113 McCaul Street, part of the Village on the Grange, and began a campus expansion (including the

---

30 Dave McGinn, "The Power of the Word 'University,'" *Globe and Mail* (Toronto, Ontario). September 8 2007, M1, https://www.theglobeandmail.com/news/national/the-power-of-the-word-university/article18145074/.

library) in anticipation of a shift to becoming a degree granting institution. Questions arose about the ability of the building's floor plate to sustain the weight of the library collection. OCAD administration assured employees that the library relocation across McCaul Street was only a temporary 5-year relocation (some 23 years ago). Conservative minister Dianne Cunningham from the Ministry of Colleges and Universities came to the grand ribbon-cutting ceremony and pronounced this public-private partnership a complete success—today it remains one of the few known examples of this questionable administrative decision.

The Ontario College of Art & Design received degree-granting status in 2002 which gave it the right to offer a Bachelor of Fine Art (BFA) degree and a Bachelor of Design (BDes) degree. As soon as this milestone was achieved, the institution launched a major capital campaign which resulted in the construction of its iconic Sharp Design Centre building on McCaul Street in downtown Toronto, which opened in 2004. In 2005 Sara Diamond was named President in 2005, and the following year OCAD was granted membership in the Association of Universities and Colleges of Canada (AUCC). OCAD then began to write and submit Briefs to the Ontario Council of Graduate Studies (OCGS) to gain permission to offer graduate degrees. In 2007, two Briefs were submitted for a Master of Fine Arts (MFA) in Criticism & Curatorial Practice, and an Interdisciplinary Masters in Arts (MA) in Media and Design. Both were approved in 2007 and launched in 2008. A Master's in Strategic Foresight and Innovation was approved by the OCGS in 2008 and launched in 2009. A Master of Arts in Contemporary Art, Design and New Media Histories was approved by OCGS in 2009 and launched in 2010. In 2010 two additional programs were approved for launch in 2011: MA, MFA, Masters of Design in Digital Futures, and Master of Design in Inclusive Design.

In January 2008, OCAD began planning for a new library facility to support the expanded curriculum, as there was a serious need for library resources. Assurances were made to the AUCC and the MCU by OCAD administration that library facilities appropriate to the new curriculum and degree granting requirements would be built. Michael Ridley, Guelph's University Librarian recommended Scott Bennett (Chicago library planning consultant) and Boston architecture firm Perry Dean Rogers were brought in to assist in "visioning" a new university library by 2012 to support graduate research and degree granting. This was an important commitment on the part of OCAD U to anticipate the construction of a new library building. After a year of work on this project, and after incurring significant consulting feeds, the library produced the report *Enacting a Learning Mission: A Consulting Report for OCAD*. In addition, there was a precedent for this project: the Toronto Metropolitan University undertook a similar timeframe by erecting a new library on Yonge Street as it transitioned from Polytechnic to a University.

OCAD began to refer to itself as the "University of the Imagination" in its 2006-2012 Strategic Plan with a one-sentence Vision Statement: "Imagination is everything!"[31] In subsequent years, the President aggressively marketed this vision along with successive promises to provide the necessary infrastructure, staffing, and resources to support both undergraduate and graduate level programs. Conceptually, this strategy was nothing more than a distorted and mirrored mantra. The idea, if you build it, they will come, was transformed into, if you can imagine it, then you may not need to come, or, more poignantly, we thought about a new library facility, so it must have happened. A favourite OCAD U "Imagination" story involves a first-year student who came to the reference desk. He looked puzzled after scanning the book collection and then asked (politely) where the Reference Library was …? I started to answer, assuming that he meant the Metro Toronto Reference Library—"it's up at 789 Yonge Street, north of Bloor Street…" Then I realized that wasn't his question. He was obviously "underwhelmed" by the scale of the Dorothy H. Hoover library, which was not that much larger than a high school library.

To understand the context and the shocking responses received when the four librarians were laid off in 2021, it is important to understand that the librarians in the Dorothy H. Hoover Library had partnered with OCAD administration in the planning and securing of University status. During the period of curricular expansion between 2002 and 2011, OCAD U followed OCGS requirements and directed the school's professional librarians to produce an independent Library Assessment Report in consultation with faculty and other stakeholders. The administration's strategic plan offered the following assurances which included an implementation timeline of 2008 to 2012:

---

31 Leading in the Age of Imagination: A Strategic Plan for the Ontario College of Art & Design 2006-2012, (Toronto: OCAD U Board of Governors, 2006), section 1, 3, accessed November 3, 2022, https://www.OCADU.ca/Assets/documents/leading-in-the-age-of-imagination-full.pdf.

OCAD has committed to developing ...a Library commensurate with its status and needs as a leading research university with a graduate studies program. A plan to develop the library will be a key priority. The costs associated with expanding print and digital collections, learning commons and technological infrastructure, staff resources and expanded facilities will be important components of future operating and capital requirements.[32]

These guarantees were repeated in other public documents. In the 2006-07 Multi-Year Accountability Agreement with the Ontario Ministry of Training, Colleges and Universities (2006-07), the University stated it would "Enhance collections to achieve greater parity with Ontario University standards."[33] In the 2007-08, the administration claimed that by June 2008, it would "Complete a Needs Assessment and Preliminary Space Program for a new Library and Archives (including collaborating units)."[34]

In response, the space plan Enacting a Learning Mission served as a tangible means for Library staff to meet these goals.[35] The document mapped a strategy for building a new library, approximately three times larger than the current one, with completion projected for 2012.[36] This timeline corresponded with the OCAD plans to become a university. In 2010, the Ontario College of Art and Design secured permission to change its name to OCAD University. When asked, in an interview with The Globe and Mail, Dr. Diamond claimed, "It's a vote of confidence... a logical step that was a statement on the part of the Ministry of Training, College and Universities (MCTU) about the quality of education at OCAD."[37] The timing of this approval proved to be consequen-

---

32 Leading in the Age, 14, section 12.

33 Ministry of Training, Colleges, and Universities, 2006-07 Multi-Year Accountability Agreement Report-Back for: OCAD, revised March 3, 2008, 7-8, https://www.OCADU.ca/site/default/files/legacy_assets/documents/2006-07-multi-year-accountability-agreement-report-back.pdf.

34 Ministry of Training, Colleges and Universities, 2007-08 Multi-Year Accountability Agreement Report-Back for: OCAD, accessed November 4, 2022, 7, https://www.OCADU.ca/sites/default/files/legacy_assets/documents/2007-08-multi-year-accountability-agreement-report-back.pdf.

35 Scott Bennett and Steven Foote, *Enacting a Learning Mission: A Consulting Report for the Ontario College of Art & Design* (Toronto, Ontario), June 27 2008, http://open research.OCADU.ca/id/eprint/10/1/Library_consultant_reprot.pdf.

36 Bennett and Foote, *Enacting a Learning Mission*, 7-20.

37 James Bradshaw, "Ontario Arts College Finally Gets its U," *Globe and Mail* (Toronto, Ontario), April 28, 2010, A13.

tial. In July 2010, OCGS moved responsibility for graduate programs to a new Ontario Universities Council on Quality Assurance, through the MTCU. Might this explain why guarantees to OCGS to triple the size of the library began to morph into increasingly smaller versions?

Space plans are usually enacted with specific locations already selected. However, in the case of OCAD U space plan *Enacting a Learning Mission* no prior spatial commitments had been made. The authors of the report *Enacting a Learning Mission*, however, were able to envision a plan based on percentages for staff, public access, and collection spaces. The critical element of the report was the recognition that librarians needed to be equal partners with the faculty as a requirement for fully enacting the mandate of a library worthy of supporting graduate-level research. Without the research-based skills of librarians in collection development and management—as represented tangibly through library collections—the capability for creating a viable academic research facility could not be realized. The document offered a clear, direct map for meeting the school's commitment to expansion. The plan, however, languished and eventually was buried by senior administration in their capital planning and the call for full faculty status for OCAD U librarians was ignored.

In 2016, when OCAD U received $27 million to develop the Creative City Campus, some of the funds were to be allocated for the "revitalization and expansion of the Art and Design Library for the Future."[38] By 2017, this had become a "renovated and expanded library."[39] In the end, none of these scenarios ever came to fruition. On June 23, 2020, OCAD U issued a news release to celebrate Dr. Sara Diamond's contributions as outgoing president. Included in the long list of her achievements was a reference to "the renewal of library space"—which never happened.[40]

---

38 "OCAD University Receives $27 Million to Develop Creative City Campus," Canada NewsWire, April 12, 2016, https://www.newswire.ca/news-releases/ocad-university-receives-27-million-to-develop-creative-city-campus-575461131.html.

39 Stefan Novakovic, "OCAD Announces Designers for 'Creative City Campus' Expansion," *Urban Toronto*, January 11, 2017, https://urbantoronto.ca/news/2017/01/ocad-announces-designers-creative-city-campus-expansion.

40 "OCAD University Celebrates Dr. Sara Diamond's Contributions as Outgoing President," OCAD U News Release, June 23, 2020, https://www.ocadu.ca/news/ocad-university-celebrates-dr-sara-diamonds-contributions-outgoing-president.

Dorothy H. Hoover Librarians

On May 5, 2021, Ana Serrano, President & Vice-Chancellor of OCAD U dispatched her bi-weekly communications to the university community.[41] She began by reporting on the creation of "a diverse Elder's Counsel...guided by the University's principles of Respect, Relationship, Reciprocity and Responsibility." [42] She then proceeded to inform the OCAD University community that earlier that morning Dr. Caroline Langill, Vice President Academic and Provost, had announced the "reorganization of the Dorothy H. Hoover Library."[43] Missing from this summary was the detail that four senior librarians had been served with layoff notices; an action conducted without prior consultation with the impacted employees, Academic Senate, nor the Student Union. In accordance with the Collective Agreement, the administration and HR had contacted the school's OPSEU Local 576 president beforehand; however, notification was conducted two business days prior to the layoffs, leaving no time to respond appropriately nor to contact the librarians being laid off. Each librarian was given a short, half hour online meeting on May 4th with no warning of their termination in the midst of the COVID-19 pandemic.

The administration's demeaning approach sent shock waves through the institution. Faculty, students, and staff were outraged by this maneuver. The impacted librarians created, managed, and administered essential services and innovative technologies in direct support of the teaching, learning, and research for the University. Work duties that directly supported the institution's academic plan, in addition to its bid to secure both degree-granting status and approvals for graduate programs, abruptly ceased. Instead of acknowledging and celebrating the contributions of these librarians, senior administration chose to use the anomalous labour environment at OCAD U to execute a reduction of professional expertise. The layoffs were intended purely as an economic means for cutting budgets and services.

On May 14th the President attempted to shift the narrative and pacify the public outcry and stop the steady flow of concerned letters coming

---

41   Ana Serrano joined OCAD U on July 1, 2020, as OCAD University President and Vice-Chancellor from the Canadian Film Centre where she was Chief Digital Officer.

42   Ana Serrano, email message to OCAD U Community, May 5, 2021.

43   Caroline Langill, email message to OCAD U Community, May 5, 2021.

from institutions across Canada. Administration issued a Statement on Library Reorganization to address the lack of due process and collegial consultation (Appendix A).[44] The Statement on Library Reorganization included the statement: "The new structure aligns with the decolonization approach by flattening hierarchies and promoting a peer-to-peer environment." [45] This resulted in immediate public ridicule: the responses were scathing. The librarian and archivist members of the University of Guelph's Faculty Association wrote: "To frame this cruel restructuring, which resulted in aggressive terminations of valued members of the OCAD U community, as aligning with 'the decolonization approach' is appalling. To invoke decolonization in this context is a gross misappropriation of the term."[46] Wilfrid Laurier University Faculty Association wrote on May 18, 2021:

> It is reprehensible that the University would use 'decolonization' in such a reductive and overly simplistic way to justify their approach to restructuring the OCAD library…. It demonstrates an alarming lack of awareness on their part to refer to decolonization in an attempt to create a smokescreen around a restructuring process…[47]

The anomalous labour environment impeded the ability to correct the situation, while ambiguity in the academic bicameral structure at OCAD U stifled the latter, which explains why Senators on May 19th were unable to compel the Board of Governors to revoke their decision to lay off the four senior librarians. In addition, the idea of peer-to-peer structures were hardly believable given the growing administrative structures at OCAD U (Appendix C and D). The internal problems were well-known and understood by OCAD U employees. Chris Thompson, Interim President of OPSEU 567 submitted a statement to the OCAD U Senate (Appendix B), which conveyed the long-standing and unresolved issues within OCAD U:

---

44 Serrano, Email to OCAD U Community, May 14, 2021; "OCAD U Issues Statement on Library Reorganization," OCAD U News, May 14, 2021, https://www.ocadu.ca/news/ocad-u-issues-statement-library-reorganization.

45 OCAD U issues a Statement on Library Reorganization; for organizational charts dated to April 2021 see OCAD University. 2021. "Organizational Charts."

46 University of Guelph Faculty Association, Open Letter, May 2015, http://www.ocadfa.ca/wp-content/uploads/2021/05/Letter-in-Support-of-OCAD-Librarians.pdf.

47 Wilfrid Laurier University Faculty Association, Open Letter, May 18, 2021, https://www.wlufa.ca/2021/05/18/wlufa-appaled-by-ocadu-lay-off-and-elimination-of-librarians/.

Like other departments predominantly filled by our members, the library has been subject to ongoing workload concerns even before the implementation of various "budget remediation plans" and hiring freezes. Such austerity measures have only served to weaken the foundations of student and faculty support across the institution, and in the library where the cracks could no longer be hidden. Instead of seeking remediation which would preserve the core curricular support and pedagogical functions of the library as embodied by four individuals with over 70 years of combined service at this institution, the administration has unilaterally redefined the structure and scope of library services in an opaque and rushed process with only a poorly conceived and communicated survey to pay lip-service to the vaguest notion of consultative process and collegial conduct.[48]

A major social media and letter writing campaign was launched with CAUT, the Canadian Association of Professional Academic Librarians (CAPAL), OPSEU Local 576, the OCAD U Faculty Association (OCADFA), and the University of Toronto Faculty Association (UTFA) to protest the layoffs. The month of May in 2021 witnessed the following events:

- On May 7th the first public notice of the layoffs was shared when OCADFA President Min Sook Lee began a Twitter campaign (@ocadfa1): "An injury to one (or 4) is an injury to all! We stand in solidarity w/ our @OPSEU 567 colleagues and won't remain silent while the academic mission of @OCAD is sacrificed in favour of capital and money-losing ventures. Shame!"[49]

- On May 10th, the OCAD U Board of Governors met via Zoom and made room on the agenda for the Interim President of OPSEU Local 576 to make a formal statement that suggested that it would be "in the financial and general interest of the institution for the administration to work in a more respectful, collaborative—and less adversarial—manner with our labour group and others."[50] The

---

48 OPSEU, Local 576, "Statements to OCAD U Senate," May 19, 2021, https://www.opseulocal576.org/news-and-annoucements-to-ocad-u-senate.

49 OCADUFA, "An Injury to One (or 4) is an Injury to all!" Twitter. 5:03 pm. May 7, 2021. https://twitter.com/minsooklee/status/1390764090205917185

50 OCAD U, Board of Governors, Minutes, May 10, 2021.

Interim President of OPSEU posted online a statement submitted to the OCAD U Senate (Appendix B).

- On May 12th, OCADFA launched a petition and letter-writing campaign, pleading for the University to reconsider its actions.

- On May 14th, a letter was sent by the Canadian Association of University Teachers (CAUT), which urged President Serrano: "to pause the restructuring plans and reinstate the four librarians until there has been a thorough review of best practices and community needs" and "to involve the University's librarians, faculty, and students in any major reorganization."[51]

- The OCADFA and OPSEU created a petition titled, "Don't Put the Hook to OCAD U Professional Academic Librarians" addressed to Ana Serrano, President, Caroline Langill, Vice President and Provost Academic, Tony White, University Librarian and Jaime Watt, Chair, Board of Directors. 1,893 supporters signed the petition.[52]

- On May 19th, actions came to a head at the Academic Senate Meeting. In a filibuster event that ran from 9:00 am to 1:00 pm, Senators created and approved a statement of dissent. The letter, however, was not considered binding.[53] It was later presented to the Board of Governors for information purposes only.

- On May 27, an Op-ed by Min Sook Lee (President, OCADUFA), Harriet Sonne de Torrens (Chair, UTFA Librarians Committee) and Terezia Zoric (President, UTFA) appears online in the Medium.[54]

- On May 31, CAUT and UTFA spear-headed librarians across Canada in an *OCAD U Digital Day of Action* on behalf of the four librarians laid-off. Tweets were shared across the country asking OCAD U to reconsider their decision.

---

51 Brenda Austin-Smith and David Robinson, "Re: Decision to Terminate Four Senior Librarians," letter to Ana Serrano on behalf of CAUT, May 14, 2021, https:///caut.ca/latest/2021/05/caut-objects-decision-lay-four-senior-librarians-ocad-university.

52 OPSEU Local 576, Petition. May 31, 2021.

53 OCAD U Senate Minutes, May 19, 2021.

54 Min Sook Lee, Harriet Sonne de Torrens, and Terezia Zoric, "OCADU's Decision to Terminate Four Librarians Reflects a Troubling Trend in the Post-Secondary Sector," *Medium*, May 27, 2021, https://utfa.medium.com/ocadus-decision-to-terminate-four-librarians-reflects-a-troubling-trend-in-the-post-secondary-4fdf11043cf1.

- On June 21s, 2021, the lay-off proceedings continued with impunity. Despite the onslaught of condemnation from the national university community, senior administration moved forward with the plan to lay-off its four senior librarians on June 1st, 2021.

More than thirty passionate and concerned letters of support for the librarians from the CAUT, Ontario College and University Library Association (OCULA), Brock University Library Council, Art Libraries Society of North America, Ontario Confederation of University Faculty Associations (OCUFA) and numerous faculty and librarian associations from across Canada were sent to the President Ana Serrano, the Vice-President, Academic and Provost, Dr. Caroline Langill, and University Librarian Tony White.[55] One letter in particular from the McMaster University Academic Librarians' Association powerfully summarizes the long-term ramifications of restructuring conducted without a due process:

> We ... speak from personal collective experience of the impacts a "restructuring" can have on a Library and its community ... our Union was formed under a not-dissimilar set of circumstances which resulted in a tremendous loss of capacity and capability for our Library and University. The debacle at McMaster in 2011 is a matter of record, but we would draw attention in particular to the catastrophic impact this process had on morale, trust, effectiveness, and the fundamental internal and external perception of the administration of the time. These effects are still being felt. For many members of our community, this became the foundational experience of their professional lives. Bluntly, and in sum: decisions like this haunt communities and poison relationships for decades. We urge, in the strongest possible terms, a re-consideration of OCAD U's process, decisions, and leadership as reflected in the current "restructuring" plan.[56]

---

55 The OCAD U Faculty Association posted all the letters of solidary that arrived from across Canada. They can be found at "Solidarity Letters in Support of OCADU Librarians Keep Pouring In," *Ontario College of Art & Design Faculty Association* (blog), accessed November 2, 2022, https://ocadfa.ca/blog/2021/05/17/solidary-letters-in-support-of-ocadu-librarians-keep-pouring-in/.

56 Myron Groover, Letter to Ana Serrano on behalf of the McMaster University Academic Librarians' Association, May 2021, https://ocadfa.ca/wp-content/uploads/2021/05/MUALA_OCADU_Letter.pdf.

Conclusion

OCAD U's dismissal of four senior librarians has now been recorded in the history of academic librarianship in Canada. This condensed overview of the historical transformation of a nineteenth-century studio-based college to a university in the twenty-first century provides insights into how the core values of an academic library and the role of academic librarianship at a university took a backseat to OCAD U administration's political and economic agendas over the decades. The case demonstrates the increased corporate mentality over research, teaching and learning in post-secondary institutions in recent decades. And lastly, most importantly for professional academic librarians is the fact that the OCAD U case exposes the precarious status of academic librarians when they choose to organize separately from their faculty association.

Bibliography

Austin-Smith, Brenda and David Robinson. 2021. "RE: Decision to Terminate Four Senior Librarians and Eliminate Two Library Positions at OCAD U." CAUT. Accessed November 4, 2022, https://www.caut.ca/latest/2021/05/caut-objects-decision-lay-four-senior-librarians-ocad-university.

Bennett, Scott and Steven Foote. 2008. *Enacting a Learning Mission: A Consulting Report for the Ontario College of Art & Design.* Toronto: Ontario College of Art & Design. June 27, 2008. Accessed November 3, 2022. http://openresearch.OCAD U.ca/id/eprint/10/1/Library_consultant_report.pdf.

Board of Governors, Ontario College of Art and Design University (OCAD U). 2006. *Leading in the Age of Imagination: A Strategic Plan for the Ontario College of Art & Design 2006-2012.* December 4, 2006. Accessed November 3, 2022. https://www.OCAD U.ca/Assets/documents/leading-in-the-age-of-imagination-full.pdf.

Board of Governors of the Ontario College of Art and Design University. 2021. *Minutes of the Board of Governors Meeting.* May 10, 2021. Accessed November 5, 2022. https://www.OCAD U.ca/sites/default/files/documents/governance/MINUTES%20Board%20of%20Governors%20Meeting%20May%2010%2C%202021(061421)(final%20-public).pdf.

Bradshaw, James. "Ontario Arts College Finally Gets its U." *Globe and Mail* (Toronto, Ontario), April 28, 2010, A13.

Bruce, Lorne. "Common School and Mechanics' Institute Libraries." In *Free Books for All: The Public Library Movement in Ontario 1850-1930.* Toronto & Oxford: Dundurn Press, 1994.

Bruce, Lorne, "Professionalization, Gender, and Librarianship in Ontario, 1920-75," *Library & Information History* 28, no. 2 (2012), 117-134.

Canada NewsWire. "OCAD University Receives $27 million to Develop Creative City Campus," April 12, 2016. Accessed November 4, 2022, https://www.newswire.ca/news-releases/ocad-university-receives-27-million-to-develop-creative-city-campus-575461131.html.

CAUT. 2013. *Open for Business: On What Terms?* Ottawa: CAUT.

CAUT. *Collective Agreement and Academic Status and Governance for Librarians.* November, 2018. Accessed November 2, 2022, https://www.caut.ca/about-us/caut-policy/lists/caut-policy-statements/policy-statement-on-academic-status-and-governance-for-librarians-at-canadian-universities-and-colleges.

CAUT and UTFA. "Digital Day of Action." May 31, 2021. Accessed November 4, 2022, https://librarianship.ca/news/may-31-OCAD U-digital-day-of-action/.

Clark, C. S. *Of Toronto the Good: A Social Study: The Queen City of Canada as It Is.* Montreal: Toronto Pub., 1898.

Fleck, Paul. "Art and Business: Ontario College of Art: A Hundred Years of Turbulence and Creativity." *Business Quarterly* 42, no. 2 (Summer 1977), 79-81.

Globe, The "Government Support for School of Art: Deputation tells Ministers that Ontario lags behind in fostering art." February 7, 1912. Ontario Society of Artists fonds, Archives of Ontario, Toronto, Ontario.

Groover, Myron. McMaster University Academic Librarians' Association (MUALA). Open Letter. May 2021. Accessed November 4, 2022, https://weloveOCAD Ulibrarians.ca/wp-content/uploads/2021/05/MUALA_OCAD U_Letter.pdf

Hoover, Dorothy Haines. n.d. "My Years at OCA." Unpublished interview by Library Director Jill Patrick. OCAD U Archives, Dorothy Hoover fonds.

Jacobs, Leona. "Academic Status for Canadian Academic Librarians: A Brief History." In *In Solidarity: Academic Librarian Labour, Activism and Union Participation in Canada*, edited by Jennifer Dekker and Mary Kandiuk, 9-38. Sacramento, CA: Library Juice Press, 2014.

Keating, Michael. "OCA Head is Forced to Resign." *Globe and Mail* (Toronto, Ontario), June 27, 1972. Canadian Newstream.

Lee, Min Sook, H. Sonne de Torrens and Terezia Zoric. 2021. "OCADU's Decision to Terminate Four Librarians Reflects a Troubling Trend in the Post-Secondary Sector," *Medium*, May 27, 2021. Accessed November 3, 2022, https://utfa.medium.com/ocadus-decision-to-terminate-four-librarians-reflects-a-troubling-trend-in-the-post-secondary-4fdf11043cf1.

McGinn, Dave. "The Power of the Word 'University'," *Globe and Mail.* (Toronto, Ontario). September 8, 2007. https://www.theglobeandmail.com/news/national/the-power-of-the-word-university/article18145074/.

Ministry of Training, Colleges and Universities. *2006-07 Multi-Year Accountability Agreement Report-Back for: OCAD.* Accessed November 4, 2022, https://www.OCAD U.ca/sites/default/files/legacy_assets/documents/2006-07-multi-year-accountability-agreement-report-back.pdf.

Ministry of Training, Colleges and Universities. *2007-08 Multi-Year Accountability Agreement Report-Back for: OCAD.* Accessed November 4, 2022, https://www.OCAD U.ca/sites/default/files/legacy_assets/documents/2007-08-multi-year-accountability-agreement-report-back.pdf.

"New Head Finds Problems Exciting: Psychologist Takes on the OCA," *Globe and Mail* (Toronto, Ontario), August 26, 1972, Canadian Newstream.

Novakovic, Stefan. "OCAD Announces Designers for 'Creative City Campus' Expansion." *Urban Toronto,* January 11, 2017. Accessed November 4, 2022, https://urbantoronto.ca/news/2017/01/ocad-announces-designers-creative-city-campus-expansion.

Ontario College of Art and Art Gallery of Ontario. *100 Years: Evolution of the Ontario College of Art.* Toronto: Art Gallery of Ontario: Ontario College of Art, 1976.

OCAD University. "OCAD University Strategic Mandate Agreement Proposal." Accountability, May 1, 2014. Accessed November 4, 2022, http://www.ocadu.ca/Assets/documents/sma-2014.pdf.

OCAD University, News Release. "OCAD University Celebrates Dr. Sara Diamond's Contributions as Outgoing President." June 23, 2020. Accessed November 5, 2022, https://www.ocadu.ca/news/ocad-university-celebrates-dr-sara-diamonds-contributions-outgoing-president.

OCAD University. "Ana Serrano, OCAD University President and Vice-Chancellor," Accessed November 4, 2022, https://www.ocadu.ca/about/president.

OCAD University. "OCAD U Welcomes New University Librarian Tony White," Accessed November 4, 2022, https://www.ocadu.ca/news/ocad-u-welcomes-new-university-librarian-tony-white.

OCAD University, *Organisation Review of OCAD University OCAD U Submission to the Minister of Colleges and Universities,* March 10, 2020. Accessed November 4, 2022, http://peqab.ca/Ontario_Public/OCAD%20U/webversion%20OCAD%20U%20Org%20Review%20Submission%20to%20PEQAB.pdf.

OCAD University. "OCAD U Issues Statement on Library Reorganization," May 14, 2021. Accessed November 4, 2022, https://www.ocadu.ca/news/ocad-u-issues-statement-library-reorganization.

OCAD University. "Organizational Charts." Accessed November 5, 2022, https://www.OCAD U.ca/services/human-resources/organizational-charts.

OCAD University, Board of Governors. Minutes, May 10, 2021. Accessed November 3, 2022, https://www.ocadu.ca/about/governance/board-of-governors.

OCAD University Senate. 2021. Minutes of the Academic Senate Meeting, May 19, 2021. Note the meeting minutes are no longer available on the Senate website. https://www.OCAD U.ca/about/governance/senate.

OCAD University. "About History." Accessed October 28, 2022, https://www.OCAD U.ca/about/history.

OCAD University Faculty Association (OCADFA, @ocadfa1). 2021. "An Injury to One (or 4) is an Injury to All!" Twitter, May 7, 2021, 5:03 pm., https://twitter.com/ocadfa1/status/1390774302698508288.

OCAD University Faculty Association (OCADFA). 2021. "We Love OCAD U Librarians", http://weloveOCAD Ulibrarians.ca (removed) but preserved at Internet Archive. Accessed November 3, 2022, https://web.archive.org/web/20210528165648/http://weloveOCAD Ulibrarians.ca/.

Ontario Ministry of Training, Colleges and Universities, 2006. *Multi-Year Action Plan for Universities*. Accessed November 3, 2022, https://www.OCAD U.ca/sites/default/files/legacy_assets/documents/ocad-multi-year-action-plan.pdf.

OPSEU, Local 576. "Statements to OCAD U Senate," (May 19, 2021). Accessed November 3, 2022, https://www.opseulocal576.org/news-and-announcements/union-statements/2021-05-19-statements-to-ocad-u-senate.

OPSEU Local 576. 2021. Petition, "Don't Put the Hook to OCADU Professional Academic Librarians," addressed to Ana Serrano, President OCADU, Caroline Langill, Vice President and Provost Academic, OCADU, Tony White, University Librarian, OCADU, Jaime Watt, Chair, Board of Governors, OCADU. Accessed November 4, 2022, https://www.thepetitionsite.com/en-ca/172/609/882/we-love-and-respect-ocadu-academic-professional-librarians-sign-our-petition-to-support-them/.

Payne, Daniel. *A Mirror of Curriculum: Art Libraries and Studio-Based Education: The OCAD University Experience (1876-2016)*. Self-published, 2020. Accessed November 3, 2022, http://openresearch.OCAD U.ca/id/eprint/1357/.

Samson, Natalie. "Across Canada, More Colleges are Transitioning to Universities," *University Affairs* (June 2018). Accessed November 4, 2022, https://www.universityaffairs.ca/news/news-article/across-canada-more-colleges-are-transitioning-to-universities/.

Schroeder, Julie. "The Bargaining Unit for the Academic Librarian." *Canadian Library Journal* 32, no. 6 (December 1975): 463-73. https://opus.uleth.ca/handle/10133/3691.

Sonne de Torrens, Harriet. "Academic Librarianship: The Quest for Rights and Recognition at the University of Toronto." In *In Solidarity: Academic Librarian Labour, Activism and Union Participation in Canada*, edited by Jennifer Dekker and Mary Kandiuk, 81-106. Sacramento, CA: Library Juice Press, 2014.

Turk, Jim. "Academic Freedom for Librarians: What is it, and Why Does it Matter?" CAUT (August 25, 2010), 1-12. Accessed November 2, 2022, www.library.mcgill.ca/mautlib/2010.08.25_McGill_Librarians.pdf.

University of Guelph Faculty Association, Open Letter, n.d. Accessed November 4, 2022, http://ocadfa.ca/wp-content/uploads/2021/05/Letter-in-Support-of-OCAD-Librarians.pdf.

Wilfrid Laurier University Faculty Association. 2021. Open Letter. May 18, 2021. Accessed November 4, 2022, https://www.wlufa.ca/2021/05/18/wlufa-appalled-by-ocadu-lay-off-and-elimination-of-librarians/.

Wolfe, Morris. 1990. "The Struggle for Equity at OCA," *Saturday Night*, December 1990. https://www.grubstreetbooks.ca/essays/oca.html.

Wolfe, Morris. 2001. *OCA 1967-1972: Five Turbulent Years*. Toronto: Grub Street Books.

Wright, Douglas T. *Report on the Organizational Structure and Administration of the Ontario College of Art*, (to the Minister of University Affairs). Toronto: s.n., 1968.

Index

academia
  expansion of market labor relations in, 4
  redefinition as a for-profit activity, 1
  strengthening of neoliberal values in, 3-4
  struggle against neoliberal influence on, 118-119
academic librarians. *See* librarians, academic
academic librarianship. *See* librarianship, academic
academic libraries. *See* libraries, academic
ACRL. *See* Association of College and Research Libraries
AI. *See* artificial intelligence
ALA. *See* American Library Association
American Library Association, 103, 104
APUO. *See* Association of Professors of the University of Ottawa
area studies collections. *See* collections, area studies
artificial intelligence, 71-72
A*SEEES* CLIR. *See* Association of Slavic East European and Eurasian Studies, Committee on Libraries and Information Resources
Association of College and Research Libraries, 10, 13-15, 17-19, 85-87, 103-105
Association of Professors of the University of Ottawa, 56-57
Association of Slavic East European and Eurasian Studies, Committee on Libraries and Information Resources, 14, 17
autonomism, 146, 152-156

CACUL. *See* Canadian Association of College and University Libraries
Canadian Association of College and University Libraries, 177
Canadian Association of Professional Academic Librarians, 125, 187
Canadian Association of Research Libraries, 44-46
Canadian Association of University Teachers, 43, 57, 58, 177, 178-179, 187-189
Canadian Knowledge Research Networks, 44, 46
CAPAL. *See* Canadian Association of Professional Academic Librarians
CARL. *See* Canadian Association of Research Libraries

CAUT. *See* Canadian Association of University Teachers
CEAL. *See* Council on East Asian Libraries
Central Intelligence Agency, 9
CIA. *See* Central Intelligence Agency
CIFNAL. *See* Collaborative Initiative for French Language Collections
CKRN. *See* Canadian Knowledge Research Networks
Collaborative Initiative for French Language Collections, 14, 17, 30-32
collection librarians. *See* librarians, collection
collections, area studies
  effects of COVID-19 crisis on, 4, 12-15
  effects of emphasis on electronic resources over print resources, 4, 10-11, 15-16
  in North America, 9-12
  scope of, 10
  spread into North American academic institutions, 9-10
  use of scholarly resources generated globally, 9, 10, 15-16
collections, electronic
  books, 4, 8-9, 11-12
  journal articles, 4, 8
collections, print, 4, 7-8
colonialism, 9
Committee on Research Materials on Southeast Asia, 14, 17, 33-37
Committee on South Asian Libraries and Documentation, 14, 17, 22, 23, 27-29, 33
CONSALD. *See* Committee on South Asian Libraries and Documentation
CORMOSEA. *See* Committee on Research Materials on Southeast Asia
Council on East Asian Libraries, 10, 11, 14, 15-16, 17, 22-25
COVID-19 crisis
  effects on area studies collections, 4, 12-15
  effects on library collection development decisions, 4, 7, 10, 12, 15-16
  effects on library operations, 7-8, 125, 148-149, 158, 169
cultural hegemony, 9

DD. *See* document delivery
document delivery, 11, 23
Dorothy H. Hoover Library, 169-171

EDI. *See* equity, diversity, and inclusivity
electronic collections. *See* collections, electronic
equity, diversity, and inclusivity, 4, 15, 17-19

Gender Decoder, 72, 77-78, 94
German-North American Resources Partnership, 14, 17, 30-32
GNARP. *See* German-North American Resources Partnership

humanities, 8-9

ICT. *See* information and communications technologies
ideology, 127-132, 138-139
IL. *See* information literacy
ILL. *See* interlibrary loan
ILO. *See* International Labour Organization
imperialism, 9
information and communications technologies, 147, 148
information literacy
  assessment tools for, 104
  barriers to, 112-117
  benefits of, 112-117
  definition of, 103
  descriptive language for, 103-104
  relationship to neoliberalism, 103-105, 106-111, 118
  scalability of, 104-105, 106-111, 119
  standards for, 103-105
  teaching of, 105
interlibrary loan, 11, 23
International Labour Organization, 126
International Studies Association, 13
ISA. *See* International Studies Association

job openings, 75
job postings
  content analysis of, 4, 74-75
  gendered language in, 4, 69-70, 83
  literature reviews about, 70-74
  stereotypical language in, 69-70
  time series analysis of, 76-77

librarians, academic
  ability to work from home, 105, 126-127
  critiques of, 1
  gender breakdown of, 125
  gradual transformation of, 1, 16
  job titles of, 125-126
  pedagogical work of, 4, 85-87
  professional autonomy of, 57
  role of neoliberalism in shaping work of, 1-4, 101-103, 125-127
  struggles with neoliberalism, 3-4
  understanding the long term ramifications of adopting electronic resources over print resources for, 4, 13-14
librarians, collection, 12-13
librarianship, academic
  collection development decisions in, 4
  critiques of, 1-4
  deprofessionalization of, 4, 16
  gender discrimination in, 4, 67
  problematization in, 4
  professional education programs for, 67
  proletarization of, 145, 161-164
  stereotypes in, 69
  transformation into service operations, 1
libraries, academic
  effects of COVID-19 crisis on, 7-8, 125
  evolution of, 144-145
  policies in, 43-46, 60-61, 127
  problematization in, 4, 39-40
  reorganization of, 4, 40, 58-59

MELA. *See* Middle East Libraries Association
metonyms, 131
Middle East Libraries Association, 14, 17, 22, 23, 26, 27, 33

Named Entity Recognition, 75, 78-83, 96-99
NCC. *See* North American Coordinating Council on Japanese Library Resources
neoliberalism
  critique of, 3, 4, 101-102
  definition of, 1-3, 101-102, 135
  in institutions of higher education, 1, 3-4, 102-103, 144-145
  objectification as facet of, 135-138
  relation to capitalism, 3
  relation to information literacy, 103-105
  relation to labor, 129, 146-152
  role in shaping academic librarians' work, 1, 103-105
NER. *See* Named Entity Recognition
North American Coordinating Council on Japanese Library Resources, 10, 11, 14, 15-16, 17, 22-25

OCA. *See* Ontario College of Art
OCADU. *See* Ontario College of Art and Design University
Office of Strategic Services, 9
Ontario College of Art, 171-180
Ontario College of Art and Design University, 4, 61, 148-149, 169-171, 180-190

Ontario Public Services Employees Union, 169, 177-179, 185-189
OPSEU. *See* Ontario Public Services Employees Union
orientalism, 9
OSS. *See* Office of Strategic Services

print collections. *See* collections, print

SALALM. *See* Seminar on the Acquisition of Latin American Library Materials
Science, Technology, Engineering, and Mathematics, 8-9, 10, 16
SCSL. *See* Society of Chinese Studies Librarians
*SEE*MP. *See* Slavic East European Materials Project
Seminar on the Acquisition of Latin American Library Materials, 10, 13, 14, 17, 20-21, 22, 23, 26, 27, 33
Slavic East European Materials Project, 14, 17, 30-32
social factory, 146, 152-156, 160
social sciences, 8-9
Society of Chinese Studies Librarians, 10, 11, 14, 15-16, 17, 22-25
STEM. *See* Science, Technology, Engineering, and Mathematics
subsumption, 156-161

Tang lexicon, 72, 75, 77-78, 95-96
technological development, 159-160
text-reader conversation, 133-134
texts, 132-134

UOL. *See* University of Ottawa Library
University of Ottawa Library, 42-43, 56-60
University of Toronto Library
  gender equity in, 68-70
  hiring practices at, 75-76, 83-85
  history of librarianship at, 67-68
  job postings at, 4, 69-70, 76-77, 88-89
  managerialism in, 85, 88
  salary equity at, 68-69
UTL. *See* University of Toronto Library

What's the Problem Represented To Be, 40-42, 46-56, 60-61
WPR. *See* What's the Problem Represented To Be

www.ingramcontent.com/pod-product-compliance
Lightning Source LLC
Chambersburg PA
CBHW050302010526
44108CB00040B/2063